Mergers & Acquisitions FOR DUMMIES®

by Bill Snow

WILEY

Wiley Publishing, Inc.

Mergers & Acquisitions For Dummies®

Published by
Wiley Publishing, Inc.
111 River St.
Hoboken, NJ 07030-5774
www.wiley.com

Copyright © 2011 by Wiley Publishing, Inc., Indianapolis, Indiana

Published by Wiley Publishing, Inc., Indianapolis, Indiana

Published simultaneously in Canada

For general information on our other products and services, please contact our Customer Care Department within the U.S. at 877-762-2974, outside the U.S. at 317-572-3993, or fax 317-572-4002.

For technical support, please visit www.wiley.com/techsupport.

Wiley also publishes its books in a variety of electronic formats. Some content that appears in print may not be available in electronic books.

Library of Congress Control Number: 2011926316

ISBN: 978-0-470-38556-2

Manufactured in the United States of America

10 9 8 7 6 5 4 3 2 1

WILEY

About the Author

Bill Snow is an experienced M&A professional. He advises business owners in the sale of their companies or the acquisition of other companies. He's the one who contacts the buyers and sellers, negotiates and structures deals, oversees the due diligence, works with the attorneys to draft the purchase agreement, and ultimately gets the deal across the finish line.

Companies that Bill has advised include (but aren't limited to) businesses in marketing services, food processing equipment, drink dispensing equipment, guarding, cleaning, staffing, distribution, data marketing, wastewater services, telecommunications, and systems integrators.

Bill has written articles for numerous online sources and self-published a book about venture capital called *Venture Capital 101*. He has been involved with World Business Chicago, the Chicagoland Chamber of Commerce, the Chicagoland Entrepreneurial Center, the Technology Executive's Club, the Midwest Entrepreneur's Forum, and DePaul University's PEN Symposium. He also hosts occasional networking events.

He has an MBA and a BS in finance, both from DePaul University, and he's a registered limited representative (FINRA series 63 and 79). You can find out more about Bill at his Web site, www.billsnow.com.

Dedication

To business owners and executives who are thinking about buying or selling a company.

Author's Acknowledgments

The genesis of this book goes back to my humble little attempt at some creative writing. Little did the subjects of those silly newsletters know that I had ulterior motives for documenting (and, uh, embellishing) those crazy years in our 20s. Sure, our little newsletter contained some funny bits, but truth to tell, I was writing it to hone my technical writing skills and to foster my creative abilities. Seriously. And you thought it was all about you!

So a big thank you to a cast of characters that include Ebbitt and that fine woman Clare, Little Lisa, Big Steve, Stevie V, Johnny V, Mariola, Jason S, Jason T, Joe, Carrie, Rogie, Rainbow, Jen, Tony, the Dold Boys and everyone at the Dold Family Compound, the brood of ungrateful Kemps (Tim, Kelly, Kerry, Karla, and Loren), and the unknowing and unwitting, creative-juice-generating granddaddy of 'em all . . . our Romanian pal Mark. I am grateful for your youthful antics, and more important, I am grateful for your continued friendship. Well, those of you who still speak to me.

A huge thanks to my mother and father, Carol and Bill Snow. I will never be able to repay you both for all that you have done for me over the years. When I find a T-shirt that reads, "We gave our kids everything and all we got was a lousy mention in a book," I'll send one to each of you. And to my sister, Laura, the first in the family to get a PhD. You made it so much easier for me to pursue this book venture: Now I can be the first in the family with a published book. You also said I was a perfect choice to write a *For Dummies* book, " 'cause they're snarky." Though I'll have you know, Ms. PhD smarty-pants, that *For Dummies* books are actually irreverent.

I'd like to thank Bob Kinsella, Bob Stutz, Louis Krzys, and Chuck Weikel from Kinsella Group, Inc., for their extremely valuable input about deal-making. I also owe a debt of gratitude to Justin Kaplan of BNY-Melon; Mark Powers of Mark Powers, PC; Keith Berk of Horwood Marcus & Berk; and Brian Krob of Ungaretti & Harris for their insights about M&A transactions.

I am greatly appreciative to Wiley Publishing for backing me in this attempt at being a *"wise old sage"* for others. I am thankful that my little treatise on venture capital somehow found its way to Michael Lewis's desk at Wiley in New Jersey. Thank you for getting the green light, and thank you, Internet; without you I never would have gotten the chance to write this book. And to my project editor, Alissa Schwipps, thank you for your sage advice and assistance. I was listening!

Lastly, to my long-lost dog park friend . . . safe travels.

Publisher's Acknowledgments

We're proud of this book; please send us your comments at http://dummies.custhelp.com. For other comments, please contact our Customer Care Department within the U.S. at 877-762-2974, outside the U.S. at 317-572-3993, or fax 317-572-4002.

Some of the people who helped bring this book to market include the following:

Acquisitions, Editorial, and Media Development

Senior Project Editor: Alissa Schwipps

Acquisitions Editor: Michael Lewis

Copy Editor: Megan Knoll

Assistant Editor: David Lutton

Technical Editor: Joelle Marquis

Senior Editorial Manager: Jennifer Ehrlich

Editorial Assistant: Rachelle Amick

Cover Photo: © Con Tanasiuk/Design Pics/ Corbis

Cartoons: Rich Tennant (www.the5thwave.com)

Composition Services

Project Coordinator: Sheree Montgomery

Layout and Graphics: Joyce Haughey, Corrie Socolovitch

Proofreaders: Melissa Cossell, Melissa D. Buddendeck

Indexer: BIM Indexing & Proofreading Services

Special Help
Todd Lothery

Publishing and Editorial for Consumer Dummies

Diane Graves Steele, Vice President and Publisher, Consumer Dummies

Kristin Ferguson-Wagstaffe, Product Development Director, Consumer Dummies

Ensley Eikenburg, Associate Publisher, Travel

Kelly Regan, Editorial Director, Travel

Publishing for Technology Dummies

Andy Cummings, Vice President and Publisher, Dummies Technology/General User

Composition Services

Debbie Stailey, Director of Composition Services

Contents at a Glance

Table of Contents

Part II: Taking the First Steps to Buy or Sell a Company................................. 61

Chapter 4: Financing M&A Deals .... .63

Introduction

*I*n every job — whether it be sales, managing retail establishments, raising capital, crunching numbers, writing, working with venture capitalists, creating online ventures, or working investment banking deals (I've done all these, by the way) — you quickly discover that you need a whole new set of rules, lingo, conventions, and nomenclature. And more often than not, what you need to know to excel at your job can be distilled into just a few salient points. If you're lucky, you bump into a wise old sage who, upon experiencing your questioning, utterly confused face, and dispirited body language, simply says, "Forget all that other stuff; here's what you really need to know." Enter *Mergers & Acquisitions For Dummies,* an inside look at the process of buying and selling companies.

Although companies change hands every day, buying and selling can mean many things and take many forms. Who or what is the Buyer or Seller? What kind of transaction is it? How will the Buyer finance the deal, and what does the Seller receive? These are only a few of the considerations in any given mergers and acquisitions (M&A) deal. It's so confusing!

As a result, business owners, some of the main participants in M&A, are often completely befuddled when the time comes to sell their businesses or make acquisitions. They don't know anything about M&A because they've been focused on their own businesses and not on the business of buying and selling companies.

That's why I wrote this book — to serve as your wise old sage as you jump into the wild M&A world.

About This Book

Although the M&A process, like any sales process, involves a step-by-step approach, I've written this book so you can simply refer to whatever section you need to read. Scan the index and table of contents and then go directly to the information you need.

When a Buyer and Seller are negotiating a deal, they're on opposite sides of the table. The Buyer wants to get the best (that is, lowest) price, and the Seller wants to get the best (that is, highest) price. This book isn't slanted one way or another. It's not pro-Buyer or pro-Seller. Deals get done only when Buyer and Seller find common ground and agree to price and terms.

During the M&A process, many of the steps and techniques I discuss in this book apply to Buyers, Sellers, or both. I highly recommend Sellers read the Buyers' information and vice versa. My hope is that this book provides some insights for both sides by helping each side see things from the other's perspective. Understanding the other side's motivation and rationale is key to getting a deal done. If you know what the other side is seeking or why she's asking for something in a particular way, you're in a better position to provide an answer that helps move the deal to a close. And closing deals, ladies and gentlemen, is what M&A is all about.

Conventions Used in This Book

I use a few conventions throughout this book to help make it more accessible:

- ✔ I format new words in *italic* and accompany them with definitions.
- ✔ **Bold text** highlights the active parts of numbered steps and signals the keywords in bulleted lists.
- ✔ Web sites appear in `monofont`. In some cases, Web addresses may have broken over more than one line during the book's printing. Just type the address exactly as you see it; I haven't added any characters to mark the line break.
- ✔ Because "mergers and acquisitions" is kind of an unwieldy phrase, I often use the abbreviation "M&A." You see it in the field all the time anyway, so why not use it here?
- ✔ One challenge in this book is that two distinct yet related groups of people (Buyers and Sellers) may read this title. When I use "Buyer," I'm referring to the individual or executives in a company seeking to acquire another company. When I use "Seller," I'm referring to the owner of a company or the owner's representatives (executives or advisors). I also use "you" to address you, dear reader, directly, even though the text in question may not apply to your specific situation. In those cases, I clearly alert you to whether I'm talking about Buyers or Sellers.

What You're Not to Read

My goal for this book was to write an easy-to-read, introductory look at the world of mergers and acquisitions. At times, however, some of the text may be a bit technical and in-depth, so turned those parts into sidebars (those shaded gray boxes) or marked them with a Technical Stuff icon. You don't need to read those parts unless you really, really, really, really want to know more.

Foolish Assumptions

I assume you bought this book for any number of reasons:

- ✔ You're a business owner or executive of a middle market or lower middle market company and are interested in selling a division, subsidiary, or entire company.

- ✔ You're an executive of a company and are interested in acquiring middle market or lower middle market companies.

- ✔ You're a business student who is interested in discovering more about mergers and acquisitions.

- ✔ You know a lot about your specific business but little or nothing about the business of buying or selling businesses.

You may be asking yourself, "Why the specific delineation of middle market and lower middle market companies?" Those two market segments, defined roughly as companies of $250 million to $1 billion in revenue (middle market) and $20 million to $250 million in revenue (lower middle market), are often overlooked by larger banks. The deals aren't as large, the companies aren't as famous or "sexy," and when you have a plethora of top-tier MBA grads all clamoring to make a million bucks a year, the smaller fees from these smaller deals just aren't of interest.

Although the lower middle market deals aren't front-page headline blockbusters, the fact is the middle market and lower middle market are comprised of many more companies than the Fortune 500, which, when you think about it, is exactly 500 companies. The owners and executives of many, if not most, lower middle market companies are wholly unfamiliar with the business of selling a business and are therefore the perfect audience for this book. But although middle market and lower middle market company execs may be this book's target audience, the information here is applicable for just about any kind of business sale transaction.

How This Book Is Organized

I organized *Mergers & Acquisitions For Dummies* in five essential parts. These parts cover the main facets of doing deals, from an introduction to the basics to the courting process to the documents and meetings involved to integrating Buyer and Seller.

Part I: Mergers & Acquisitions 101

Part I gives you the lowdown on M&A's foundations. Chapter 1 introduces you to some of the basic building blocks in the M&A world: words, phrases, decorum, players and their motivations, and generally accepted steps to buying and selling companies. Chapter 2 analyzes the rationale and motivations of Buyers and Sellers so that you can better understand the folks on the other side of the table (and maybe get some insight into your own goals as well). In Chapter 3, I provide an outline of the generally accepted M&A process; you have a much better chance of making a successful deal when you know what steps to follow.

Part II: Taking the First Steps to Buy or Sell a Company

When you actually want to do deals, as opposed to merely thinking about doing deals, Part II gets you started on the first steps. You need money (or seashells, cigarettes, or some form of consideration that the Seller finds acceptable), and Chapter 4 offers some thoughts about financing M&A deals. Every deal-maker needs a little (well, a lot of) help, so Chapter 5 lays out the advisors you need in order to successfully buy or sell companies. M&A is really a form of dating, except with meetings, boring documents, and grueling travel. Chapter 6 provides you with colorful tips for successfully approaching Buyers or Sellers and explains why M&A is one of the few industries where selling is easier than buying.

Part III: Starting the Deal on the Right Foot

In this part, I show you how to get going on a deal. Chapter 7 quietly discusses the cloak-and-dagger world of confidentiality. Chapter 8 deals with the offering document, which is basically the story a Seller tells a Buyer about the company, as well as how to write it and what to look for when you review it. M&A requires a certain level of discretion, and that level is high! In Chapter 9, I introduce you to the form and function of the indication of interest (IOI — this field loves its initialisms) that Buyer offers Seller when Buyer's ready to move from talking about doing a deal to providing specific thoughts on an actual deal. (What can I say? M&A loves crafting documents, too.) The next steps are the management meetings between Buyer and Seller; Chapter 10 helps you navigate these meetings, which don't have fancy abbreviations but can be tricky.

Part IV: Firming Up the Deal

When Buyer and Seller agree to do a deal, what's next? Part IV's topics, that's what! First, Buyer and Seller have to agree to terms; M&A deals involve layer upon layer of complexity that you can and should negotiate. Chapter 11 takes you to the smoke-filled back rooms where deals are made; all cigar-chomping is figurative.

Chapter 12 plows the fields of valuation for you and reaps an answer to that most nagging of questions: What the heck is this company worth?

When Buyer and Seller want to stop playing the field and get married, they move on to the letter of intent (LOI). Chapter 13 takes you through the ins and outs of this key document. Due diligence is the next key phase; it's where Buyer and Seller confirm certain facts from the other side just to be safe. Chapter 14 fills you in on what to expect during the confirmatory due diligence phase. Chapter 15 provides insight about converting the LOI and the results of due diligence into a final, binding purchase agreement.

Part V: Closing the Deal . . . and Beyond!

Part V helps you successfully conclude the deal. In Chapter 16, you get the insider's look at that important day. Chapter 17 details all the sordid adjustments one side or the other makes after the closing. After the deal is done and a new day has risen, Buyer and Seller must integrate and learn to live together. Integrating Buyer and Seller can be a difficult proposition that many people don't think about, so Chapter 18 tackles this hidden issue.

Part VI: The Part of Tens

The Part of Tens is a *For Dummies* classic, so of course this book includes it as well. Chapter 19 clues you in to important questions to ask before signing an LOI. In Chapter 20, I warn you against mistakes that can sink a deal, and Chapter 21 offers ways to come to an agreement on valuation. I also give you an appendix full of resources such as a due diligence checklist, helpful online sources, and some sample M&A documents.

Icons Used in This Book

I use the following four icons throughout this book to help draw your attention to particularly important or salient bits of information (and let you know what bits aren't essential):

This icon denotes info that can save you time and/or hassle as you work through a deal.

The Remember icon flags important points and concepts worth searing into your memory banks.

The text next to this icon is useful but not vital to the topic at hand; you can skip it if you're in a hurry or just want the need-to-know information.

I use this icon to highlight potential M&A disasters you want to avoid.

Where to Go from Here

No matter your immediate interests or needs, I highly recommend reading Chapter 3, which provides an overview of the process. An understanding of the typical steps involved in a business sale can help you as you read other specific sections. From there, you can dive in and out of this book as you please.

Beyond this book, the best advice I can offer for anyone who wants to buy or sell companies or work as an advisor in the M&A industry is to get off your duff and get in the game. Books are great, and I certainly hope you find *Mergers & Acquisitions For Dummies* to be an extremely valuable resource, but the fact remains that the best way to learn something is to do it yourself. The only way you can truly get a handle on buying and selling companies is to actually buy and sell companies.

I'm a big believer in "ground up" learning. No, I'm not talking about deli meats; I'm talking about getting your hands dirty and learning business from the ground up. You're going to make mistakes, but finding out what doesn't work is the best way to learn. If you want to be successful in M&A (as a

Buyer, a Seller, or an intermediary), you're best served if you can talk from a level of actual experience. Those experiences should ideally include successfully selling a product or service, interacting with customers, hiring and firing employees, merchandising, marketing, working in human resource compliance, banking, making a payroll, filing taxes, and bookkeeping. (Mopping some floors and scrubbing a few toilets won't kill you, either.) You don't want to be the only one at the table who hasn't dealt with real-world business issues and problems. Being the least-qualified person in the room is never a good thing!

One of the big ironies for the investment banking world is that most people who do what I do didn't start their careers with the plan of being an investment banker. I'm often asked how to get into the investment banking industry. I always say the same thing: "Most of us who do this didn't choose this career. Go do something else. Get involved in a business first, and then segue into investment banking."

One final thought: One of the keys to M&A is accounting. If your accounting skills are suspect (or nonexistent), you need to take a class, stat! Most community colleges offer accounting classes, and you can probably audit the class instead of taking it for credit.

Part I
Mergers &
Acquisitions 101

The 5th Wave   By Rich Tennant

THE END IS NEAR

"Isn't that our bookkeeper?"

In this part . . .

This part delves into the basics of M&A: The players, their motivations, the terms, the nomenclature, the conventions of the industry, and the rules and regulations. I also discuss reasons to buy or sell a company, and I walk you through the generally accepted process of buying or selling a company on a step-by-step basis.

Chapter 1

The Building Blocks of Mergers and Acquisitions

In This Chapter

▶ Becoming familiar with the main vocabulary of mergers and acquisitions

▶ Understanding the rules of the road

▶ Opening your eyes to potential costs

▶ Figuring out where your company fits

Mergers and acquisitions is a complicated field, so this chapter provides a basic overview: an introduction to the basic terms and phrases, a discussion of decorum and the basic M&A process, a look at the players and the category of deals, and my handy-dandy guide to helping business owners determine what kind of businesses they have.

Defining Mergers and Acquisitions

Mergers and acquisitions (or *M&A* for short — the M&A world is rife with acronyms and initialisms) is a bit of a catchall phrase. For all intents and purposes, M&A simply means the buying and selling of companies. When you think about it, mergers and acquisitions aren't different; they're simply variations on the same theme.

In the strictest sense, a *merger* is a combination of two or more entities where each merging entity has an equal stake in the new enterprise and each merging entity has a very clearly defined role in the new entity. This ideal is the vaunted *merger of equals*. Daimler's 1998 combination with Chrysler was a merger of equals. In a more practical sense, so-called mergers of equals are rare; one side usually ends up controlling the enterprise. For example, the years following the Daimler-Chrysler merger showed that Daimler executives planned all along to control the combined entity.

Although actual mergers do occur, most of the activity in the M&A world centers on one company buying another company, or the acquisitions category. I like to think using the word *merger* keeps the uninitiated on their toes; plus, talking about combining two companies as equal partners rather than about committing a hostile takeover sounds much more egalitarian.

Mergers are far less common than acquisitions. An *acquisition* is when one company buys another company, a division of another company, or a product line or certain assets from another company. Actually, an acquisition is when any kind of business purchases another part (or all) of another business. Although some companies grow *organically* (from within by creating and selling products or services), an acquisition allows a company to bypass the growth stage by simply buying existing sales and profits. Starting up a new product line may be less expensive than buying an existing one, but the market may take a while to adapt to the new product, if it does at all. For this reason, buying other companies rather than relying on organic growth may make sense for a particular company.

The fact that one can transfer a company's ownership through a sale often comes as a bit of surprise to many people (including many business owners, believe it or not). Business owners, especially owners of middle market and lower middle market companies (with revenues between $250 million and $1 billion [middle market] and between $20 million and $250 million [lower middle market]), have spent their careers building a company, so the process of selling a business is often something new and foreign to them.

In addition to being an activity, M&A is an industry. As this book illustrates, the steps to doing a deal, the names of documents and processes, the conventions, and the sundry tips and insights I provide are all based on de facto industry standards that have developed over time, and my humble hope is that this book helps introduce you to those standards and conventions.

Introducing Important Terms and Phrases

Like any topic, M&A has a language that you have to get a handle on to understand the field. Although I introduce many more terms and phrases throughout the book, the following words are part of the basic building blocks of M&A.

The *lingua franca* of M&A is an amalgam of accounting and banking terms sprinkled with initialisms, acronyms, and words and phrases adjusted and twisted to suit certain needs at certain times. Pay close attention to the terms I define throughout the book. Although some are tricky, I use them all for a reason.

Buyer

You can't sell something unless you have a buyer for it. Although Buyers (both potential and actual) are typically companies or entities, I often refer to them as individuals for clarity.

In documents and contracts and agreements, you usually see *Buyer* as a defined term, which means it's capitalized. When you read those documents, *Buyer* looks like the name of a person. In fact, to make it seem really formal, M&A professionals often drop the word *the* from *Buyer*.

"Buyer" isn't a one-size-fits-all category. A Buyer may acquire all or part of a company, the stock of the company, or certain or all assets and even assume some of the liabilities. Despite this wide variety of possibilities, Buyers typically fall into four broad types:

- ✔ **Strategic Buyers:** These Buyers are other companies planning to combine operations of the two companies to some extent (as opposed to buying strictly for financial reasons). For example, when Oracle buys a company, Oracle is considered a strategic Buyer because it buys companies that have some sort of synergy to its business.

- ✔ **Financial Buyers:** *Financial Buyers* are funds of money that buy companies. Financial Buyers of middle market and lower middle market companies are typically private equity (PE) funds, which are essentially large pools of money (see Chapter 4 for more).

- ✔ **Other companies backed by PE funds:** The company will be the new owner of the acquired company, but another entity (the fund) is providing the dough to do the deal.

- ✔ **Individuals:** Although it happens, an individual buying a middle market or lower middle market company is rare. When individuals buy companies, those companies tend to be small retail shops, consulting firms, or construction companies. Typically, these companies have revenues of less than $1 million.

As a Seller, know that who's on the other side of the negotiating table may change the way your M&A process works. Are the Buyers experienced deal people, or are they new to the process? For example, if your Buyer is a PE firm, rest assured that the people you're negotiating with know exactly what they're doing.

Seller

You can't buy something unless you have a Seller. Like Buyers, Sellers usually aren't individuals, though I often refer to them in the singular here for clarification purposes. *Seller* is a defined term, meaning it's capitalized for the purposes of documents and contracts.

Here's a quick look at the types of Sellers you may find in the world of M&A:

✔ **The spinoff:** A company may be divesting a division, a product line, or certain assets.

✔ **The change of control:** This company is selling enough of itself (more than 50 percent) to result in a change of control. In these cases, the owner or owners most likely receive the money. Colloquially, this approach is called *taking some chips off the table.*

✔ **The recap:** Sometimes an owner wants to take some chips off the table without giving up control of the company. This situation is called a *recapitalization,* or *recap* for short.

✔ **The growth capital:** A Seller may issue more stock for the purposes of raising capital to invest in the business. In this case, the owner isn't actually selling the company but rather selling more stakes in the company. The money from the sale doesn't flow to the owner; instead, the company retains the money to fund growth.

Remembering why the Seller is selling the company, how much of the company he or she is selling, and where the money goes is key. Follow the money.

Transaction (also known as the deal)

The *transaction* is when Buyer sells a company to Seller. It's an abstract concept, as in, "We're working on a transaction that will sell ABC to XYZ." It can also refer to the finished sale: "We completed the transaction yesterday." (Don't confuse the transaction with the *purchase agreement,* a contract that memorializes the transaction. See Chapter 15 for more on this document.)

Transaction is a more formal version of *deal;* most documents, agreements, and contracts use the word *transaction* (often capitalized as a defined term), but conversations and e-mails may use *deal* and *transaction* interchangeably. Think of *deal* as *transaction's* popular cousin from the wrong side of the tracks.

M&A personality types

Regardless of whether you're buying or selling, one helpful trick for getting deals done is to assess the personality of your negotiating counterpart. Based on my experience, you're liable to run across the following types of people:

✔ **The highly motivated:** This person has to get a deal done or he's doomed. He's so desperate to do a deal that he may — strike that, *will* — leave dollars on the table.

✔ **The ruler-of-the-universe business magnate:** He's from Experienced, Wily, and Cagey, Ltd.; he's made countless deals and knows exactly what he's doing. If you find yourself matched against this person, look out. The worst thing you can do is to turn into the highly motivated (see the preceding bullet); you'll get your clock cleaned.

✔ **The know-it-all who's never sold a company:** This person is one of the potential problem children of the M&A world. Quite often, he's an expert in one field and thus thinks he's an expert in everything. The best way to counteract this type of person is by asking questions, reasoning, and getting him to explain his point of view. Avoid simply saying "no" if you don't like his proposal. Challenge him. Your only hope of changing this person's mind is getting him to change it himself.

✔ **Mr. Irrational:** Mr. Irrational is the insane twin of the know-it-all, except without the strong logic skills. As a result, employing logic and reason doesn't work. An irrational person is difficult to work with, so your ability to get a deal done is limited. Give it your best shot and then walk away when the proceedings begin to get petty and frustrating. Interestingly enough, these irrational people often come to their senses after the heat of the battle fades. Don't fuel their irrationality with endless negotiating and discussions.

✔ **The earnest first-timer:** The country cousin of the know-it-all and Mr. Irrational, this person is so intent on doing everything letter-perfectly that he misses the proverbial forest for the trees. Work to get this person to do as you want, or he'll end up irritating you to no end.

✔ **The professional:** Typically, this type is the best person to work with. He's a deal pro who's been around the block many times, leaves emotion out of the negotiation, and works to close a deal on mutually beneficial terms.

✔ **The chronic negotiator:** This exhausting individual negotiates and fights for excruciatingly minor details over and over again. Although attention to detail is important and worth the hassle, endlessly negotiating those details eventually evokes the law of diminishing returns — you put in more time for smaller and smaller advancements. At some point the nit-picky details aren't worth the hassle. This person blasts through that point.

✔ **The renegotiator:** Don't confuse this person with the chronic negotiator (though the same person can be both). This guy's MO is to wait until the deal is seemingly done before asking (or demanding) that you change the terms. Don't give in; changing the deal at the last minute comes back to haunt you because you may be needlessly agreeing to concessions. Don't let the rush of closing a deal cloud your decision-making.

Consideration

Consideration is what Seller receives from Buyer as a result of selling the business. In its most obvious form, the consideration is cash, but cash is not the only way to pay for a business. Buyer may issue stock to Seller in exchange for the business. Seller may accept a note from Buyer (Buyer promises to pay later). Or perhaps the price of the business is contingent, and Buyer pays Seller an *earn-out* based on the performance of the business after the transaction's completion.

Consideration is not an either-or situation. In other words, the consideration may consist of some cash at closing, stock in the acquiring company, and an earn-out. Or perhaps the consideration is a note plus an earn-out. No single right or wrong way to structure a deal exists. Structuring a deal by using various forms of consideration is similar to twisting the knobs on a stereo: To get it just right, you may have to increase the bass and turn down the treble. Chapter 4 provides a much deeper dive into the ways Buyers can finance deals.

Consideration is usually a defined term and therefore capitalized in documents and so forth.

EBITDA

EBITDA (earnings before interest, tax, depreciation, and amortization) is one of those horrible business jargon terms, but it's unavoidable in M&A. EBITDA (and its variations) forms the basis for most deals.

EBITDA is the cash flow of a company without accounting for interest payments or interest income, tax bills, and certain noncash expenses (depreciation and amortization). In other words, EBITDA measures the cash generated from doing what the company is supposed to do: sell its goods or services.

Why is this number so gosh-darn important? EBITDA is often (but not always) the basis a company uses to determine its valuation (see Chapter 12) and is often a defined term in the agreements and contracts. Banks quite often include EBITDA as one of the covenants for making a loan.

EBITDA is commonly pronounced *ee*-bah-dah. And in case you're wondering, EBITDA is not a generally accepted accounting principles (GAAP) term. (Neither is adjusted EBITDA, which I cover in the following section.) However, both EBITDA and adjusted EBITDA are perfectly acceptable terms for the purposes of M&A activities.

Adjusted EBITDA

Adjusted EBITDA, which is EBITDA's wild and crazy cousin, is simply EBITDA with adjustments! For example, a business owner often takes a salary larger than industry standards, so a Buyer may want to add back part of that salary to arrive at a more reasonable level of earnings. Say the owner of a company with $20 million in revenue receives total compensation of $500,000 when the industry standard for the president of a like-sized company is $250,000. In this case, adding $250,000 (plus the pro-rated amount of income tax) back to the EBITDA figure makes sense.

Other adjustments to EBITDA may include add backs for other owner-related expenses (cars, gas, cellphone, country club, health club, and so on). If certain employees won't be part of the business after the deal is complete, adding back their salaries (and corresponding payroll tax and benefits expenses) is appropriate.

No set standard exists for adjusted EBITDA; adjusted EBITDA is whatever Buyer and Seller agree it is.

Although running certain personal expenses through a business may be common, the practice may run afoul of the IRS. Consult with your tax advisor for the proper treatment of personal expenses.

Closing

Closing is what Buyer and Seller dream of! It's why we M&A folks do what we do. In fact, it's so important that I devote an entire chapter (Chapter 16) to closing. In a nutshell, closing is the day when Buyer hands over the consideration to Seller and Seller hands over the company to Buyer.

Adhering to Basic M&A Rules and Decorum

Knowing the M&A language is important (see the earlier section "Introducing Important Terms and Phrases"), but understanding the rules of the M&A game and the decorum for its participants is equally important. Much like a poker game, the actions, the inactions, the movements, the gestures — in other words, the "tells" — are hugely important in the world of buying and selling companies.

If you're going to get into the M&A business, you have to know what to do and what to expect. Those caught off guard are those who won't be successful. Simple as that. Inadvertently (and incorrectly) broadcasting yourself as an M&A amateur can be hazardous to the health of your deal.

Follow the steps to getting a deal done

Remember that the M&A process is a serial process — transactions follow a step-by-step process. The following list gives you an overview of that process; I strongly encourage you to check out Chapter 3, where I discuss the steps in more detail.

Even though M&A follows a step-by-step process, the process often isn't linear. It goes through unforeseen twists and turns, so you have to be able to adjust.

1. **Compile a target list.**

   For Sellers, this means creating a list of potential Buyers, and for Buyers, this means a list of business owners who may be potential Sellers.

2. **Make contact with the targets.**

   Reach out to an executive or owner of a company on your list from Step 1. I prefer to make phone calls when contacting Buyers and Sellers.

3. **Send a "blind teaser" if you're selling or ask for an executive summary if you're buying.**

   If both sides (Buyer and Seller) have some level of interest in exploring a deal after the initial contact, Seller provides Buyer with a little bit of info in the form of an anonymous *teaser*. That way, Buyer isn't inundated with too much info, and Seller maintains confidentiality and anonymity.

4. **Sign a confidentiality agreement.**

   In this legal document, Buyer promises not to disclose Seller's private information or even the fact that conversations about a potential transaction are ongoing.

5. **Send an offering document if you're selling, or review the offering document if you're buying.**

   The *offering document* is the deal book, the document that contains the information about the company for sale. A well-written offering document should contain enough information for Buyer to make an offer.

6. **Ask for an indication of interest if you're selling or submit one if you're buying.**

   Buyer submits a simple letter expressing his interest in doing a deal. If the indication meets Seller's approval, she invites Buyer to a meeting.

7. **Conduct management meetings.**

   Management meetings give Buyer and Seller an opportunity to meet face to face. Seller provides Buyer with updated figures from when the offering document was written, and based on this update, Buyer may or may not submit a formal offer.

8. **Ask for a letter of intent (LOI) if you're selling or submit one if you're buying.**

   The *LOI* is the formal offer. However, it's still nonbinding, so each party can still walk away from the deal at this stage.

9. **Participate in due diligence.**

   Due diligence occurs after Buyer and Seller come to terms. During this step, Buyer reviews, examines, and inspects Seller's books, records, contracts, and more to verify that all the Seller's claims are accurate.

10. **Craft a purchase agreement.**

    During due diligence, Buyer and Seller write a purchase agreement to finalize the deal both sides negotiated. This document is final and legally binding.

11. **Attend closing.**

    After due diligence is complete and the purchase agreement is drafted, Buyer and Seller close the deal. Seller turns over the keys of the business to Buyer; Buyer forks over money to Seller.

12. **Deal with post-closing adjustments and integration.**

    A deal is not done the day it closes! In most cases, Buyer and Seller have some post-closing adjustments to navigate, and Buyer has the task of integrating the two companies.

Understand M&A etiquette

If you aren't careful, you can easily give off the wrong signal inadvertently during your M&A proceedings. Failure to follow up quickly, return calls, and give complete answers is an easy way to turn off the other side and kill a deal. Show interest in doing a deal. If you're not interested in pursuing a deal, communicate that to the other side. Here are a few more quick pointers to help you make the best impression:

✔ **Respond to a direct question with a direct answer.** Sellers most often break this rule. Instead of addressing a basic question like "What were revenues last year?" with a simple answer, Seller decides to dive into a 15-minute monologue about something that sounds impressive. In this case, Seller doesn't impress Buyer; Buyer merely gets bored and may even wonder what Seller is hiding.

✔ **Don't put on airs.** Sometimes one side is so intent on impressing the other side that it instead looks foolish, childish, and amateurish. The best course of action? Just be yourself. Don't think you need to go out of your way to impress someone. Trying to impress someone rarely works and often backfires.

✔ **If you don't know something, just say you don't know it.** You're not going to impress the other side by talking about things you don't know. If you're not sure, simply say, "I need to check into that and get back to you."

✔ **When you say you're going to do something, follow through and do it!** No explanation needed.

Know what to tell employees — and when

Ambiguity is no one's friend. The disclosure to the outside world that a company is for sale can be a devastating bit of news. Competitors may pounce and try to steal customers by implying that the sale may impact product quality or through some other scare tactic. For this and many other reasons, news of a potential business sale should be a very closely guarded secret known to only a select few until the time is right to make the announcement.

Likewise, revealing a sale or impending sale to employees is a delicate, critical matter. The timing of such an internal announcement often depends on your situation and whether you're doing the buying or the selling. The following sections give you some insight into this important topic.

When you're selling your company

If employees find out that their employer is for sale, they may get twitchy and nervous. The news that a company is for sale can cause key people to begin looking for work elsewhere. For this reason, Sellers should tell employees about a potential sale on a strictly need-to-know basis.

Staggering the release of the business sale news is acceptable. Not everyone needs to learn the news at the same time.

For example, key executives and managers need to know before lower-level employees. Exactly who that is depends on the specifics of each company. Generally, the CFO needs to know, and depending on the size of the firm, she may need to let certain key employees in on the secret. Financial disclosure is very important, and people in the accounting department can usually figure out when something is going on — they're suddenly inundated with very unusual and exacting requests for financial data!

If an employee asks you about a rumor that the company is for sale, neither confirm nor deny the rumor, but never lie. If you tell the employee that the company is not for sale and then the company makes a sale announcement two months later, that employee will feel betrayed and her trust will be broken. Instead, tell her that the owners are exploring some options, including bringing in investors to help take the company to the next level.

When you're buying companies

For Buyers, letting employees know that the company is seeking acquisitions has little downside. Think about it: How much harm can come from your competitors finding out that your company is so successful that you're exploring making acquisitions?

Treat the confidentiality clause in the confidentiality agreement very seriously. Loose lips sink ships. A sure way to scuttle a potential deal is for Buyer to talk about it with people who aren't part of the process. See Chapter 7 for more details about confidentiality.

Considering the Costs Associated with M&A

Although the main cost in any M&A transaction is most likely the cost to acquire the company (or assets), both Buyers and Sellers incur other costs. These costs range from the retinue of advisors needed to close deals, paying off debt, adjustments made after the close, and, regrettably, taxes.

Tallying advisors' fees and other costs

As I explain in Chapter 5, M&A deal-makers can't do the job alone. Any Buyer or Seller should retain a capital M&A advisor (investment banker), a lawyer, and an accountant. These people don't work for free, so their charges are part of the expenses of doing a deal. Of course, advisor fees vary based on the deal and how much work the advisor does, but here are some very general guidelines:

- ✔ A lawyer may charge anywhere from $25,000 to more than $100,000.

- ✔ An accounting firm may charge anywhere from $25,000 to $75,000.

- ✔ Investment banking fees vary, but in a very general sense, you should expect to pay roughly 3 percent to 10 percent of the transaction value.

Some deals involve other costs as well, including a real estate appraisal, an environmental testing, a database and IT examination, and a marketing analysis. Fees vary, of course, but all these functions likely cost anywhere from $10,000 to more than $100,000 apiece.

This section may seem a bit wide open, but nailing down the costs without knowing the deal is impossible. The best way to get a concrete estimate of a particular deal's fees is to speak with advisors and ask them to ballpark their expenses.

If you're worried about fees spiraling out of control, negotiate a flat fee, or a capped fee, from your advisors if possible. Not all will be willing to do this arrangement. If you get pushback, you can always agree that if the advisor does the work for a flat fee now, you'll give him the ongoing legal or accounting work post-transaction.

Paying off debt

One of the areas that Sellers often overlook is the debt of the business. Unless stipulated, a Buyer doesn't assume the debt. If a company has $5 million in long-term debt and the company is being sold for $20 million, the Seller needs to repay that debt, thus reducing the proceeds to $15 million.

Post-closing adjustments

Another area that Sellers often don't think about is the adjustments made to the deal after closing. Most often this is in the form of a *working capital adjustment,* which occurs when the *working capital* (receivables and inventory minus payables) on the estimated balance sheet Seller provides at closing doesn't match up with the actual balance sheet as of closing that the Buyer prepares at a later, agreed-upon date (usually 30 to 60 days after closing). Buyer and Seller do a working capital adjustment to *true up* (reconcile) their accounts; this adjustment is typically (though not always) minor. If the actual working capital comes in lower than the estimate, Seller refunds a bit to Buyer (often by knocking some money off the purchase price). If the figure comes in higher than the estimate, Buyer cuts Seller a check.

Say Buyer agrees to pay $10 million for a business and that Buyer and Seller agree that working capital has averaged $2 million. If Seller's estimated balance sheet shows working capital to be $1.5 million, Seller has to provide Buyer with $500,000. With a working capital adjustment, Buyer just pays Seller $9.5 million rather than $10 million.

Why take working capital adjustments? Simply put, working capital is an asset, and if less of that asset is delivered at closing, Buyer is due a discount from the agreed-upon purchase price (and vice versa). Without a working capital adjustment, Seller would have every incentive to collect all the receivables (even if done at deep discounts), sell off all the inventory, and stop paying bills, thus inflating payables. Buyer would take possession of a business that has been severely hampered by the previous owner. Buyer then has to spend money to rebuild inventory and pay off the old bills and doesn't have the benefit of receivables.

Sigh . . . talking taxes

Sellers often forget that they likely face capital gains tax on the business sale. That's one reason Sellers generally prefer stock deals; a stock deal likely has a lower amount of tax. For many (but not all) Sellers, an asset deal exposes them to double taxation: The proceeds are taxed at the time of the sale at the company level, and then the owner pays again when the company transmits the proceeds to her. (Chapter 15 gives you the lowdown on stock and asset deals.)

Speak to your financial advisor about your specific tax situation.

Determining What Kind of Company You Have

As I state throughout the book, *Mergers & Acquisitions For Dummies* is primarily for Sellers or Buyers of middle market and lower middle market companies. But what exactly constitutes those types of companies, and how do you define other company types? The distinction has to do with size, most often revenues and profits.

Then you have the issue of critical mass. *Critical mass* is a subjective term, and it simply means size: Does the company have enough employees, revenues, management depth, clients, and so on to survive a downturn? Smaller businesses most often do not have enough critical mass to be of interest to acquirers. Capital providers who may be able to help finance acquisitions will have little or no interest, too. Although critical mass differs for different companies, in a general sense a company with $30 million in revenue and $3 million in profits has a better chance of surviving a $1 million reduction in profits than a smaller firm with only $500,000 in profits.

If you're thinking about chasing acquisitions or selling your business, understanding where your business fits is important. Who may be interested in acquiring it?

Definitions vary, but for the purposes of this book, I've divided the market into sole proprietorship, small business, lower middle market company, middle market company, and large company (and beyond). Table 1-1 defines these companies at a glance; the following sections delve into more detail.

Table 1-1	M&A Company Types		
Company Type	*Annual Revenue*	*M&A Advisor*	*Number of US Companies*
Sole proprietorship	Less than $1 million	Business broker	6 million
Small business	$1 to $10 million	Business broker	1 million
Lower middle market company	$10 to $250 million	Investment banker	150,000
Middle market company	$250 to $500 million	Investment banker	3,000
Large company (and beyond)	$500 million+	Bulge bracket investment banker	3,000

Source: www.census.gov/epcd/www/smallbus.html

Sole proprietorship

Sole proprietorships are companies with revenues of less than $1 million. They're your neighborhood pizza joints, corner bars, clothing boutiques, or small legal or accounting practices.

Although these businesses are viable *going concerns* (aren't facing liquidation in the near future) and often trade hands, they're too small to be of interest to PE firms and strategic Buyers, as well as corresponding service providers who assist in M&A work. (Flip to the earlier section "Buyers" for more on these kinds of Buyers.)

Why are sole proprietorships of little or no interest to an acquirer? Simply put, buying a $1 million business and a $100 million business requires about the same amount of time and the same steps and expenses, so if you're going to go through the trouble of buying a company, you may as well get your money's worth and buy a larger concern. Making dozens of tiny acquisitions is just not worth the time or expense.

Small business

Small businesses usually have annual revenues of $1 million to $10 million. These businesses are larger consulting practices, multiunit independent retail companies, construction firms, and so on. Unless the company is incredibly profitable (profits north of $1 million, preferably $2 million or $3 million), small businesses are too small to be of interest to most strategic acquirers and PE funds.

Although PE funds and strategic acquirers are usually not interested in smaller companies, they occasionally make exceptions if a company has a unique technology or process. In these cases, the acquirer can take that technology or process and deploy it across a much larger enterprise, thus rapidly creating value.

Middle market and lower middle market company

Lower middle market companies are companies with $10 million to $250 million in annual revenue; *middle market companies* have revenues of $250 million to $500 million. These companies typically have enough critical mass to be of interest to both strategic acquirers and PE funds. Also, because these deals are larger than small business and sole proprietorship deals, M&A transaction fees are large enough to justify the involvement of an investment banking firm.

Large company (and beyond)

Companies with revenues north of $500 million are considered large, huge, gigantic, and, if revenues are well into the billions, Fortune 500. Although transactions are typically very large, the fact is very few companies are large. The middle and lower middle markets are far larger.

Firms in this category typically use *bulge bracket* investment banks. These entities are the largest of most sophisticated of investment banks. They also charge enormous fees.

The term *bulge bracket* originates from the placement of a firm's name on a public offering statement. Public offerings of securities typically involve multiple firms, and the largest firms, or managers of the offering, want their names to the left, away from the names of the smaller firms. The placement of the names looks as if they were bulging, hence the moniker.

Chapter 2

Getting Ready to Buy or Sell a Company

In This Chapter

▶ Knowing why companies often sell or buy other companies

▶ Preparing your company to engage in M&A

*O*n Seller's side, the conversation begins with any one of numerous comments: "I think it's time to retire," or "I've taken this company as far as I can take it," or maybe even, "This company is about to crater; I want to get out."

On Buyer's side, the conversation also begins with any one of numerous comments, but comments of a slightly different variety: "Organic growth isn't enough. We need to consider growth through acquisitions," or "I think buying that product line might be easier and less expensive than building one from scratch," or maybe even, "Those guys are killing us; let's see if we can buy them out."

These conversations are often held with advisors — lawyers, accountants, wealth managers — or other executives. Most often, a set of questions follows: "How do we do this?", "What's the first step?", and finally, "Do you know anyone who can help us?"

The decision to sell a business or to make an acquisition is often confusing, frustrating, time consuming, and expensive. But never fear; in this chapter, I break down the early considerations for selling or buying a company so that they feel less intimidating.

Considering Common Reasons to Sell

Many people, including many business owners, think the cash flow from a business is the only source of wealth creation. They overlook the (quite often stunning) wealth that company ownership can create. This section explores the reasons an owner may want to sell his business.

Trying to *time the market* — that is to say, trying to set your transaction to close when the economy is roaring — rarely works. Instead of trying to guess when Buyers are going to pay high prices, Sellers should focus on running the business, increasing sales, controlling costs, and improving profits. The best time to sell a company is at the intersection of salability and the need/want to sell the business and not necessarily when the market is booming.

Retirement

Retirement is one of the top reasons business owners decide to sell their businesses. The older some people get, the more they hear the siren call of Florida or Arizona. Or the Carolinas. Or . . . well, any place that doesn't involve work sounds enticing. When an owner is considering moving on to the next phase of life, that phase of life often is fueled by the proceeds from selling his business.

So the question then becomes, "How do I know when it's time to retire?" Here are some typical issues business owners consider when deciding whether to head off into the sunset:

- ✔ **Family:** Where are the kids? At home? In college? On their own? Are you still supporting them, or are they financially independent?

- ✔ **Lifestyle:** What do you want to do? Get involved with charities? Golf? Boat? Travel? Spend time with the grandkids? How much vacation time are you taking each year? If you're spending increasing amounts of time away from the business and the business can operate without you (a good thing if you want to sell it), retirement time may be nigh.

- ✔ **Finances:** Do you have enough saved to fund the lifestyle you want? Have you actually figured out that number with a professional planner, or are you just guessing?

  As far as funding retirement, business owners usually have a rough, back-of-the-envelope number in their heads. Many times, that number is little more than a guess, and that guess often is a gross overstatement of what the owner really needs to fund his retirement. Sit down with a qualified wealth manager and talk about exactly what you want to do in retirement. That wealth manager should be able to determine what you'll need to retire and live exactly as you want to live.

- ✔ **Your personal drive:** Be honest: How's your energy and drive? Yeah, I know, that sounds like one of those pharmaceutical commercials, but in all seriousness, are you still the go-getter who originally built the business? Admitting that your drive isn't what it once was and that you're putting aside your ego to think about what's best for the business and your employees is no cause for shame.

If your position is no longer necessary to support the family, you have enough to retire, your lifestyle interests are increasingly outside the confines of work, and you've simply lost your mojo and desire for work, perhaps you're ready to think about selling the business and retiring.

Buyer, you can ask a reluctant Seller if she has planned her retirement with a qualified professional. Getting an owner to create a concrete retirement plan with an advisor can be a way to bridge a valuation gap (see Chapters 12 and 21 for more on valuation and bridging valuation gaps).

Let someone else take the company to the next level

Some owners choose to sell because they've determined that they've taken the business as far as they can take it. They may not want to retire, but they also may not want to run the same company anymore. This situation happens for a few reasons:

- ✓ **Capital needs:** A growing company, even a highly profitable company, usually requires more capital than the business generates from operating cash flow. Why is that? For most companies, cash flow lags behind revenue recognition, and revenue recognition lags behind expenditures required to support that revenue. A growth company that constantly needs to reinvest in the business (new employees, equipment and supplies, and so on) essentially has the capital needs of a much larger enterprise. Owners often decide they're no longer willing to put their money at risk, and as such, they're ready for another owner, perhaps a larger and better-capitalized entity, to swoop in and take the company to the next level.

- ✓ **The segue:** I'm not talking about those fancy two-wheeled scooters here. The *segue* refers to a natural phase during the life cycle of a company: the gradual shift from a entrepreneurial company to professional company.

  As a company grows, it needs more people to manage, oversee, and support the company's new, larger size. With each new hire, the dynamic of the company changes; the entrepreneur/owner's influence on the corporate culture is diminished. This move isn't a bad thing; it's normal. The company, by necessity, has to shift from a centralized, seat-of-the-pants, CEO-is-in-on-every-decision organism into a diverse, decentralized, and highly structured entity.

  Many successful entrepreneurs simply don't have the ability (or interest) to design, implement, and run a highly structured company and thus begin to pine for the days of yore. At this point, bringing in a larger, professionally run entity may be the best way for the company to continue its upward growth.

- **Chairman of the bored:** The major battles are won, the company is on a great footing, and everyone knows his job and does it well. So where's the problem? Believe it or not, many business owners, especially those of the entrepreneurial stripe, grow exceedingly bored with a well-run company. In this situation, both the company and the owner may be better off if another, more-engaged entity takes over.

An owner selling his business so that someone else can take it to the next level isn't indicating that he can't run the business; he may be setting his sights on his next business venture. He may be one of the vaunted serial entrepreneurs you've undoubtedly heard about. The world of M&A is rife with them, and everyone is better off as a result because entrepreneurs create jobs, new products, and better services.

Divesting a division or product line

An owner doesn't have to sell the entire company; selling a division or a product line is a very common M&A activity. Some of the reasons to divest a division or product line include

- **A bad acquisition:** Here's a bit of irony for a book about M&A: Bad acquisitions are often the reason companies sell businesses, thus fueling a less-than-virtuous cycle (for Buyer's shareholders) of making acquisitions at high prices and then selling them off at low prices, over and over and over. Sometimes Buyer is too large and the acquired company gets lost in the shuffle and declines from lack of focus and support from the parent. Other times, the acquired company suffers as a result of bad decisions by Buyer. I've seen far too many acquired companies go downhill because Buyer decided to cut costs by firing the sales staff! Getting rid of the sales staff often has the effect of — surprise, surprise — reducing revenue. As the acquired company declines because of these bad decisions, it may start to lose money to the extent that Buyer eventually seeks to cut its losses by divesting the acquisition.

- **An overleveraged Buyer:** Sometimes Buyer borrows too much money to finance the acquisition, and the slightest hiccup in the economy can impair the acquired firm, thus forcing Buyer to sell off the acquired company. Actually, Buyer's lending sources most often force the issue when Buyer is unable to service the debt incurred to finance the acquisition. Buyer has to sell the acquisition (often at a bargain- basement price), or worse, the creditors may end up taking over the acquired business, resulting in a total loss for Buyer.

- **A money-losing division:** The decision to sell a weak division is often very easy and straightforward, especially if the rest of the company is strong. Losses can drag down an otherwise-strong company, so instead of throwing good money after bad, a company may simply spin off a money-losing division to get rid of it and its offending losses.

> ✔ **A lack of synergy:** Sometimes one plus one equals three. Many other times the grand plan of combining two entities doesn't pan out. For example, say a marketing services company starts up a janitorial services division. Most likely, the parent company will discover two divisions in disparate markets are spreading the company too thin. The best course of action may be to sell off one of the offending divisions and focus on the core strengths of the company.

In the hands of the correct owner, divested divisions often rebound quickly. Far from being the bad gift that just keeps on giving, selling off a division or product line that doesn't fit with Company A may be a perfect fit in the hands of Company B.

The industry is changing

The decision to sell a company in the face of a changing competitive landscape is often a very smart move. But it's a difficult move because forecasting the future is so darn difficult. When people wanted to forecast the future in days of old, they would observe the flight patterns of birds . . . and then make up something. Today, folks read newspapers and the Internet, follow their gut instincts, and try to guess what's going to happen next.

Timing the market can be a dangerous pursuit, but if a business owner believes the future involves technology developments that will render his company a has-been, or worse, obsolete, he may be ready to exit the industry by selling the business.

For Buyers, changes in the industry are always a risk. Just ask any newspaper about how the Internet changed the way news is disseminated.

I've got troubles, troubles, troubles

In the "How did I get here?" file, you find the troubled children of the M&A world, often known as *troubled companies, special situations, challenged companies,* and *turnaround opportunities.*

Troubled companies run the gamut from handyman's specials that just need a little TLC to those that should be in bankruptcy. A company that is suffering from poor management decisions but remains a *going concern* (liquidation is not on the horizon) may make a suitable acquisition for an acquirer well versed in turnaround work. On the other end of the spectrum, a company that is no longer a viable going concern should probably be liquidated by an orderly bankruptcy.

Although the reasons a company becomes troubled are virtually limitless, you can pool them into three distinct buckets:

- **Changes in the macro-economy:** A general downturn in the economy, much like the one experienced in the latter years of the first decade of the new millennium, often has a chilling effect on many companies, including those that are fundamentally sound. An otherwise healthy company that has been beaten up by the market (suffered declining revenues and profits) is often a great acquisition for a savvy acquirer.

- **Managerial mistakes:** Companies can suffer a downturn at the hands of poor management. Bad managerial decisions may or may not be tied to the general economy, and include overextending the company's operations by opening too many new locations (often, the second location constitutes "too many"), making bad hires, neglecting to reinvest in the company, throwing company resources after a bad idea, and failing to participate in a new trend in the industry.

Is this company worth the trouble?

In addition to considering the nature of the target's downturn (macro-economic, managerial, or changes in customer preferences — see the nearby section), a wise Buyer also looks at a few other key considerations when determining the value, if any, of a troubled company:

- **Is the target still profitable?** If profits are down (perhaps even greatly down) but the target is still break-even or better, a Buyer will be able to ride out the storm (because the acquisition is not burning cash) and wait for the economy to pick up. After the economy turns around, the acquired company's bottom line will be in position to snap back to its previous higher levels.

- **What are the target's trends?** Is the target continuing on a downward slope, or does it appear to be on the rebound? If the worst is behind the company, a Buyer will be in good position to pick up a bargain.

- **What's the target's top line revenue?** Even if a target is suffering losses, that company may still have a great deal of value if revenues are large enough. What's "large enough" depends, of course, but in a general sense, a $40 million revenue company has far greater residual value than a $3 million revenue company. A Buyer may be able to move the target's operations to a new facility and/or eliminate duplicate positions, thus rapidly improving the bottom line of the acquired company.

- **Does the company have a recognizable brand name or other intangible qualities?** These factors are notoriously difficult assets to value, but if a company has a recognizable name within in an industry or has done a good job of differentiating itself from the pack, that intangible may have value for the right Buyer. On the flip side, a company that's essentially a faceless name in a sea of interchangeable companies probably doesn't have much intangible value.

The good news is a company that has made managerial errors similar to those listed here may make a great pickup for the smart acquirer. The bad news is a company suffering through a series of near-fatal managerial mistakes may have burned bridges with its customers or suppliers. Consider yourself warned!

✔ **Changes in customer preferences:** In the world of troubled companies, those affected by this situation are the most troubled of them all. Think of the proverbial story about buggy whip manufacturers in the wake of the advent of the automobile. Sometimes, technology passes by a product; regardless of the product's quality, companies can't do much to regain market share when customers move on to new and better products. The word for this phenomenon is *disintermediation.*

If you own a troubled company, speak to your attorney and an M&A advisor about how to proceed with a potential M&A transaction. You may need to consider accepting a deal below your dream price because holding out for a better, future deal is risky. That better deal may never materialize, and the clock is ticking on the longevity of a troubled company.

Selling a piece of the company

Business owners don't need to sell the business and then retire or move on to other pursuits. The following sections explore some of the common reasons a business owner may want to sell a piece of the company.

Needing capital for growth

A growing company often needs more cash than it can generate from operations. If the owner doesn't want to put her own money into the company or sign a personal guarantee for a bank loan, she can raise money from an outside investor. Outside investors come in two basic flavors, control and non-control:

✔ **Control investment:** A *control investment* simply means the investor has control of the company. This situation occurs when an investor, often a venture capital or private equity fund, invests money in exchange for stock in the company. (Well, maybe stock, maybe something else. See the nearby sidebar "Structuring equity investments.") In most cases, this investment is in the form of a majority equity investment — that is, the new investor owns more than 50 percent of the equity in the company, or the bylaws of the entity are amended to grant effective control to the investor.

✔ **Non-control investment:** A *non-control investment,* often called a *minority equity investment,* is similar to a control investment, except the investor doesn't have control of the company.

Structuring equity investments

In the minds of most people, especially M&A novices, an investment comes in the form of *equity* — an investor buying stock in the company. This kind of investment makes the most sense when the company has publicly traded stock and the stock has a large-enough average daily volume to make the investment liquid.

But investments in private companies are highly illiquid because the shares don't trade on a public stock exchange, so investors are wise to structure the deal in the form of *convertible debt,* debt that they can convert to equity, usually at the time of their choosing. This way, if the company goes under, the investor gets repaid before equity holders, but she also has the option to covert her debt into to stock in the event the company goes public.

Why structure the deal this way? In the world of accounting, debt holders are higher up on the food chain that stock owners. Say a company has two investors: One person loaned $1 million to the company, and the other person owns 100 percent of the stock. If the company fails and selling the assets recoups $500,000, that money reverts to the debt holder, and the stockholder is wiped out. On the other hand, if the company is wildly successful, turning the debt into stock can be quite lucrative. Say that same company sells for $25 million. As a debt holder, the investor gets her $1 million (plus any outstanding interest) back, but as a stockholder, she'd receive the remaining $24 million.

As you may guess, Sellers tend to prefer the non-control investments, while Buyers prefer control investments. The control investor has greater recourse to change management and affect the direction of the company. The non-control investor simply goes along for the ride, with little or no recourse to exit the investment.

Diversifying assets: Take some chips off the table

Many business owners have nearly all their wealth tied up in their companies, so their finances are in serious jeopardy if the company fails. Selling a piece of the company to an investor allows an owner to create liquidity in an otherwise illiquid holding. This maneuver is called a *recap* (short for *recapitalization*).

With the right investor, an owner who has recapped her business also has a capital source for further investment in the business and/or for acquisitions. In other words, the investor may also be willing to pony up more money to invest in the business or pay for acquisitions. One of the many challenges for most business owners is the age-old question, "Do I pay myself a big fat dividend or reinvest that dough back in the company?" By selling off a piece of the company, the owner is essentially able to pay herself that big fat dividend and have a source of capital for growth.

Lastly, a recap sets up the owner to get a "second bite of the apple," that is to say, to generate a second *liquidity event* (realizing a gain from an investment by selling shares for cash) when the company is sold to another acquirer. For an owner who's looking to retire in five to ten years, the recap can be a great way to lock in a certain amount of wealth and allow herself some additional time to continue to run and grow the company, setting up a potential second payday when she sells off her remaining shares and retires or goes off to another venture.

Bringing in an outside investor to buy out a partner

Partners are a great way to build a business: One person deals with one area, such as sales, and the other handles another (say, the back-office administration and accounting). That's a good coupling. The downside to having partners is that they sometimes stop seeing eye to eye, and one of them needs to leave the business.

For a closely held business, this situation can be a problem; the partner who wants to stay may not have the money to buy out the partner who wants to leave. Bringing in an outside investor is a way to solve this problem.

Planning Ahead to Ensure a Smooth Sale

If you're thinking about selling your company, a division, or a product line, you can take a few steps to make your asset more attractive to potential Buyers. This section tips you off to some areas to look at before you sell (or even decide to sell) so that you can avoid common pitfalls.

If Seller is unable to institute operational improvements prior to a sale process, she should inform Buyer where he can make additional improvements. Getting Buyer to pay for the improvements he's bringing to the table is often a difficult proposition, but it's usually worth a try. At a minimum, Buyer will view the suggested list of improvements as a sign of goodwill, thus increasing the odds of a successful closing.

Clean up the balance sheet

One of the biggest obstacles to getting a deal done is a messy balance sheet. Now, don't freak out about the accounting. Repeat after me: Accounting is your friend.

One of the key figures on a balance sheet is the *current ratio,* or the difference between current assets and current liabilities. Anything labeled *current* on the balance sheet is essentially the same thing as cash. So what are these cash or almost-cash items?

✔ **Assets:** Cash, accounts receivable, inventory, deposits, and prepaid expenses

✔ **Liabilities:** Accounts payable, accrued expenses (those not yet paid), and the current portion of any loans (interest, and perhaps some principal)

The current ratio measurement is important because if the current liabilities exceed current assets, the company is considered *illiquid,* which means that if all the current creditors demand immediate payment, the company doesn't have enough current assets to pay those demands. And if you're trying to sell a company, that's not going to endear you to most Buyers.

To fix up your balance sheet in preparation for a sale, follow these steps:

1. **Collect your receivables.**

   Buyers check to see whether Sellers are diligent about this collection (at least, they should). If the terms are *net 30* (that is, money is due within 30 days), as a Seller you should be collecting those receivables within that time frame. If customers are taking longer to pay, that's effectively a use of cash.

   Slow collections on receivables may mean Buyer has to obtain a *revolver loan*, a loan designed to help companies with fluctuations in cash flow. Loans aren't free; therefore Buyer may demand to reduce the purchase price to help defray the cost of that loan.

   Buyer will likely assume your working capital, namely receivables and payables, as part of a transaction. Buyer will probably want all the receivables but may make you grant a discount on overdue accounts. Buyer will also only assume payables if they're current or *within terms.* For example, if a vendor gives you net 30 days terms but you've been paying net 45 days for years without complaint from the vendor, you can make a case that the actual (or *de facto*) terms are 45 days.

2. **Make sure inventory is all saleable.**

   If you have obsolete or slow-moving inventory, talk to your accountant about how best to write off this inventory. Writing off inventory decreases the company's earnings, so you want to get this step out of the way before you go through a sale process. If you write off any inventory prior to a sale process, you should be able to discuss the rationale you used for those write-offs as well as the steps you've taken to prevent future build-ups of excess or obsolete inventory.

   You put yourself in a precarious position as Seller if, during the due diligence phase, Buyer discovers a boatload of obsolete inventory that isn't reflected on the valuation. In this scenario, Buyer will likely attempt to *renegotiate* (that is, argue for a different deal, probably with a lower price) because earnings are now effectively lower in light of the inventory the company needs to write off.

If you want more information about the wonderful world of accounting, check out *Accounting For Dummies,* 4th Edition, by John A. Tracy, CPA (Wiley). Or you can talk to your accountant.

Pay off debt

Another hurdle in selling a company is taking care of your long-term debt. Many Sellers either "conveniently" forget about the debt or hope/assume that Buyer will simply assume the debt no questions asked. Here's a little bit of expert advice: That ain't gonna work! The long-term debt of the business is Seller's obligation.

Don't despair if your business has unattractive long-term debt; you have some options: Retire that debt now, make a plan to retire that debt before closing, or retire that debt at closing. Although Buyer can assume the long-term debt of an acquired company, Buyer will probably simply deduct the amount of debt from the proceeds of the sale. For all practical purposes, if Buyer assumes the debt, Seller is retiring that debt at closing.

If you're worried that your company's long-term debt may block a sale, here's a tip for negotiating with the lending source. Call the lender, explain that a deal to sell the company is on the table but may be in jeopardy because of the company's debt load. Ask whether the lender would accept a percentage of the amount owed (60, 70, 80, or whatever) within a certain time period (such as 45 days) and then consider the debt paid in full if you meet those new terms. Tell the lender that if you fail to meet the terms of this new agreement, your deal reverts to the original 100 percent. The lender, if it accepts the deal, gets the benefit of getting part of its money repaid right away (or in the near future), and if that immediate repayment doesn't materialize, the lender hasn't lost anything. It's an offer some lenders won't be able to refuse. If the lender agrees to this gambit, be sure to memorialize the agreement in writing.

Address legal issues

A wise business owner settles any outstanding lawsuits before a sale and is prepared to talk about those lawsuits and their outcomes. Planning to gloss over or omit mention of lawsuits, or simply expecting Buyer to uncover a lawsuit (or criminal investigation) by itself, isn't smart. These actions indicate that you're negotiating in bad faith, which means you've just kneecapped your credibility. Ideally, you want to be able to honestly say, "We are not aware of any pending lawsuits or investigations."

The other major legal issue for many deals is the legal organization of the company. In other words, is it an LLC or a corporation (and if it's a corporation, is it an S-corporation or a C-corporation?). These distinctions are important because they affect the taxation of the business.

An LLC and an S-corporation allow for a single layer of taxation, which means the government taxes a sale of assets once, most likely at the prevailing capital gains rate.

The Seller of a C-corporation, on the other hand, gets hit with two layers of taxation. First, she pays on the proceeds of the sale at the corporation level, and then when the remainder of those proceeds is distributed to the shareholders, the shareholders also pay tax, most likely at the capital gains rate. This double-whammy means the shareholders of a C-corporation many be looking at receiving less than 50 percent of the gross proceeds. Ouch.

Sellers should speak with their tax advisors prior to pursuing a business sale and set a plan well in advance of the decision to sell. Depending on the company's legal organization, converting to a different legal entity may make sense tax-wise. But starting early enough is key: When converting from a C-corporation to an S-corporation, you may need a full decade before the full benefit accrues. And don't forget to talk to a wealth manager before the decision to go through a sale process. An able advisor can provide you with a structure for a deal that minimizes your tax burden. Don't wait until after the deal closes to talk with a wealth advisor, or you may be unhappily surprised.

Trim staff and cut dead weight

If you want to maximize the company's valuation, you need to maximize the company's profits. One way is to reduce and eliminate wasteful expenditures, and because the largest expense of most businesses is personnel, you may have to make some difficult decisions.

Please don't read this suggestion as a license to be capricious or cruel. Don't start firing staffers simply for the sake of cutting positions. Make a determination of what personnel you need to run the business and simply execute on that decision.

Don't be afraid to be tough. No one likes to let people go; it's difficult. But if certain employees aren't pulling their weight or aren't performing up to expectations, you need to lay them off. If an otherwise-good employee is in a low/no value position, either move that employee into a productive role or bite the bullet and let him go.

If some staffers are on the edge, give them a chance to improve. Set realistic goals and give them the tools to succeed. My experience has been people respond to this challenge in one of two ways: Either they step up and improve their performance to a tolerable level or they quit. Either option is a suitable outcome.

Increase sales

The other side — and happy side — of the "improve profits" coin is higher revenue. The profitability of your company improves when revenues increase and expenses stay the same. It's simple math, of course, but you can't follow the road to higher revenues until you push your salespeople and perhaps provide a different (that is, more lucrative) commission plan.

Don't settle for short-term fixes that will likely go away when the new owner takes over. That's why permanent plans, as opposed to a one-time, short-term stimulus plan, pay better dividends over time. Set the stage for long-term success. A savvy Buyer sees a short-term gimmick for what it's worth and argues for a lower transaction price.

Quantify owner's expenses and other add backs

Most business owners and executives are familiar with the term *generally accepted accounting principles,* or GAAP. Closely held businesses often utilize a different version, colloquially called FAAP, or *family accepted accounting principles.* Owners of closely held businesses often run personal expenses, such as car, country and other clubs, travel, cellphone, meals, and any other expense that isn't really a business-related expense, through the company. If you're one of those owners, talk with your accountant about how best to quantify and present those expenses.

These owner expenses are add backs to the all important EBITDA calculation. Providing these *add backs*, or a "roadmap of value" as I like to call it, helps provide Buyer with the ability to see the true value in the business and helps improve his willingness to pay for that value.

Although this section shows an owner or executive how to treat owner expenses prior to a sale, I don't actually advocate running personal expenses through a business. If the business is audited by the IRS, those expenses may be disallowed and the owners may face penalties.

In addition to owner expenses, you may have other add backs to account for, including one-time expenses such as severance, a lawsuit settlement, or a once-in-a-lifetime capital investment (for example, buying equipment with an extremely long useful life). The proverbial "acts of God" also fall into this category.

The rule of thumb when analyzing whether an expense is one time is simple: What are the odds of this expense happening again? The higher the odds, the less the ability you'll be able to claim it as one time. If the so-called one-time expense happens year after year, it's not a one-time expense, and you'll have a difficult time arguing for that add back.

Owner, make thyself expendable

Companies with the greatest value to Buyers are those companies where ownership is completely, totally, and utterly replaceable. Not surprisingly, that's a spiky pill for many owners to swallow. Heck, the thought of being utterly replaceable is spiky for almost anybody! But ego aside, think of the issue this way: How can you expect to get top dollar for selling your company if the company can't operate without you?

Here are a couple ways you can make yourself replaceable as an owner:

- ✔ **Train other managers to run the company without you.** Empower them to make decisions, and trust them to work independently and make their own decisions.

- ✔ **Design and implement systems that remove any ad hoc decision-making systems.** You're not trying to cripple the decision-making of others; instead, you're providing a framework for employees to make decisions so that they can do so without constantly running to you.

Exploring Typical Reasons to Acquire

Since time immemorial, mankind has grown through acquisitions. Granted, those early acquisitions were really conquests, but in recent years, empire-building has focused on acquiring companies.

As I note in Chapter 1, an acquisition allows a company to skip the growth stage and buy existing sales and profits. For this reason and those in the following sections, a company may choose to buy other companies instead of relying on organic growth.

Make more money

Make no mistake: The pursuit of money is a main reason for making acquisitions. Although it may be the most base and crass of reasons, it's an extremely valid one. Making more money is a noble pursuit. Profits make shareholders happy and therefore keep the vultures from descending upon high-flying executives' careers.

Gain access to new products and new markets

Acquiring a company with a similar product allows the acquirer to increase its share of the market. Being a larger player in an industry can have benefits, such as the ability to negotiate better prices or terms from suppliers and vendors, increase awareness to customers (larger companies typically are better known than small companies), and raise prices.

Buying a company may also allow the acquirer to introduce its products into new markets, as well as introduce the acquired company's products into Buyer's markets.

Implement vertical integration

Vertical integration means buying a supplier or an end user of your product. An ice cream manufacturer that buys a dairy farm is vertically integrated. The benefits may include better pricing (the ice cream manufacturer doesn't have to pay the dairy farm's markup) and control of raw materials.

The downside is that the acquired company may service other competitors. If that dairy farm also supplies other ice cream manufacturers, those competitors may balk at buying from their rival. This situation is a *channel conflict*. (And you thought that was when you and your spouse argue over what program to watch!)

Take advantage of economies of scale

You're likely to hear this term countless times. *Economies of scale* simply means that as a company grows larger, the fixed expenses stay the same (or increase far more slowly than the top line revenue). Therefore, the larger the company becomes, the more profitable it becomes.

Buy out a competitor

If you can't beat 'em, buy 'em! If Company A is killing a Company B in the marketplace, Company B may determine simply buying Company A is the best way to make the competition go away.

Prepping before an Acquisition

A company thinking about making acquisitions just doesn't wake up one day and close a deal. Successfully acquiring other companies takes some planning and preparation; I cover the vital considerations in this section.

Determine the appropriate type of acquisition

How much revenue does the target need to have? Does the target need to have a minimum profitability level, and if so, what is it? Are you willing to consider acquiring a money-losing operation? Should the acquired company be a product extension or a new product? Should the acquisition allow you to vertically integrate? (See "Gain access to new products and new markets" and "Implement vertical integration" sections earlier in the chapter for more on these topics.) These are only a few of the possible questions to consider when choosing a potential acquisition.

Unless you have a clear idea of what you want to buy, you probably won't successfully close a deal. Many strategic and financial Buyers often take a "show me everything" approach when looking for acquisitions. The odds of finding the right fit are exceedingly low when you haven't defined the parameters of a right fit.

Get your company's balance sheet in order

How's your balance sheet? No, really, be honest. How is it? If your balance sheet is a mess, your company isn't ready to do deals. Companies able to successfully do deals have strong cash positions and little or no debt. Working capital should be positive, and the current ration should be at or above the industry norm. (The "Clean up the balance sheet" section earlier in the chapter gives you some balance sheet basics.)

Have the money lined up

Have your sources of cash ready to go before you begin the acquisition process. Sure, a strong balance sheet with lots of cash is very helpful, but an acquirer doesn't necessarily have to use its own money to fund 100 percent of a deal. Depending on the acquirer's situation, a line of credit from a bank, a *mezzanine fund* (a lender subordinate to the bank loan), and/or a private equity fund may be able to help with the financing.

Although you don't have to have a private equity fund or mezzanine fund as a financial partner to make an acquisition, failure to line up your sources of financing ahead of time may mean you're unable to close a deal, resulting in wasted time for both you and Seller. Also, reputations travel because people talk. A Buyer unable to close a deal because of a lack of forethought sullies its reputation.

Set up an acquisition chain of command

In order to successfully complete acquisitions, you need to determine who's taking what role. If you're handling the acquisition internally, give team members specific jobs: compiling the target list, making the calls, negotiating and structuring the deals, and so on. If you're bringing in an outside firm to perform some or all of these tasks, appoint an internal person to be the main interface with the intermediary. Following this chain of command at all times helps the acquisition process go smoothly and efficiently by eliminating poor communication and duplicate steps.

Designate a specific individual as the deal point-person to have all of the interaction with Seller or Seller's representative. All requests and questions go through this one person to prevent poor communication, duplicated steps, and a frustrated Seller.

Buying a Company from a PE Firm

In some situations, you may consider acquiring a company from a *private equity* (PE) *firm,* a pool of money that buys companies with the intention of reselling them later for a sizable profit. PE firms can be very motivated Sellers. But be warned: They're also extremely crafty deal-makers. After all, buying and selling companies is their industry. They're experts. (Head to Chapter 4 for the lowdown on PE firms.) The following sections offer some considerations to keep in mind as you look at dealing with a PE firm.

Understanding why PE firms sell

Because PE firms are in the game to make money (and who isn't?), a PE firm will eventually be looking to exit its investment (which may now include some add-on acquisitions).

PE firms also hear the constant ticking of the *internal rate of return* (IRR), one of the key metrics they like to flaunt when raising capital. In a nutshell, the longer a PE firm holds an investment, the greater the chance the IRR will be lower than the PE firm prefers.

Evaluating a PE firm's portfolio company

I provide plenty of factors to consider in acquisitions throughout this book, but here are a few specific suggestions to look at for a PE firm's portfolio companies.

✔ **Does the company fit with your goals?** This question is pretty basic, of course, but as Buyer, take care when evaluating the fit of a portfolio company with your company. Despite the great case the PE firm may make for the portfolio company, a company that doesn't fit your goals isn't that great a deal.

✔ **How will the company's earnings affect your earnings?** If the acquired company's earnings increase your earnings, they're *accretive;* if they decrease your company's earnings, they're *dilutive.* Decide whether a potential earnings hit matters to your company. Consider also whether the acquired company will eventually be able to generate higher earnings for the entire firm if earnings take an initial hit.

✔ **Is the company actually an integrated set of other companies?** PE firms often cobble together multiple companies into one integrated firm. This setup is perfectly fine, and PE firms often do a wonderful job of integrating, but you need to be wary of just how well organized formerly disparate companies have been integrated.

✔ **How long has an integrated company been operating (since the last acquisition)?** If the acquired company is actually a group of formerly independent companies, don't make an acquisition too quickly. Waiting awhile (at least a year) to make sure these formerly independent companies are operating as a cohesive unit is a good idea.

Chapter 3

Previewing the Generally Accepted M&A Process

*A*lthough the truism "always be prepared" applies to just about everything in life, it's especially true in mergers and acquisitions. To the uninitiated, the world of M&A may seem to be a Wild West of sorts: chaotic, bizarre, and full of strange nomenclature and acronyms. But believe it or not, the buying and selling of companies has a clearly defined process. To be a successful Buyer or Seller, you need to understand how that process works so that you can think many steps ahead and plan accordingly — just like a chess game, but without the checkered board.

In this chapter, I break down the phases involved in a typical M&A deal as well as define the two methods of selling a business: auction and negotiation. I also look at the constantly changing power balance between Buyer and Seller in a deal and provide suggestions on preserving as much power as possible in less-than-ideal circumstances.

Take Note! The M&A Process in a Nutshell

You don't wake up one morning and suddenly decide you want to buy or sell a business. A good deal of planning occurs before Buyer or Seller can undertake the process of buying or selling a business, let alone successfully close a deal.

The number of steps in the M&A process may vary depending on the type of deal you're negotiating (a quick auction versus a drawn-out negotiated sale, for example), but overall the process more or less remains the same. That's why being well versed in the generally accepted steps in the following sections is so important. M&A professionals have honed these steps over the years, and each step has a specific purpose.

The process to buy or sell a company isn't as linear as you may think, and it often takes longer and costs more than you expect. These steps aren't carved in stone, nor are they the be-all and end-all. Don't become rigid in your approach to doing deals; feel free to riff on these steps and write your own variations on a theme. The key points are to disseminate information in a timely, orderly, and appropriate manner and to close mutually beneficial deals.

To keep the process moving along, Seller needs to create a line in the sand by instilling due dates. The first due date will be for indications of interest. Buyers will almost always be late in submitting their indications, so Sellers are wise to allow for a little padding of time.

Step 1: Compile a target list

If ownership decides to sell or make acquisitions following discussions with advisors, family, friends, and management, the process begins by identifying prospective Buyers or Sellers. The key word here is *prospective;* these businesses may or may not be interested in doing a deal. You begin to make that determination in the following steps. Chapter 6 provides a much deeper dive into the process of researching, compiling, and culling a list of targets.

For a successful acquisition or sale campaign, I strongly recommend having at least 75 prospects, and preferably more than 100. Having a small universe of prospects simply lowers the odds of finding the right deal, but a list of many more than 150 targets gets untenable.

Step 2: Make contact with the targets

If the target list seems viable enough to warrant going through an M&A process (see the preceding section), Seller or Buyer begins to reach out to the targets. Some people prefer a passive approach (e-mails or letters), while others prefer a more assertive approach (phone calls). I prefer making calls when contacting Buyers (believe me, most of them are literally sitting by the phone waiting for a Seller to call). Contacting Sellers is far trickier. Check out Chapter 6 for more on contacting Buyers and Sellers.

Avoid hyperbole at all costs. Although I'm a big fan of creating a sense of urgency and having a call to action in my correspondence, telling prospective Buyers they need to act quickly or else they'll lose out on the greatest thing since sliced bread makes you sound like a snake oil salesman.

Step 3: Send or receive a teaser or executive summary

If Buyer wants to learn more about the company for sale, Seller will forward a teaser to Buyer. The *teaser* (sometimes called the *blind teaser*) is an anonymous document that provides just enough nonconfidential information to pique the interest of Buyer. As the name implies, the teaser is designed to tease Buyer into a frenzied state of wanting to know more.

An *executive summary* is similar to a teaser but isn't anonymous. These documents are the doorway that leads to the other steps in the process. Chapter 8 provides a lot more information on these documents.

Step 4: Execute a confidentiality agreement

If, after reading the teaser (discussed in the preceding section), Buyer is interested in learning more about Seller, the two parties often execute a *confidentiality agreement* (CA). (On planet Let's Use More Words, this document is called a *nondisclosure agreement* [NDA]). Essentially, Buyer promises to not share any of Seller's confidential and nonpublic information with anyone other than Buyer's advisors. Chapter 7 offers a detailed look at all the ins and outs of confidentiality.

The confidentiality agreement doesn't just extend to confidential information. As part of the agreement, Buyer usually agrees to not even mention that M&A discussions are ongoing.

Step 5: Send or review the confidential information memorandum

If the confidentiality issue in the preceding section is socked away and settled, Seller provides Buyer with a boatload of information, usually in the form of a book known as an *offering document, deal book,* or some similar title. The offering document provides a huge amount of informational about Seller: financials, customer info, employee info, products, marketing, operations, legal, real estate and fixed assets, and more. The offering document should provide sufficient information for Buyer to make an initial offer. I cover offering documents further in Chapter 8.

Step 6: Solicit or submit an indication of interest

If the Buyer reviews the offering document (see the preceding section) and is interested in pursuing a deal, Buyer indicates that interest in the aptly named *indication of interest* (IOI). An IOI provides a valuation range (not a specific price) Buyer would consider paying for the company, as well as some other basic info (estimated closing date, source of funds, basic composition of the purchase price, and so on). An IOI is nonbinding, which means it can't be enforced in a court of law. See Chapter 9 for more.

Step 7: Conduct management meetings

When the Indication of Interest covered in the preceding section is acceptable to Seller, the next step is for Buyer to meet with Seller's management team. Seller conducts the meeting, which provides a financial update as well as updates to any other issues that may be pertinent for Buyer, such as new customers, lost customers, new hires, new product launches, litigation, and so on. The meeting also allows Buyer and Seller to interact and engage in question and answer sessions — and to gauge whether both sides can play well together. Chapter 10 gives you the lowdown on these meetings.

Step 8: Write or review the letter of intent

If Buyer's management has met Seller's management as noted in the preceding section and is interested in making a firm offer, the next step is the vaunted *letter of intent* (LOI). The LOI is a nonbinding document that forms the basis of the final deal. It contains a specific purchase price (rather than a range) and provides the steps needed to close the deal. The LOI usually includes an *exclusivity clause,* which means Seller can no longer negotiate with other Buyers. Flip to Chapter 13 for details on making and receiving offers.

Exclusivity is an enormous issue! Grant it carefully.

Step 9: Perform due diligence

When Seller accepts Buyer's LOI (see the preceding section), the process moves to *due diligence,* where Seller discloses all its contracts, financials, customer info, employee info, and much more to Buyer. These days, the due diligence info is usually provided in a secure, online data room. Seller's investment banker manages this process, which I cover more thoroughly in Chapter 14.

Step 10: Draft the purchase agreement

If due diligence (see the preceding section) is progressing reasonably well, the parties draft a purchase agreement. The *purchase agreement* is the final document, which means it's the binding document (at long last!). The lawyers for Buyer and Seller work out the details of the purchase agreement; see Chapter 15 for more.

When drafting the purchase agreement, make sure the lawyers hammer out the legal details and *only* the legal details. All of the business particulars should be handled by the investment bankers. Lawyers should never, ever, upon pain of death, negotiate a single business term! It's not their job. Lawyers aren't the deal-makers; they're the people who make sure the deal-makers don't agree to something illegal or unenforceable in a court of law. Business and legal issues are two separate worlds and each should be handled by the appropriate party.

Step 11: Show up for closing

When the parties are ready to wrap up the deal, both sides meet (usually in a lawyer's office) to close the deal. It's mainly a sign-this, sign-that kind of a day, much like the closing for buying a house. After all the documents are signed, the money is wired to the appropriate parties, and the deal is done! Chapter 16 provides more info on closing.

Step 12: Deal with post-closing adjustments and integration

After the deal actually closes, the real work begins: tying up the loose ends of the deal in the post-closing adjustments and integrating the acquired company into Buyer's company. See Chapters 17 and 18 for more on how to do just that.

For those of you who successfully complete the M&A process, there's a special Step 13, a hidden track on the M&A CD, if you will: enjoying your success. One of the benefits of successful deal-making is the money, the wealth creation, and the self-actualization that comes from success. Before you think that's merely a joyful ode to money making . . . well, okay, it is. But more than that, successfully doing deals means creating wealth and opportunities for others. A consummate deal-maker expands the economy as she improves her personal balance sheet. The best deals, where both sides make money, come from the value creation of hard work and ingenuity and the hardnosed ability to negotiate mutually beneficial deals. If you don't believe that — if you can't sleep well at night because engaging in M&A activities bogs you down with some sort of guilt — you may want to find a new line of work.

Exploring Two Types of M&A Processes: Auction versus Negotiation

The world of M&A breaks down into two large camps: negotiated sales and auctions. Although they're similar (they both follow the same steps outlined in "Take Note! The M&A Process in a Nutshell" earlier in the chapter), auctions and negotiated sales have a few key differences.

✔ An *auction* is a business sale process where a group of Buyers makes their final and best bids and the company goes to the best bid. So what does best bid mean? In most cases, the *best bid* is the highest price, although Sellers do examine other factors, including Buyer's ability to close a deal, how much of the sale price is in cash, and when Seller will receive that cash.

For example, say Seller is examining two bids. One bid has a total deal value of $10 million, with $1 million in cash at closing and $9 million in the form of a *note* (a promise to pay later). The other offer is for $5 million, all cash at closing. Which is the better deal? Perhaps the first bid ($10 million total value) makes the most sense; after all, it's more money. But depending on the situation, the second bid, although lower, may make more sense; perhaps Seller is willing to forgo a higher potential price for the certainty of more cash today.

✔ A *negotiated sale* occurs when Seller (or Seller's advisor) talks with each Buyer and perhaps tailors the pitch to highlight those benefits that will be most appealing to each individual Buyer. A negotiated sale still has elements of an auction (numerous participants making bids), but a negotiated sale involves a lot more hand-holding of the Seller.

Which process is better depends on the situation. An auction usually works best for larger, well-known companies. In these cases, Buyer may be willing to pay a premium for a famous company.

A negotiated sale works best for smaller companies or companies with losses or thin profits.

Some Buyers shy away from auctions. Although an auction can be a great way to sell a company, the auction may result in an unintended consequence: no bids!

Who Has It Easier, Buyer or Seller?

Anyone who has worked a sales job has probably dreamed about being on the other side: the buyer, the person who seemingly has all the power. Buyers, after all, are the ones who pick and choose. They get to interview numerous possible vendors and pick the one that delivers the best combination of price, quality, and, often, the intangibles of an interpersonal connection.

But in mergers and acquisitions, that scenario gets flipped on its head. Buying companies is actually more difficult than selling companies because the M&A Buyer plays the role of vendor; Buyer has to market its deal to Seller the way a traditional salesperson would sell his or her product. The following sections look at each of these positions.

Selling is easy if you know what you're doing

M&A is a strange industry because it's one of the few that I can think of where the selling functions are in many ways easier than the buying functions.

Simply put, quality companies with critical mass are in demand. (For more on what that means, see the nearby sidebar.) Suffice it to say that after a company gets above a certain revenue level and especially a certain profit level, Buyers of all shapes and sizes start chasing it. When an owner decides she wants to put her company up for sale, she stands a good chance of being in the driver's seat. Assuming she follows the proper M&A process (as I outline in the earlier section "Take Note! The M&A Process in a Nutshell"), she'll likely have multiple offers, thus putting her in a position of control.

Although I call selling "easy" earlier in the chapter, keep in mind that that's a relative term. Selling is typically easier than trying to make acquisitions, but selling a company is fraught with challenges, difficulties, ups and downs, and sheer white-knuckle poker playing. For more on actually navigating a sale, check out Chapter 11.

What's a quality company of critical mass?

Although definitions vary from Buyer to Buyer, *critical mass* simply means a company that has size, scale, and scope. In other words, it isn't a start-up or an unprofitable company selling a product indistinguishable from the competition.

In a very general sense, critical mass may mean any of the following:

✔ **Revenues north of $10 million (and the farther north, the better):** Larger companies usually have more critical mass than smaller companies because they're often able to withstand an economic decline. They have more company to go around! Nothing is particularly magical about $10 million other than the fact that it's larger than, say, $1 million. But after companies pass this threshold, they're often considered lower middle market companies, which simply means they're not a small company anymore. An unprofitable company with enough revenue may even have value to the right Buyer. Think of it this way: Say two companies each have an annual loss of $2 million. Everything else being equal, would you rather take Company A with $5 million in revenue, or Company B, with $100 million in revenue?

✔ **EBITDA north of $2 million:** Similar to revenues, the higher the EBITDA (earnings before interest, tax, depreciation, and amortization), the more critical mass for the company. Companies with large-enough profits will always be in vogue with Buyers. A company with only $500,000 in EBITDA may be more susceptible to an economic downturn than a company with $5 million in EBITDA.

✔ **Access to C-level decision-makers at clients:** *C-level executives* are the top-ranking (CEO, CFO, and the like) executives at companies. Selling products or services into the executive ranks is often a coveted level of access, and companies that lack that sophistication may be willing to pay a premium for it. Wouldn't you rather have the CEO, CFO, or some other high-ranking official than some low-level flunky as your decision-maker?

✔ **A strong name, good reputation, and/or brand awareness:** Many Buyers are interested in obtaining these intangibles. In fact, a solid brand and reputation can help an otherwise troubled company generate a good price during a sale.

Buying is difficult even if you know what you're doing

Believe it or not, buying a company is more difficult than selling one. Owners of companies are bombarded on an almost daily basis from all sorts of Buyers. I'm constantly amazed by the fact that these would-be Buyers, be they private equity firms or investment bankers working for a strategic Buyer, are often oblivious to the fact that a Buyer is little more than a commodity to the owner of company with $10 million or more in revenue. Buyers are a dime a dozen.

An added difficulty in buying a company is that Sellers fall into two basic camps: those who know they want to sell and those who don't want to sell. Deals offered by those who know they want to sell are difficult deals for Buyers because a wise Seller has gone through the M&A process I cover in this chapter and has hopefully generated interest from multiple parties, thus putting her in the enviable position of having options.

Those who have no interest in selling are difficult deals because they aren't looking to do a deal! They aren't selling their business. Period. And if the company has critical mass — that is to say, sizeable revenues or profits or a strong brand name — the owner is tired of receiving a constant barrage of phone calls, e-mails, and letters from Buyers of all shapes and sizes who all say the same thing: "We have money, we're different, and we want to buy your company."

Even worse, many of these so-called Buyers aren't seriously looking to buy and instead are on fishing expeditions and have entrusted the cold-calling to the lowest-level executive they can find. Many times, the person making the phone call is fresh out of business school, which means he probably hasn't yet learned any real-life business lessons.

Buyers, take note: Never say "We have money, we're different, and we want to buy your company." Everyone says that! For tips on how to better entice an otherwise uninterested business owner, see Chapter 6.

Another obstacle for Buyers looking for acquisitions is that targets are quite often the Buyers' competitors. Understandably, the owners and executives of these companies are extremely reluctant to talk to a competitor, let alone give up sensitive information such as revenues, profits, customer data, sales compensation, and the like.

Following the Power Shifts in the M&A Process

During a typical M&A process, the power shifts from Buyer to Seller and back again many times depending on which party has more riding on a particular stage of the deal. This swing in motivation, plus a little poker-esque bluffing and tell-reading, means the power balance in a deal is constantly shifting.

Being cognizant of the power issue is extremely important as the savvy deal-maker navigates the sea of deals because, as negotiations progress, who's in power one day may not be who's in power the next.

Looking at the factors of motivation

The most motivated party in a deal is the one most likely to cede power to the other side to make sure the deal goes through. But what exactly provides this motivation? Several factors:

- ✔ **Interest:** The side that has the most interest in doing a deal probably has the least power because that party will be most willing to compromise in order to get a deal done.

   Although you don't want to appear overly interested to do a deal, you don't want to inadvertently appear blasé, either. Failure to show interest, respond to requests, and answer questions may cause the other side to call a halt to the process because it's concluded you're not interested.

- ✔ **Desperation:** Nothing spells "weak negotiating position" like the smell of a desperate owner who is desperate to do a deal desperately quick! Desperation often indicates an impending business failure, thus greatly increasing the willingness of the owner to accept a deal, any deal.

- ✔ **Boredom:** A business owner who is bored and wants to move on to something else can unwittingly become a highly motivated Seller. Broadcasting that boredom to potential Buyers puts those Buyers in a huge power position.

- ✔ **Time:** Time is the wild card in the motivation game. A Seller who wants (or needs) to do a deal right now will likely cede power to Buyer. Conversely, the longer the process takes, the more the power may flow back to Seller because Buyer becomes the one who has invested time and money and increasingly needs to get the deal across the finish line.

- ✔ **Money:** Deals don't get done for free. Buyer and Seller have to retain advisers. The more money one side spends, the more that side (often Buyer) wants to get a deal done so as to not waste that money. Buyers are most often guilty of overspending.

   The more money a side spends during the process, the greater the odds are that that side will want to get a deal, any deal, across the finish line. No one wants to spend money and have nothing to show for it.

Understanding who has power

Typically, Seller has a lot of power early in the process. As the party being courted, Seller controls whether meetings occur and whether information is exchanged.

One way Buyers can get more power early in the process is by submitting a *pre-emptive bid*, making a bid before other Buyers have made their bids and knocking out all other possible suitors. Eliminating competition is a boon for any Buyer and puts Seller in a vulnerable position. If Buyer subsequently decides against closing a deal, Seller has lost time otherwise spent talking with multiple Buyers and thus finds itself back at square one.

Even without a pre-emptive bid, the power balance swings toward Buyer when the parties sign an LOI with an exclusivity clause. (You can brush up more on these terms in "Step 8: Write or review the letter of intent" earlier in the chapter.) At this point, Seller can no longer speak with other Buyers.

If Seller accepts a pre-emptive bid from Buyer, Seller should insist on removing the exclusivity clause from the LOI. Short of that, Seller should include language in the LOI that ends the exclusivity period and allows the Seller to speak with other Buyers in the event that Buyer attempts to change the price or terms of the deal.

From the signing of the LOI through closing, Buyer most often calls the shots. However, the longer the due diligence and purchase agreement drafting takes, the more the power may shift back toward Seller because Buyer is investing more and more money as the process goes on.

Some Buyers, most notoriously private equity (PE) firms, retain advisors whom they pay after the deal closes. The longer the process takes, the more those bills accumulate. PE firms typically pay those bills with the proceeds from the closing. And guess what? The PE firm managers making all of these decisions probably don't have the money at ready access; they need to request cash from various sources (the fund itself, the fund's limited partners, and other lending sources such as banks).

If a deal falls apart and doesn't close, the firm employees working that deal probably don't have the ability to simply write checks. They have to go back to their bosses, tails between their legs, and ask for money. The employee's spiel goes something like the following (apologies to Monty Python's "Dead Parrot" sketch):

> Hi, boss. Bad news. The deal is no more. It has ceased to be. The deal expired and has gone to meet its maker. It's an ex-deal. Can I have a couple hundred grand to pay off all the professional services firms that did all kinds of work on this deal that turned out to be all for naught?

As you can imagine, that's not an enviable position to be in.

To give you a visual of all these power shifts, Figure 3-1 details who has the power in the various steps of the M&A process. For more on the steps themselves, check out "Take Note! The M&A Process in a Nutshell" earlier in this chapter.

	Who has control?			
	Seller's Process		Buyer's Process	
	Seller	Buyer	Seller	Buyer
Step 1: Target list	X			X
Step 2: Contact with targets	X		X	
Step 3: Teaser	X		X	
Step 4: Confidentiality agreement	X	X	X	X
Step 5: Confidential information memorandum	X		X	
Step 6: Indication of interest		X		X
Step 7: Management meetings	X	X	X	
Step 8: Letter of intent		X		X
Step 9: Due diligence	X		X	
Step 10: Purchase agreement		X		X
Step 11: Closing		X		X
Step 12: Post-closing adjustments and integration		X		X

Figure 3-1:
Following the power during the M&A process.

Reading the other party's situation

Whether you're a Buyer or Seller, in any sale process you want to be able to read your opponent like a poker player. You want to know whether you're in a strong position or a weak position. The stronger your position, the greater your negotiating leverage.

The four positions are as follows:

- **You have a strong position and your opponent knows it.** This situation is where you may need the most skill. You have the upper hand, but if you push too hard, you lose the deal or get a less-than-ideal return. In poker, if the table knows a person has a great hand, all the other players fold. Although he wins that game, the strong hand can win bigger by downplaying his hand and keeping the other players betting for longer.

- **You have a strong position and your opponent doesn't know it.** Being underestimated is a great thing! Hubris is the great enemy of getting deals done, so let your opponent crow and brag. Check your ego at the door and play the simpleton. Remember, what people think of you during the process isn't what's important; how the deal ends is. And if it ends in your favor, what do you care about what other people think?

- **You have a weak position and your opponent knows it.** This position is the danger zone. Your options are limited, and the other side is calling the shots. In this situation, your best bet is to move as quickly as you can and close the deal. Take your lumps, lick your wounds, and move on. The longer you linger, the worse your deal may get.

- **You have a weak position and your opponent doesn't know it.** Time to test your poker-playing skills and bluff. I'm not saying you should lie, but you have no reason to say (or show) you're in a precarious position simply because you are. Finding that out is the other party's job, and you don't need to make the other side's argument.

So short of having ESP, how can you ascertain the strength or weakness of the other party's position? Here are a few pointers:

- **Ask questions and shut up.** Let the other person talk. You may be amazed how much someone divulges when given a chance to talk.

- **Find out about the other party's personal interests and likes.** What seems like an innocent discussion about hobbies may reveal that the guy on the other side can't wait to sell the business and pursue his real passion (be it sailing, travel, golf, volunteer work, or whatever).

- **Pay attention to details.** For example, observe the faces of the employees when you visit the other party's office. Are they generally upbeat and happy, or do you see a lot of long faces? How clean and orderly is the business? Messes, clutter, water stains, burned-out bulbs, mold, and so on are often the signs of a business in decline. The employees (and ownership) no longer have the pride of a well-run business, and they simply may be ready to give up.

Keep an eye out for these *tells* (those subconscious habits or mannerisms that belie your true position) on your end as well. After all, you don't want to unintentionally give away helpful information either.

Although this section helps you get as much negotiating power as possible, keep in mind that negotiating isn't about taking advantage of other people. Deals only get done if Buyer and Seller find a mutually agreeable deal.

Maintaining as much power as possible when disclosing undesirable news

At some point or another in a deal, you may find that you need to give the other party a piece of information that gives that party more power over you. These suggestions can help you control all that you can.

- ✔ **Don't lie.** It's an old adage, but it's true: Honesty is the best policy.

- ✔ **Deliver the news in a matter-of-fact manner.** Although being honest is vital, *how* you present your information is also key. If you have bad news to share, don't editorialize or tell a long, drawn-out story. Simply say what you have to say as neutrally as possible.

  You may be surprised by the other side's reaction. An issue you think is problematic may turn out to be no big deal for the other party. However, if you phrase the news in the form of a negative editorial, you may transfer that negative vibe and thus turn a nonissue into a weapon your opponent may use against you. As I note earlier in the chapter, never make your opponent's argument.

- ✔ **Disclose everything early.** If you have a disclosure to make, do it sooner rather than later. And if you think you can hide negative or bad news, remember that those kinds of skeletons usually come to light during due diligence.

What to Tell Employees and When

Informing employees that a company is in the process of being sold is a tricky proposition. If employees find out about a potential sale that doesn't eventually occur, the management/ownership may lose face in the employees' eyes. Worse, employees may begin to leave because they think, correctly or not, that the company is in some sort of trouble. A failed sale process can become a self-fulfilling prophecy of doom for an otherwise-healthy company. For some thoughts on what to say to employees after the deal closes, see Chapter 17.

Keep news of a sale process confidential

Simply put, the greater the number of people (even employees) who know about a pending business sale, the greater the chance someone will inadvertently spill the beans to someone else, who will mention it to someone else, who will talk about it in a public place where anyone can overhear.

The first concern is a competitor learning of the sale process. A competitor may use knowledge of a business sale as leverage to steal clients by spooking the clients into questioning the company's future. The second concern is gossip among employees. In the absence of fact and communication, people can be extremely creative as they attempt to fill in the blanks with some sort of guesswork. Ambiguity is never a friend to business.

Never lie

If an employee asks if the company is for sale, don't lie and say, "No, absolutely not." A better option is to simply say the company is exploring bringing in a financial partner to help take it to the next level. That's a true statement.

A staggered release

If a business is going through a sale process, certain employees need to know about the business sale at different times. The owner doesn't need to inform everyone at the same time. The controller (or similar accounting employee) should be taken aside and told of the sale process. Because financial documents are one of the main items collected during the sale process, accounting employees usually figure it out on their own. However, talking with the controller ahead of the process reduces the odds that she tells other employees. Other than accounting employees, the remaining employees should be told about the potential sale on a need-to-know basis. If at all possible, tell the employees after the deal has closed.

Part II
Taking the First Steps to Buy or Sell a Company

The 5th Wave   By Rich Tennant

"Can you explain your loan program again, this time without using the phrase 'yada, yada, yada'?"

In this part . . .

Part II examines the steps necessary to start the deal-making process. One of the first orders of business for Buyers is to make sure the necessary capital is available. Because M&A can be a complex activity, Buyers and Sellers alike need advisors to help advance and close the deal, so I devote a chapter to helping you assemble your team. And because it takes two to do the M&A tango, I show you how the sides can find each other in the first place!

Chapter 4

Financing M&A Deals

· ·

· ·

*B*efore discussions between Buyer and Seller heat up — and possibly burn out due to lack of planning — Buyers need to line up their financing for acquisitions, and Sellers should ascertain Buyers' ability to actually come up with the dough.

In this chapter I explore the various methods that help Buyers finance the acquisition of companies, including where Buyers get the necessary capital, what exactly they're buying, and what those transactions look like.

Exploring Financing Options

To many, buying a company means an exchange of cash: Seller gets some dough, and Buyer gets the company. This transaction implicitly states that the payment is currency, to be paid now, and the price is fixed. Although that's one way to finance a deal, it's not the be-all and end-all of M&A transactions. Timing, currency, and even the amount of payment all affect a deal's financing.

Although cash, especially the all-time favorite "cash at closing" variety, is the preferred payment, it's not the only way to pay for a company. A better word for what Buyer pays Seller for the company is *consideration*. Consideration can be anything that a Seller is willing to accept in exchange for the ownership of her company, such as land, another company, or, yes, cash (be that dollars, pounds, Romanian leu, or whatever). Basically, consideration is anything of value (or, more accurately, anything that someone considers valuable). Heck, if Seller accepts a pizza, some seashells, and small island in the Caribbean as consideration for her company, that's a deal, too!

Traditionally, the consideration used in M&A transactions consists of some combination of cash, stock, notes, and contingent payments (head to Chapter 12 for more on noncash payment options). For example, say a deal has a valuation of $15 million. Buyer may not actually be paying Seller $15 million cash at closing. Instead, the consideration may look like the following:

- ✔ $5 million cash at closing
- ✔ $5 million in a three-year note at 10 percent
- ✔ $3 million in stock in the acquiring company
- ✔ Up to $2 million in an earn-out, with the amount actually received based on acquired company achieving certain results

This setup is just one example of virtually limitless permutations of structuring a deal.

Consideration is limited only by your imagination, which is why creativity is so important during the deal-making process. I'm a firm believer that Buyer and Seller can almost always find a mutually beneficial transaction. Think of it as turning knobs on a stereo: You have a virtually infinite number of ways to twist a multitude of knobs. The following sections lay out a few such options.

Buyers, don't provide Sellers with your financials, even if they ask. Instead, offer some sort of proof of your ability to complete a transaction. A letter from Buyer's senior leader expressing support for Buyer's acquisition strategy goes a long way on this front.

Buyer uses his own cash

The most obvious source of capital is for Buyer to use his own money. The benefits are obvious: a Buyer using his own money has total control over the situation. A third-party lender usually institutes hoops for the Buyer to jump through; using his own money removes those external limitations.

The downside is that money isn't a bottomless pit, and a company putting money into an illiquid asset such as an acquisition ties up that capital such that the money can't go toward other important expenses such as payroll and other operating expenses.

Using his own capital to finance 100 percent of an acquisition also means the Buyer is assuming 100 percent of the risk. Bringing in outside capital helps Buyer spread the risk.

Many Sellers incorrectly assume that Buyers are using their own money, and worse, that Buyers have an endless stream of money they're willing and happy to throw around with little or no planning. Mentally spending someone else's money like this is one of the biggest errors anyone can make. Being carefree with someone else's wallet is easy, but think about how you'd feel if someone told you, "You have money; just pay more."

Buyer borrows money

Because using up precious cash and assuming 100 percent of the risk of an acquired company often makes little sense for Buyers, many Buyers borrow money to help finance the transactions. Borrowed money comes in three basic flavors: senior debt, subordinated debt, and lines of credit. See "Understanding the Levels of Debt" later in this chapter for more on how debt plays into a deal.

Debt, or *leverage*, is a double-edged sword: It can help a company diversify its risk and make an acquisition easier to swallow. But the borrowing Buyer becomes beholden to the creditor and has to jump through hoops to obtain the capital and keep from defaulting on the loan down the road. If the Buyer's business declines, he may not be able to the meet loan terms, and a Buyer who can't repay the loan at that time may lose the business — the entire business, not just the acquired company.

Sellers should keep in mind that Buyers may have limited ability to adjust price or conditions of the acquisition; the Buyer's overlord, the lending source, has an enormous say in these transactions.

Buyer utilizes Other People's Money

Although I warn against spending someone else's money earlier in the chapter, getting other people to give you money to finance a deal is actually a good strategy. Securing Other People's Money (as I like to call it) is easier said than done, of course; no Other People's Money shops exist, so you have to be creative.

Private equity (PE) firms can be a good source of Other People's Money. A Buyer unable or unwilling to utilize bank sources of capital may be able to turn to a PE firm to help with the acquisition, although PE firms often exact a high price in return for using their money.

A PE firm often wants a controlling interest in the entire company (not just the acquisition) in exchange for helping finance the deal. If the acquisition goes wrong, the PE firm may be able to take over the entire company.

Bringing a PE firm also means bringing in debt. Although the PE firm acquires an equity stake in the business in exchange for providing the capital for making the acquisition, the company's balance sheet becomes loaded with debt. The benefit is that the company can essentially borrow money on the PE firm's credit, thus opening a world of finance previously unavailable to the company.

Buyer seeks financial help from the Seller

Seller financing — why would a Seller do such a thing? Oh, that's right: to help get a deal done! A Seller willing to provide financing to a Buyer gains the benefit of being able to move on to the next phase of life — retirement, hobbies, charity work, or perhaps starting another business — while receiving consideration as the result of the sale.

Although cash is always king, a Seller who wants to get out of running the business may find that extending financing (in other words, accepting a promise from Buyer to pay Seller later) helps achieve that goal. Seller financing also can be a way for a Buyer and Seller to conclude a transaction where Buyer is having difficulty obtaining outside capital. Instead of paying back a third-party lender (a bank, for example), Buyer pays back Seller. Seller is taking on the role of the lender.

The typical forms of Seller financing include

- ✔ **Seller note:** Seller effectively loans money to the Buyer in order to help with the financing of the acquisition. Money doesn't flow from the Seller to the Buyer and then back again. Instead, Seller agrees to allow Buyer to pay a certain portion of the transaction price at some later date. Typically, these notes earn interest, either paid on a regular schedule (such as monthly, quarterly, or annually) or accrued and added to the loan, thus repaid when the loan is repaid.

- ✔ **Earn-out:** Any kind of payment tied to some future measure of the acquired company's performance is an *earn-out*. If Seller believes the company is worth more because she believes future earnings will reach a certain level, Buyer may agree to pay that higher price if the company achieves that certain goal. Earn-outs may be based on top line revenues, operation profit, EBITDA, gross margin, gross profit, sales increases, and so on (see Chapters 12 and 21 for possible earn-out options).

If you agree to an earn-out, keep it as simple as possible. Overly complicating an earn-out is a sure recipe for a disagreement. For Sellers, the best measure of an earn-out may simply be sales. Post-closing, Seller won't have any control over expenses or allocated expenses, so any target based on profitability will be tough to measure.

✔ **Delayed payments:** Because time is effectively a part of consideration, delaying payments may be a way for Seller and Buyer to bridge a valuation gap. Simply allowing Buyer to make payments over time affords the Buyer with the ability to pay the price that the Seller wants to receive. Although as Seller you'd prefer $10 today, perhaps you'd be inclined to take $1 per week for the next 15 weeks.

✔ **Consulting agreement:** An effective way to increase the deal value to Seller is to offer her a consulting agreement that pays her money over some period of time.

Any or all of these plans may be good options for a highly motivated Seller who trusts Buyer to hold up his end of the bargain.

As a Seller, accepting any kind of contingent payment involves an element of risk because you can't be as sure you'll be paid in full as you can when the cash is in your hand at closing. To mitigate some of that risk, demand some sort of premium for accepting it by making the contingent price higher. Simply put, pay me $10 million today, or $5 million today plus another $10 million in three years.

Determining whether a Buyer is legit

Sellers, take some time to determine whether a Buyer is a legitimate Buyer and not just dabbling in acquisitions. If Buyer is a publicly listed company, its financial statements are publicly available. Pay close attention to the balance sheet in particular. How much cash and how much debt does Buyer have? If the company has little or no cash and has a high debt load, Buyer may have a difficult time financing an acquisition. If Buyer is privately held, you can ask for the company's financials, though most privately held Buyers don't provide Sellers with financials. But what the heck? Asking never hurts.

If you can't get financials from Buyer, remember that the advent of the Internet has been a great leveler in finding information about companies.

A routine online search may yield answers as to whether Buyer is legitimate or not. If Buyer is a privately held but large, well-known company that regularly does deals, it's probably a legitimate Buyer. If Buyer is not well known, and doesn't share financials with you, determining Buyer's legitimacy can be a trickier affair.

Tip: As Seller, don't agree to a *financing contingency* (an agreement that says Buyer who can't arrange financing can back out of the deal) with any Buyer, especially one whose financials/general standing you can't verify. Be skeptical of a Buyer who insists on a financing contingency, particularly if that Buyer purports itself to be a successful and financially flush company.

Understanding the Levels of Debt

Debt can help Buyer make an acquisition by leveraging Buyer's existing capital. The following sections cover the different types of debt common in M&A, so dig in!

Surveying senior lenders and subordinated debt

A *senior lender* is usually a bank that lends a company money, often for the express purpose of financing an acquisition. As the name implies, this lender is *senior* to all other lenders, which means that the senior lender gets paid before the other lenders in the event the borrower goes bankrupt. A loan from a senior lender is called a *senior loan.*

Subordinated debt, often called *sub debt,* is a strip of capital similar to senior debt; however, the lender purposefully agrees to take a back seat to the senior lender. A lender willing to subordinate itself to the senior lender does so in exchange for a higher rate of return. *Mezzanine debt* (or simply *mezz*) is a form of sub debt that usually has some sort of equity component (usually in the form of a *warrant,* which is the right to buy stock in the future at a low price).

Leverage

Simply put, *leverage* is debt — borrowed money — that helps Buyers make acquisitions. Instead of putting all of their money into play, leverage allows Buyers to spread their money further and make more acquisitions.

Say Buyer has $10 million to invest in acquisitions. Without leverage, he can make a single $10 million acquisition. However, if he borrows another $10 million, he can use the borrowed money to make more acquisitions. In this case, that same $10 million enables Buyer to make two $10 million acquisitions, so he now has $20 million of investments under management. Because he borrowed money to finance half the acquisition amount, he's used 50 percent leverage. Back in the good old crazy days of the mid-2000s, some Buyers were able to put down just 10 percent, meaning that same $10 million could finance $100 million in acquisitions.

PE firms, in particular, like to utilize as much leverage as possible. The less equity a firm has to use, the higher the (potential) return on equity after the investment is sold.

Leverage gives you more bang for the buck as Buyer, but don't use debt excessively; the greater the debt load, the less likely a company will be able to withstand a downturn in the economy. That warning aside, and to paraphrase Alexander Hamilton, leverage, as long as it is not oppressive, will be a blessing to your company.

Looking at lines of credit

A *line of credit* (LOC) is simply a loan from a bank, often used to help finance acquisitions. Unlike a senior loan (see the preceding section), the borrower pays interest on the amount it has used. A company may have a $5 million LOC, but if it has only tapped $2 million to help pay for an acquisition, the company only pays interest on the $2 million, not the full $5 million available.

A *revolver* is a type of LOC designed to help with the short-term cash flow needs of a business. A revolver is helpful to a company whose cash reserves are low (perhaps because it just spent some money making an acquisition) and that needs to pay bills even though its clients are a wee bit slow in paying. Making payroll is usually the main reason for establishing a revolver.

To help during a cash crunch, a company may establish a revolver with a bank. If the company needs cash, it utilizes the cash on its revolver and then repays the revolver as clients remit payment to the company.

Taking a Closer Look at Investors

Investors come in all shapes and sizes. Sometimes they're *institutions* (other companies, often called strategic investors), and sometimes they're people. In this section, I detail the ins and outs of working with institutional and individual investors.

Institutions versus individuals

Most often, Buyers of middle and lower middle market companies are institutions (PE firms or strategic Buyers). Individuals can certainly buy these companies, but due to the size of the companies and the amount of money needed to buy them, individuals buying companies in these markets are somewhat rare.

Individuals seeking to acquire a company may be little more than dreamers with no money. Sellers should take appropriate steps to ensure individual Buyers can back a transaction.

Institutions usually have more money than individuals, greater access to other sources of capital, and a certain level of sophistication as compared to most individuals. The executives at a company or PE firm probably have more experience doing deals, more experience running a business, and greater financial acumen than an individual. Not always, of course, but usually.

Following the financing food chain

Investing in a company isn't as simple as buying stock. Investors may opt to put their investment in the form of debt, which comes in myriad options with varying risk levels. The higher up the food chain the investor's place on the balance sheet is, the more likely that investor gets paid in the event of failure, bankruptcy, or liquidation.

If a business fails, it faces liquidation, meaning its assets are sold to repay its debts. In an ideal world, the value of the sold assets would cover the value of the debts, but often that's not the case. Because of that bitter reality, bankruptcy laws are very clear about who gets what and when. In the US, the liquidation order is as follows:

- ✔ **Employees:** Employees, rightfully, are at the top of the list. In the unfortunate event of a business failure, employees who are owed back wages get paid first.

- ✔ **The IRS:** Not surprisingly, Uncle Sam wants his cut, too, so any unpaid taxes must be paid in full before any of the remaining money is kicked down the food chain.

- ✔ **Secured creditors:** After the employees and Uncle Sam are taken care of, secured creditors are next. *Secured* means the creditor has a lien or personal guarantee against assets, both of which mean that the creditor can go after the owner's personal assets (home, cash, cars, and so on).

- ✔ **Unsecured creditors:** Any money left over after the secured creditors are repaid goes to the unsecured creditors. These folks typically include vendors and suppliers.

- ✔ **Preferred and common stockholders:** If all the creditors are repaid, any money left goes to the equity owners of the business. Preferred stockholders are repaid first, and then what's left (if anything) goes to the common stockholders.

That setup paints a rather ugly picture for common stock, so why would anyone want to own common stock? Answer: Common stock is the only security that affords the owner unlimited upside potential.

Say a company is being liquidated and everyone else in the food chain is owed a collective $20 million before the common stockholders see a dime.

Although that sounds like a huge hurdle, and it is, suppose the assets sell for $100 million. In this scenario, the common stockholders receive $80 million.

Remember: Please note that for simplification's sake, I haven't included the numerous layers of secured and unsecured creditors, some of whom take precedence over others, or the fees of lawyers and other advisors.

Note, however, that a wealthy individual may be able to act more quickly than a company. An individual Buyer has far less bureaucratic red tape than an institutional investor Buyer.

An important distinction is an executive backed by a private equity firm, a situation that's really closer to a PE Buyer than an individual Buyer. In this case, the individual essentially has the financing lined up and is simply seeking the right acquisition.

Private equity (PE) firm

A *private equity firm* (sometimes known as a *private equity fund*) is a pool of money looking to invest in or to buy companies. For all intents and purposes, the firm has no operation other than buying and selling companies, which go into its *portfolio*.

PE firms raise money from limited partners (LPs). LPs often include university endowments, pension funds, capital from other companies, and *funds of funds* (which are simply investments that invest in other funds, not in companies). Wealthy individuals also invest in PE firms.

As Seller, don't assume a PE firm has money to burn. PE firms aren't bottomless pits of money; they're using Other People's Money, so executives are beholden to their LPs.

General partners (GPs) manage the money from the LPs. The GPs oversee the day-to-day operations of the firm, making investor decisions and managing the acquired companies (which become known as *portfolio companies* after acquisition).

PE firms make money by charging an annual management fee of 2 percent to 3 percent of the money under management and then taking a cut (called the *carry*) of the profits when they sell portfolio companies. Most often, the PE firm's carry is 20 percent. The LPs get their original investment back plus 80 percent of the profits.

Getting the founder of a company "out of the way" is often an underappreciated role of PE firms. The PE firm can step in and help bridge a company's transition from an entrepreneurial firm to a company that better fits with a large acquirer. This role is especially important when the acquired company is a closely held company run by the founding entrepreneur because in that case the transition can be too big to otherwise handle.

Sellers, take time to understand the nature of any PE firm you're dealing with. Not all PE firms are the same. Some investors are actually *fundless sponsors,* or Buyers without money. They look for a company to buy, work out a deal with the owner, and then they try to find the money to close the deal. These groups can and do complete deals, but most often, a fundless sponsor adds a layer of complexity to an already-complex subject.

The following sections clue you in on a few common types of PE firms.

Traditional (buy and sell)

A *traditional* PE firm wants to make an acquisition and perhaps fix up the company by streamlining operation, cutting wasteful spending, increasing sales, and maybe making some add-on acquisitions, all on a three- to five-year timeline. The traditional PE firm finances transactions by putting in as little of its own money as possible. In fact, I'm convinced the ultimate fantasy of most PE firms is to make acquisitions without having to use a dime of their own money!

Traditional PE firms need to eventually sell their portfolio companies. This sale is called a "liquidity event." Why? Because the firm is taking an illiquid asset (ownership in the company) and exchanging that ownership for some sort of equivalent store of value, commonly called *money*.

Although PE firms talk about holding their investments for a few years, in reality, all their portfolio companies are for sale at all times, for the right price. The GPs love to brag about their return rates (see the later section "Internal rate of return"), so an early sale with a great return is fine by them.

Family office (long-term holders)

These firms work in a similar fashion to traditional PE firms, except the money usually comes from one or an extremely limited number of LPs. Most often, the LP is an extremely wealthy family that set up an office to manage a portion of the family's wealth.

Family offices are usually long-term holders of their portfolio companies. In fact, the term is so long that these entities are often called *buy and hold.* If you ask the typical executive at a family office when the firm expects to sell a portfolio company, the typical answer is a curt, "Never." For this reason, a family office can make an idea financial partner for a Seller who is concerned about the company being bought and then rapidly flipped or otherwise dismantled.

What's the difference between PE and VC?

Private equity (PE) firms differ from their more famous cousins, venture capital (VC) funds, in terms of the types of investment each fund pursues. PE firms typically invest in profitable companies, while VC funds invest in start-ups. The PE firm usually makes the acquisitions by loaning the company money (and/or arranging the injection of debt in to the company), while a VC fund typically buys equity in the start-up.

A PE firm wants its portfolio company to continue to grow, so it may add on other synergistic acquisitions and then sell the company to another firm within a few years. Although enormous growth rates are usually desirable, most PE firms are realistic and don't expect their portfolio companies to grow by quantum leaps. They aren't seeking exponential growth but rather good, solid geometric growth.

A VC fund is betting the start-up will rapidly bloom into an enormous company (eBay, Microsoft, Sun, Google, and Apple are all examples of venture funded start-ups). The VC fund expects its investments to experience exponential growth; it needs to have this kind of return because many of the investments fail.

Strategic Buyer

Strategic Buyer is simply a fancy term for *corporate Buyer*. As I discuss in Chapter 2, companies make acquisitions for a slew of reasons: growth, new markets, new products, buying out a competitor, and more. Strategic Buyers often focus their acquisition activity on companies that are a fit for their current (or future) strategic plans, often buying from PE firms (see the earlier section "Private equity (PE) firms").

Strategic Buyers are often the end Buyer after a PE firm has made an acquisition. PE firms may be willing to get their hands a little dirtier than a strategic Buyer is; that is, a PE firm may be willing to take on a deal with some moving parts, replace management, fix operations, add on other acquisitions, and so on.

After the PE firm has spruced up the portfolio company, a strategic Buyer may have great interest in making an acquisition. Much of the heavy lifting, such as turning an entrepreneurial company into a professionally managed company, has been done by the PE firm, and a strategic Buyer recognizes and pays for that value.

Aside from the added value of professional management, strategic Buyers pay more for companies for a few reasons:

- ✔ **They need specific pieces for their puzzles.** As the name implies, "strategic acquisition" is exactly that. The acquirer is buying a company that has an important strategic fit, so the acquirer may be willing to pay a premium to keep a valuable company out of the hands of a competitor.

- ✔ **They're often not bound by the same limitations as PE firms.** The investors in PE firms agree to invest only if certain parameters are part of the deal; not paying too much for a portfolio company is often part of the PE mandate. Strategic Buyers have more freedom to spend what's necessary to get what they need.

- ✔ **They may be looking for a long-term investment.** Strategic Buyers may be willing to pay a higher price because their strategy is to buy and hold long term. They aren't seeking to earn a return on the investment; they're seeking to earn a return on the cash flow of the acquired company's operations.

Striking the Right Type of Deal

M&A transactions are basically variations on a theme: How much of the company is being sold, and what is Buyer buying — stock or assets? The following sections delve into these issues.

Exploring the differences among buyouts and majority and minority investments

When Buyers make acquisitions, those purchases can take the form of a complete, 100-percent buyout (mainly for PE firms), a majority investment, or even a minority investment.

As the name suggests, a *buyout* occurs when 100 percent of a company is sold to another company. A buyout results in a change of control, and although 100 percent of the outstanding stock may be acquired to effect the transaction, it's possible for Buyer to acquire Seller's assets (instead of buying stock) and still have a buyout. In other words, buying 100 percent of the stock means you buy 100 percent of the assets, but buying 100 percent of the assets doesn't necessarily mean you buy any of the stock. Head to the following section, "Choosing an asset or a stock deal: What's Buyer buying?", for more.

The new owners may allow the management of the acquired company to acquire the new shares either for a discounted price or as a part of some sort of stock option plan.

A *majority investment* is when Buyer acquires greater than 50 percent of the company. A *minority investment* is when Buyer acquires less than 50 percent of the company. Regardless of whether the transaction is a majority or minority investment, in most cases Buyer buys the stock of Seller. If the acquired stock is sold by an existing shareholder, that transaction is called a *recapitalization.* In this case, no new shares are being created; existing ones are simply changing hands.

If the acquired stock is the result of a new issuing, however, the money raised from selling those shares goes to the company. This setup is often called *growth capital* because the company retains the money for the purposes of facilitating growth.

Choosing an asset or a stock deal: What's Buyer buying?

One often-overlooked area of M&A is the question of what exactly Buyer is buying. Companies themselves aren't really sold, per se; instead, Buyer is acquiring either certain assets of the company (in an *asset deal*) or the company's stock (in a *stock deal*).

Buyers prefer asset deals over stock deals because the former are a lot cleaner logistically. The assets involved may or may not constitute the entire company and often include intangibles such as company name, domain names, customer lists, work in progress, sales pipelines, and so on.

Asset deals are cleaner because Buyer is essentially picking and choosing what she wants to buy. She picks the good assets and leaves behind the bad assets and some (or perhaps all) of the liabilities. Most often, Buyer does assume certain liabilities relating to working capital. A smart Buyer makes sure any assumed liability is *current* (or within terms).

The big perceived advantage for Buyer in an asset deal is *successor liability*. If Buyer acquires the stock, any past misdeeds of the company are a liability for the new owner. In some cases, an asset deal may help shield Buyer from the past misdeeds of Seller, but that's not always the case. Stringent representations and warranties (see Chapter 15) and an escrow account help mitigate this concern, but the risk never completely goes away.

The *assignability of contracts* (Buyer's ability to enforce contracts originally signed by Seller) is often in question with asset deals. Buyer may want to consider the risk of losing contracts as the result of an asset deal. The contract is with the company, not the assets!

Sellers usually don't like asset deals because those deals pose the risk of double taxation. Proceeds from the sale first go to the company, which may have to pay a capital gains tax on those proceeds. The remainder of that money is then paid out to Seller, who in turn may have to pay tax on that after-tax amount.

For that reason, Sellers prefer stock deals. In a stock deal, owners of the company's stock sell those shares to Buyer and in most cases face just one layer of tax (which is hopefully the capital gains rate). Unless Buyers want to increase the purchase price to offset the higher taxes of an asset deal (and some Buyers will do that), they need to get themselves comfortable with the possibility of stock deals.

Regardless of which side you're on, talk to your legal and tax advisors, who can advise you appropriately on a case-by-case basis.

Examining the All-Important EBITDA

In addition to being fun to say (I had a client who once referred to it as "EBITDA dabba do!"), EBITDA is a key M&A metric. Heck, it's a key metric in all things business. *EBITDA* is a measure of a company's profitability for doing what that company is supposed to do: selling a product or service. EBITDA effectively removes the profit-distorting effects of taxes, interest income, and expense and eliminates the effects of making capital investments in the firm. In other words, EBITDA is a measure of a company's financial performance if that company were in a bubble, sheltered from the real world.

Because EBITDA helps measure the company's underlying profit, banks and other sources of capital tend to use EBITDA when determining how much money they can lend. These institutions measure that amount in *turns;* one turn is equal to the business's EBITDA. For example, if the business is generating $3 million in EBITDA, one turn of EBITDA is $3 million. If a company is being sold for $15 million, the Buyer needs to come up with five turns of EBITDA.

Buyer doesn't necessarily come up with all the necessary turns from one lender. A senior lender may be willing to extend, say, two turns of EBITDA to Buyer ($6 million in this example). If Buyer gets a subordinate debt of one turn ($3 million) and chips in three turns itself, the acquisition financing is complete. (Flip to "Understanding the Levels of Debt" earlier in the chapter for more on senior lenders and subordinate debt.) Most acquisitions follow a financing model along these lines.

In years past, a Buyer may have been able to make that acquisition using less of its own money, but with the tightening of the credit markets in 2008 and the downturn in the economy from 2001 to 2010, most Buyers now find they need to put in more equity than in years past. As of the time of this book's writing, these estimations are accurate and are subject to change as the economy changes; as always, check with your advisors for your own situation.

Making Buyers' Return Calculations

Make no mistake: Buyers don't act solely because of feel-good business-book babble like "the right fit" and "synergy." They make acquisitions for one simple reason: profit. Besides EBITDA (see the preceding section), Buyers measure profitability in various ways. The following sections present the main methods.

Return on equity

Return on equity, or ROE for short, is simply the amount of income divided by the total amount of the company's equity. If the company has $1 million in after-tax income and $10 million in equity, the ROE is 10 percent.

ROE is a measure of how well a company is able to generate profits from invested capital. It helps Buyers measure each acquisition's profitability and continue to monitor whether acquired companies remain profitable enough. If the ROE is too low, management may decide that it can more profitably use the capital tied up in the company elsewhere and that selling the company is the best option.

Return on investment

Return on investment (ROI) is similar to ROE (see the preceding section), except it accounts for the acquisition price and the sale price of a business. You calculate it by subtracting the sale price from the acquisition price and dividing that difference by the acquisition price; the result is a percentage. If you acquire a company for $10 million and sell it for $15 million, the ROI is 50 percent.

Internal rate of return

Internal rate of return (IRR) is a favorite of PE firms and is the main metric investors use when comparing one fund to another. It's a discounted rate of return; that is, the anticipated future earnings of a company are discounted. A dollar today is worth more than a dollar next year, so the more time that expires, the lower the potential IRR. That's why PE firms are often very open to selling off a portfolio company sooner rather than later; keeping it may not be beneficial if the IRR is likely going to decline.

Financing a Problem Child

Not all companies go up for sale in the rosiest of circumstances. Sometimes, Sellers need to unload debt-laden or money-losing businesses. Working out financing for these so-called problem children is trickier than finding financing for healthy companies, but it's not impossible. The following sections present some problem situations and suggest ways you may be able to finance such deals.

Debt is greater than purchase price

When the external debt of a business exceeds the purchase price Buyer is willing to pay (known as being *underwater*), Seller is in a sticky situation. To accept the price means Seller literally has to write a check for the honor of selling his business. Short of getting Buyer to pay more (always an option worth trying!), Seller has a couple of options for selling his underwater company:

✔ **Ask Buyer to pay more.** Seller should explain the situation to Buyer; if Buyer is hot enough for the deal, she just may be willing to pay enough to cover all the outstanding costs and debts of the business.

✔ **Negotiate with creditors.** This situation is tricky because informing a creditor that a company is in financial trouble may cause that creditor to put place a lien on the business or force a bankruptcy on the company. The key is to not say the creditor will get nothing but rather that the creditor will get something. If Seller in financial straits can get major creditors to agree to accept less than the full amount owed, he may be able to extract himself from this precarious position without having to bankrupt the business.

Buyers of troubled companies shouldn't let Sellers repay all creditors. Instead, Buyers should take complete control of the situation, ask Sellers to submit a complete list of all the business's creditors, and directly pay all outstanding debt of the business at closing.

The business has operating losses

If a business has operating losses, Seller is wise to ask Buyer to pay for the assets of the business, which may have more value than the business. Sellers are strongly encouraged to speak with their accountants and lawyers before pursuing this course of action.

Another method of selling a business with losses is to determine the *contribution,* essentially revenues minus direct costs associated with those revenues (typically cost of goods sold, salespeople, marketing, and so on).

Say Seller has $30 million in revenue and $32 million in costs, resulting in $2 million in losses. Assume the direct costs associated with those revenues is $22 million. Therefore, the total nonsales and marketing administrative costs are $10 million ($32 million – $22 million). In this example, Seller would provide $8 million in contribution ($30 million – $22 million = $8 million) to Buyer, assuming Buyer has sufficient existing administrative overhead to absorb Seller without needing Seller's $10 million of nonsales and marketing administrative costs.

In this example, the question Seller should ask Buyer is, "What value does my company's $30 million in revenue and $8 million in contribution have to your company?"

For the right Buyer, all or most of Seller's $8 million in contribution would go to the bottom line. Even if Buyer figures it would need $7 million in overhead to handle Seller's revenues, that still leaves $1 million that would fall to the bottom line. Any investment banker worth his salt should be able to make that case!

Chapter 5

With a Little Help from Your Friends: Working with M&A Advisors

....

In This Chapter

▶ Noting advisors you need when buying or selling a company

▶ Establishing effective communication with advisors

....

Ringo Starr nailed it. Well, actually John Lennon and Paul McCartney nailed it; Ringo just sang it. But it's true: Everyone needs a little help from his or her friends, whether those friends are genius writers of timeless pop music or the lawyers, accountants, and business advisors who help you engage in M&A activity. This chapter helps you pinpoint those advisors and ensure strong communication.

Choosing Wisely: Identifying Ideal Advisors

Whether you're a Buyer or Seller, successfully completing M&A transactions requires a skilled team of advisors who have negotiating experience, the right temperament to deal with many different personalities, and the willingness to listen to you whine and pout.

At the core, a deal is very simple: A Buyer gives a Seller money or some other store of value in exchange for a company. But a deal isn't just about numbers; it's about the personalities of the Buyer and Seller. Those personalities, along with the myriad motivations, needs, and wants on both sides that go hand in hand with putting together a deal, are what make completing a deal complicated.

The M&A deal-maker (Buyer or Seller) should be a *generalist* (have a broad knowledge of all the deal's aspects). The advisors should be the specialists for specific issues, such as accounting or negotiating business or legal issues.

Ideally, your deal advisors should have the following traits:

- ✔ **Depth of correct experience:** Clearly the most important aspect of any advisor is his experience! But don't stop simply at area of expertise. In addition to being an expert in law, accounting, tax issues, or whatever, make sure the person is an expert in M&A deal-making. For example, the attorney who wrote your will or disputed your property taxes may not be the person to advise you during an M&A transaction because that lawyer's professional experience probably doesn't translate to M&A prowess.

- ✔ **Confidence and self-assuredness:** You don't want an advisor who's a pushover. You need someone with a backbone, someone who's willing to challenge you and tell you when you have a bad idea. After all, if your advisor can't or won't tell you your idea is bad, how can you know when you legitimately have a good idea? Challenging you is just half the equation, of course; your advisors should be able to stand up to the other side as well. Wavering is fine in your gelatin, but it's a poor quality in an advisor, especially in M&A.

- ✔ **Tact and professionalism:** Your advisor shouldn't be so self-confident that he forgets to be polite. Negotiations during the sale of business can often become contentious and frustrating, thus devolving into name-calling and recrimination. An M&A professional should always refrain from letting business decisions and discussions become personal.

- ✔ **Ability to serve as a sounding board:** A good advisor should be able hold your hand (figuratively, of course) as you navigate the ambiguities of M&A. You also want an advisor who can offer you a shoulder to cry on when things get difficult or frustrating, an ear to listen when you vent, and a firm hand to slap you back into reality when you need it.

- ✔ **Logic and reason:** Negotiating doesn't mean forcing your will upon the other party. It involves understanding the needs and wants of the other side and working together, in good faith, to craft a mutually beneficial agreement. The ability to reason and logically explain your rationale is a key consideration for an advisor, and someone adept at the Socratic method is ideal.

The *Socratic method* is a process of using questions and answers to determine whether ideas, suggestions, and so on are logical and reasonable.

✔ **Calmness:** Advisors need to be calm, cool, and collected rather than prone to being overly emotional. (Think the Fonz, not Richie Cunningham.) Emotions can run hot in mergers and acquisitions. A company often represents a Seller's life's work, and dissecting that through the M&A process often makes Sellers feel open and vulnerable as they look back on mistakes they may have made and how those errors are affecting the proceedings. Buyers worry about financing and whether they're making a good buy; a bad acquisition can ruin a career. When you're in that kind of state, a team full of drama queens isn't very helpful.

✔ **Creativity:** A creative brain is a huge asset for an advisor. Just like skinning a cat, there's more than one way to pull off an M&A deal. If one plan doesn't work, you want an advisor who can jump in with another idea.

✔ **Willingness to negotiate:** Deals rarely get done if one side is digging in its heels. Advisors who are willing to negotiate and try different ideas are what often get deals across the finish line.

✔ **Perseverance and foresight:** A good advisor, especially one of the "been there, done that" variety, knows that deal-making is often a marathon, not a sprint. It inevitably has ebbs and flows and ups and downs, and the advisor's ability to see long term, anticipate problems and the other side's next move, and stick with the deal is an enormous boon to getting deals done.

 When hiring consultants ask for referrals from other members of your M&A team, interview more than one candidate, and don't be afraid to ask about fees. Specifically, consider asking whether a consultant, especially the legal or accounting type, would be willing to work on some sort of flat-fee basis. You can always offer those consultants the long-term relationship in exchange for a lower rate or flat fee now.

Utilizing Inside Advisors

The most obvious set of team members for deal-makers is the *inside* team — that is to say, those employees who already work for the company. Working with inside advisors makes sense because they don't represent any additional dollar cost for the company. The company is already paying them, so it may as well use them!

However, utilizing inside advisors means a company incurs another kind of cost: opportunity cost. Having an employee devote all or some of her time to selling the company or finding acquisitions means you're taking that person away from the regular business of the company. In the following sections, I highlight some of the main inside-team members.

CFO or other financial bigwig

The CFO or other key finance person at a company is usually an integral part of the M&A process. For Seller, that person is responsible for assembling, preparing, and presenting the company's financials and explaining, justifying, and examining any *add backs* (nonrecurring, one-time, or owner-related expenses). For Buyer, she's also the person who interacts with the bank, lines up the financing, makes sure money is wired or received, and runs financial models to make sure a given offering price makes economic sense for the company.

Corporate development people

Some companies (often those that do a lot of acquiring) have employees specifically tasked with engaging in M&A. These folks usually have the phrase *corporate development* in their titles, such as *Director of Corporate Development, Corporate Development Manager,* or even *Vice President of Corporate Development.* That's a big one.

Whatever that person's title, I'll just call her the Corporate Development Dude. (The title *Dude* has no gender in M&A.) The Dude is the liaison between the company and the target or the target's outside advisors (see the following section).

Do you need an in-house lawyer?

Sound legal advice is vital in deal-making regardless of which side you're on. A deal attorney negotiates the legal aspect of the deal, including representations and warranties, amount of money held back in escrow, employment agreement, non-solicitation agreements, and all sorts of other important legalese. Whether a company needs an in-house attorney to handle these functions or whether it should hire outside counsel is usually a function of the size of the company.

In other words, if you don't already have an in-house attorney, you probably don't need to hire one just to conduct M&A deals.

Remember: Much like buying a private jet, if you need to ask about the cost of hiring an in-house attorney, your company probably can't afford it. Retaining a capable attorney for certain discrete tasks is a better use of your company's resources.

Hiring Outside Advisors

Having someone to look at a situation from a distance, to be able to consider that situation from a perspective of a detached outsider, can often be the greatest benefit to a person who is buried in the minutiae of day-to-day operations and worries. In other words, an outsider just may be the help an M&A deal-maker needs to successfully complete deals.

Both Buyer and Seller need the following advisors:

- ✔ An attorney to draft (or edit/revise) the purchase agreement (assuming you don't have an in-house lawyer qualified to do so; see the sidebar "Do you need an in-house lawyer?" for more)

- ✔ Accountants to audit or review the numbers and more importantly, to interact with the other side's accountants

- ✔ Advisors to negotiate the deal and to make sure it gets across the finish line. These folks are usually called investment bankers.

And depending on the complexity of the deal and other factors, Buyer may also need marketing, environmental, and perhaps IT/database consultants.

Here are some other considerations to keep in mind when hiring outside advisors:

- ✔ **Don't be afraid to manage your outside advisors and hold them accountable.** At the same time, let them do what you hired them for. They're deal experts.

- ✔ **Find the right-sized firm for your company.** M&A transaction experience is a must, of course, but an advisor should specialize in working with companies the size of your company.

Consulting wealth advisors when you're ready to sell

A *wealth advisor* is a person who manages other people's money. But I don't merely mean a stockbroker. Most financial services firms have a specific department or division designed to work with wealthy people. These advisors consult their clients on a wide array of issues, ranging from investment choices to estate planning to tax strategies.

Selling a business can generate a great deal of personal wealth, and working with a trusted advisor to help manage and shepherd that wealth is an important consideration during the M&A process. An advisor worth his salt can advise Seller on a preferred structure, one that minimizes taxes and/or moves wealth to the next generation.

Sellers should sit down with a wealth advisor before embarking on the M&A process, especially if they're contemplating retirement. As amazing as it may sound, Seller may discover that the lifestyle he wants to lead post-sale requires less money than he previously thought with some specific planning rather than back-of-the-envelope guesswork.

Pick your wealth advisors very carefully. The dirty secret of many firms, even the largest, most well known, household name firms, is much of the work is done by junior people who don't have any wealth, don't know much about investing, and may not even care that much about your goals and plans and desires. Because managing wealth isn't so much about your future but rather the future of your children, grandchildren, and charities — your legacy, in other words — choose your advisors carefully.

Considering an intermediary

An *intermediary* is a person who represents Buyer or Seller in an M&A transaction. Commonly called *investment bankers* or *business brokers,* this breed of M&A advisors is essentially salespeople, and what they're selling is a company. The intermediary is often the quarterback during the M&A process, and Buyers or Sellers thinking about hiring an intermediary should look for deal experience, demeanor, confidence, business understanding, creativity, and accounting skills when hiring that quarterback. The following sections look at how intermediaries operate for each side and how the two main varieties differ.

Understanding an intermediary's role

For Seller, an intermediary is the one who helps execute the M&A process I lay out in Chapter 3, including contacting buyers, structuring the deal, and performing due diligence. The intermediary can also be the voice of reason for an otherwise-emotional Seller. The business sale is likely to be the largest transaction of Seller's life, and he needs someone who isn't emotionally tied to the business to represent him. (That's why Sellers should never represent themselves in a sale.)

For Buyer, an intermediary is the one who does the most difficult of jobs: contacting Sellers (flip to Chapter 6 for more information) and getting the appropriate information for Buyer's offering document (see Chapter 8) and due diligence (see Chapter 14). Depending on the needs of the client, the intermediary may also help with the negotiating and structuring of a deal, although many Buyers who utilize an intermediary for help with finding targets prefer to do the negotiating and structuring themselves.

Most Buyers (and their advisors) these days review the copious amounts of data generated by due diligence in a secure, online data room, so when hiring an intermediary, make sure that person is well versed in online data rooms.

What the intermediary doesn't do is hammer out all the details of the purchase agreement (that's for the lawyers) or go through all the books in order to perform a comprehensive financial analysis (that's the job of the accountants).

Buyers should note that Sellers are usually extremely reluctant to speak to a competitor or a company they perceive as a competitor. For that reason, using an intermediary can be a very useful buffer when contacting Sellers. A Seller is more apt to talk with an intermediary and quite often more willing to open up and provide quite a bit of information.

Knowing the difference between a business broker and an investment banker

Intermediaries come in two flavors: investment bankers and business brokers. An *investment banker* likely provides a fuller service for a Seller, but that fuller service usually means higher fees. Investment banking firms are more expensive because they have more overhead. In other words, they have more professionals (including specialized employees such as business development teams, researchers, and a host of analysts) and often fancier offices in fancier buildings. All those extras cost money.

In a very rough sense, the revenue threshold for working with an investment banking firm is $10 million. Companies with revenues north of $10 million will most likely be able to afford the fees associated with a full-service firm.

For companies under $10 million in revenue, a business broker probably makes the most sense; transactions that small probably won't interest an investment firm.

A *business broker* does much of the same work as an investment banker does, just with fewer people and lower overhead. In some cases, the broker is the person who signs the new client, writes the offering document, conducts the research, develops the target list, makes the calls, organizes the meetings, and negotiates the deal. The broker can charge a lower fee and still make a good living, but the extent of the service won't be the same as a larger firm, simply because the larger firm has more resources.

Brokers are more apt to work on a *contingency basis*, meaning they're often willing to only get paid if a deal successfully closes. Investment bankers probably will require an initial retainer, monthly fees, and a success fee.

Due to recent changes in securities laws, both Sellers and Buyers should work with an intermediary that is affiliated with a regulated investment firm (called a *broker-dealer*). Any individual involved in transacting an M&A deal needs to be registered with the Financial Industry Regulatory Authority (FINRA). Basically, this entity makes sure people involved in securities transactions haven't committed financial crimes and also have a certain level of financial proficiency. To become registered, an individual needs to pass a couple of securities exams — usually, the series 7 (or 79) and series 63.

When hiring a firm to conduct an acquisition search make sure you ask who is making the calls to business owners: an experienced professional or some kid straight out of business school? Some M&A firms that focus on acquisition search work are little more than what I call "dialing for dollars shops." Often these firms utilize the boiler-room approach — that is, packing a slew of young people into a room and having them make call after call after call with little or no thought about what they're saying or to whom they're speaking.

Don't allow one intermediary to represent both sides. Representing both sides is a conflict of interest. Anyone who offers to represent both sides is inept and/or is acting in a highly unethical manner.

Lawyering up on both sides

Legal issues are always at the forefront. The lawyer is a very important advisor to both Seller and Buyer. Similar to the intermediary (see the preceding section), each side has its own lawyer. The lawyer should be someone who is well versed in M&A; only use an attorney who has actually engaged in M&A transactions.

The lawyers for both sides work together and craft the details of the purchase agreement. These agreements are very complex and often utilize arcane terms and phrases, so I can tell you from experience the best thing you can do is to let the lawyers do their lawyerly alchemy and craft a document they think makes sense. Stay out of their way, but always stay abreast of the situation.

Here's why you want to stay on top of what the lawyers are doing: Many law firms turn over the mind-numbing exercise of negotiating the myriad legal points to junior associates. These associates often can be sweet, caring, and utterly passive creatures. As a result, one lawyer will mark up the purchase agreement (called a redline") and e-mail it over to the other side.

Redline refers to an edited document that retains the edited text. Edited text is crossed out and the new text is easily identifiable because it's blue, green, or, surprise surprise, red!

The other side's junior associates, also sweet, caring, and utterly passive creatures, undo the changes and revert back to the original text. This passive e-mailing can continue *ad infinitum* because these passive creatures often prefer the easier e-mail route to having a conversation. Coincidently or not, this back-and-forth also results in running up the legal fees of Buyer and Seller.

Of all the advisors, lawyers are prone to try to take over the process. Keep your lawyer focused on negotiating the legal terms of the purchase agreement, and leave the negotiating on business terms to your investment banker. You're paying the lawyer, so don't be afraid the tell her to stand down.

Check out the later section "I'm the tax man!" for more on issues that fall under the jurisdiction of both the lawyer and the accountant. (And for more on accountants, head to the following section.)

Looking at accountants and auditors for Buyers and Sellers

Accounting is another issue that can cause a deal to crash and burn. Accounting may be a science, but the application of accounting, especially in companies utilizing family-accepted accounting principles (FAAP; see Chapter 8), can become an art. A capable accounting advisor is a must.

Accountants and their bean-counting brethren, auditors, are hugely important during the M&A process. Wading through enormous amount of data, especially financial statements, inventory reports, and bank statements, and then applying and double-checking arcane accounting rules, regulations, and conventions against that pile of data is mind numbing, dreadful work, so be thankful you have someone willing to do it!

Your fancy investment banker isn't going to sit still long enough to do all that counting, and your lawyer will provide you with dozens of equally boring legal reasons, replete with references, why he can't count up all the numbers.

Perhaps the best thing about accountants, beyond the fact that they gleefully jump into a world of monotony, is the fact that they don't complain and rarely try to hijack the negotiations. See the following sections for some duties accountants share with lawyers regarding taxation.

I'm the tax man!

In the not-too-distant past, the U.S. tax code contained more than 4 million words and almost 200,000 lines of rules, regulations, exceptions, exemptions, thinly veiled threats, overt threats, twists, turns, and a writing style that can make your eyes glaze over in massive pronoun confusion. Oh, and just for good measure, the code tosses around arcane and bizarre language like a sailing vessel slammed by a rogue wave of bureaucratic tomfoolery. So you definitely need the advice of a tax expert.

Taxes are the bane of doing deals. Yeah, they're a necessary evil, I get it, but of all the deals I've worked on that ultimately didn't close, taxes were the number one reason for the failed transaction. Sellers are often unaware of the full effect of the taxes their sales generate, so having a tax expert on the team helps insure the best-possible tax treatment of the transaction.

The issue of taxes straddles the expertise of the attorney and the accountant (see the preceding sections). Ideally, Seller works with an accounting firm that is large enough to have a dedicated tax expert on staff.

Tax evasion (not paying taxes owed) is illegal. *Tax avoidance* (merely avoiding transactions or structures that trigger taxes or higher taxes) is not.

Recruiting more consultants to Buyer's team

Buyers may need to enlist the services of additional outside advisors including environmental consultants, database/IT consultants, and marketing consultants. However, these consultants are farther down the food chain and aren't part of every deal.

Technology

If the acquired company utilizes technology (such as the contents of a customer information database or some proprietary software designed and built by Seller) as any component of what Buyer is buying, Buyer should strongly consider hiring an appropriate consultant to test and confirm the strength of the technology. Testing the technology is important because many (if not all) of the decision-makers aren't computer programming experts. Bringing in an outside expert to test the software may be the only way to determine whether the software truly is as strong as Seller claims.

Marketing

Getting a marketing consultant's third-party opinion on a company's marketing strategy may make sense for Buyer as a way to determine where it can make improvements in marketing post-acquisition. However, using this report to argue for a price reduction is a dubious practice Buyers should avoid.

Environmental

Buyers should hire an environmental consultant especially if they're acquiring land and/or have reason to suspect the site of the business may be on contaminated land.

Responsibility for contaminated land is a hot-button issue as of late. The Environmental Protection Agency (EPA) can make Buyer's life miserable if it discovers after a transaction closes that land acquired as part of the deal has an environmental problem.

Some key questions the Buyer's consultant should ask include

- ✔ **What was the land used for prior the being home to Seller's business?** Specifically, was it a gas station, a recycling facility, or a manufacturing facility?
- ✔ **Were heavy metals previously fabricated on these premises?**

The due diligence pertaining to land comes in two types of phases:

- ✔ **Phase I:** A Phase I is basically a review of records from local, state, and any pertinent regulatory agencies, focusing on the current use and past use of the real estate in question. The review includes photos, maps, and an examination of aerial pictures, as well any information pertaining to the local water table. A Phase I usually includes a walk-through of the premises and lands. The examiner is looking for tanks (oil, gas, chemical, and so on) and other visual evidence of some sort of problem or issue.
- ✔ **Phase II:** If, based on the findings in the Phase I review, the examiner believes the property may have issues, a Phase II may occur. A Phase II is a more in-depth, on-premise review and analysis. Some of the problems the Phase II tries to uncover include nasty things such as radon, asbestos, and other hazardous materials.

Buyer may include an environmental assessment as part of due diligence, but it may make sense for Seller to go ahead and conduct a Phase I prior to the M&A process. If the Phase I is clean and relatively recent, Buyer may be able to skip further environmental testing, thus saving time.

Depending on the consultant's findings, Buyer may be in a position to demand strong representations and warranties as part of the deal if the land presents an environmental problem. Speak to your attorney for more advice.

Seeking friendly advice: Using friends and family as informal advisors

Friends and family are the whipping boys of the business world. Emotional pals and relatives call on them to fund all manner of crazy start-ups. Then the loved ones want free advice! Luckily, friends and family are usually willing to offer advice and thoughts about doing a deal.

Friends and family probably aren't helpful guides for all the small details and tiny nuances a deal-maker encounters while delving in to the world of M&A. But even though they may not be M&A experts, they probably know the deal-maker better than most people and can therefore be a good source of opinion about the big issues (such as whether the potential Seller should sell).

Skipping business appraisers

Business appraisers are people who offer the "service" of valuing a business. Sometimes this service is offered as part of another advisor's product offerings; for example, many investment bankers and business brokers (which I discuss earlier in the chapter) also offer the "service" of appraising a business and determining valuation.

I put "service" in quotation marks for a simple reason. In my humble opinion, business appraisals aren't helpful. They merely put a valuation number in Seller's head, and that number quite often doesn't make any sense because the appraiser's valuation techniques are mostly guesswork. Sure, the guesswork can have impressive methodology — I'll be generous and call it an academic exercise — but the only true measure of a company's worth (what someone else will pay for it) is missing from any and all academic exercises.

Beyond providing a number rooted in no rational basis, the appraisal may raise Seller's expectations and cause him to reject the market value of his company. Worse, the actual market value of a company may be perfectly suitable to fund Seller's desired lifestyle, but that high appraisal number may lead him to opt against selling the business.

I have firsthand experience in how business appraisals can be counter-productive, if not downright destructive, to wealth creation. A company I approached for my client, an acquisition-minded Buyer, ultimately had to pass on our offer. The owner was interested in selling, and the offer price was suitable for his needs, but because the company had an employee stock ownership plan (ESOP), it was required by law to have an annual appraisal. The last appraisal valued the company at 15 times EBITDA, which was significantly above our offer price of five times EBITDA. Because the owner had a fiduciary responsibility to his employees (because of the ESOP), he was unable to accept our offer.

As a result of an inflated and ultimately arbitrary appraisal price, the owner was unable to do a deal. The upshot was that an illiquid asset remained illiquid, no taxes were paid as the result of the sale, no fees were earned by the advisors, and the business didn't receive a new owner who would have invested in the business, possibly creating more opportunities for the existing employees and employees yet to be hired.

What do Buyers think of an appraiser's valuation? They don't. The valuation an independent appraiser, someone with no skin in the game other than the fee he's charging Seller, is of zero value to Buyer. People in the M&A industry may say otherwise, but they're just being nice. A business appraisal isn't worth the paper it's written on.

Bottom line: Sellers should let the market decide the value of their businesses.

Keeping Everyone on the Same Page: Avoiding Communication Breakdowns

To steal Strother Martin, Jr.'s, immortal line from *Cool Hand Luke*, "What we've got here is failure to communicate." Well, I think Strother drawled it "cahmun'kate," but you get the idea. Communication breakdowns may make fine fodder for rock 'n' roll songs, but a failure to communicate can be major problem and even a death knell for the M&A process.

Communication problems typically come in one of three flavors:

✔ **Purposely communicating incorrect information:** You may know this better as *lying*. Unfortunately, many people conveniently forget the benefits of honesty, which is why due diligence is a necessary part of the M&A process. (Chapter 14 gives you more info on performing due diligence.)

✔ **Not communicating information:** This version is lying by omission. Seller has the obligation to divulge any information that may be construed as *material* (important).

✔ **Inadvertently communicating incorrect information:** Unintentionally signaling the wrong information can weaken one side's bargaining strength because the other side may think it has an advantage where it didn't know it had before. But in some cases, it can prove fatal to a deal because the other side may think something is wrong and bow out of the a deal.

To keep your team of advisors on the same page, here are three tips to avoid communication breakdowns:

✔ **Establish a chain of command.** One person should be the point-person when dealing with the other side. All requests for data, meetings, follow-up questions, and so on should be routed through that person.

Although this suggestion may sound like creating more busywork and bureaucratic layers, a failure to institute and follow a chain of command results in cross-communication, duplicated steps, and general frustration such that emergency conference calls and meetings become necessary to get the process back on track.

✔ **Assign specific roles and tasks to each team member and hold each member accountable for fulfilling that assigned role.** Some of the specific tasks the deal-maker needs to determine are

- Who makes the calls to the prospective Buyers or Sellers?

- Who is responsible for structuring the deals and making sure the deal makes economic sense for the company?

- Who is the final authority for green-lighting a deal? In other words, who has the final say-so?

- Who is the point-person with outside advisors?

- Who makes site visits?

- Who leads management meetings with the other side?

Clearly deciding who does what helps ensure your side follows through with its promises, which is important for maintaining credibility with the other side.

✔ **Don't fall into the trap of communicating only by e-mail.** E-mail is a wonderful tool and should be utilized, but because it's a passive form of communication, it may not be the best method to communicate. It's certainly an easy solution to *call reluctance* especially when a particularly difficult bit of information needs to be conveyed or when a delicate question needs to be asked, but in those situations, my million-dollar advice is always the same: Pick up the phone and have a conversation.

The problem with e-mail is that it doesn't pick up on nuance or read the other side and adjust its tone or delivery. E-mail can be abrupt, and the reader may interpret unintended harshness in an otherwise innocuous note. As a result, e-mail can inadvertently derail a process. When negotiations have bogged down and both sides are merely sending e-mails back and forth, it's time to get on the horn.

Following up a conversation with an e-mail is a perfectly acceptable method to memorialize the conversation. Delicate conversations should be handled in person or by phone, but the nuts and bolts of a deal are often best hammered out through e-mail. This way, you have a record of what the other side said or agreed to.

Getting Your Banker Involved

The decision to sell a business means the owner eventually has to tell his banker of the transaction or pending transaction. The first step is to review the loan covenants for any guidance as to when the bank needs notification. Barring any specific requirements (such as Seller alerting the bank when he hires an intermediary to sell the business), the right time to make the announcement often depends on whether the company in good financial health. If the company is in good shape, the announcement of a possible sale probably won't trigger any warning signs in the banker's eyes, so Seller can sensibly wait until he's accepted an offer from Buyer (usually in the form of a signed letter of intent, or LOI, which I cover in Chapter 13).

The banker's main concern in a business sale is the loss of the credit; the new owner probably has its own banking relationships. Although such a loss is unfortunate for the banker, that shouldn't be Seller's concern. As harsh as it may sound, the guiding principle in this situation is, "Don't let someone else's problem become your problem."

If a company is challenged, the news of a potential sale can cause the banker to get nervous about the company's prospects, and by proxy, the credit extended to the company. As Seller, you should speak with the banker in a very frank and honest manner. Selling a troubled company actually means the banker has a better chance of being repaid than if the company were to simply shut down. Remind a nervous banker that calling the company's loan right now will kill the company; giving the company some time to conclude a deal will result in the bank getting its dough.

Don't panic if a nervous banker calls the loan in the wake of learning about the potential sales transaction. Talk to the banker. Ask for an extension or a waiver, but don't let the calls from the banker go unanswered.

Chapter 6

Finding and Contacting Buyers or Sellers

· ·

In This Chapter

▶ Creating Buyer and Seller lists

▶ Navigating the phone labyrinths of large companies successfully

▶ Dealing with people who can't help you

· ·

*A*ny acquisition or sales process depends on having an appropriate target list. Not having enough targets lowers the odds of a successful closing; having too many makes it an unwieldy process. Selling a company is probably the only time a sales call is easy; buying a company is a trickier affair. Business owners get tons of buy offers, so as a Buyer, standing out from the crowd can be difficult. Luckily, knowing whom to talk to, how to get to that person, and what to say when you do can make a world of difference.

In this chapter, I introduce you to the target list — specifically, how to create one and then use it to make contact with potential Buyers or Sellers. I also show you how to avoid wasting time on the phone with people who can't help you.

Creating a Target List

Before you can have a conversation about selling your company or acquiring someone else's company, you need to have someone to speak to! It's one of those crazy things about mergers and acquisitions. If you want to find a Buyer or Seller, you have to seek it out, and that starts with a *target list* (list of potential deal partners).

Getting started

Creating a target list starts with basic brainstorming of any and all companies that you would like to buy, merge with, or be bought by. As with any brainstorming session, no idea is a bad idea. Even if you think of a company that isn't a right fit, merely mentioning that company may cue your memory (or someone else's memory) of another type of company that is a suitable fit. Consider this your shortlist.

The most obvious targets include competitors, but vendors and customers may also make suitable M&A targets. You need to weigh the relative merits and risks of contacting competitors, vendors, and clients; every situation is different, so working with an experienced M&A advisor, who also probably has a shortlist of possible targets, is so important. (Head to Chapter 5 for more on picking advisors.)

Spending time on the Internet is important. You can learn a lot about a company by reviewing its Web site and searching for news articles. I also recommend using proprietary databases to conduct research. A couple of my favorites include CapitalIQ (www.capitaliq.com) and OneSource (www.onesource.com).

After you complete the basic brainstorming, you're ready to compile a target list.

Buyer: Considering what kind of business you want

For Buyers, the job begins by defining the "whats" of the target:

- ✔ **What type of business do you want to acquire?** A product extension? A new product or service? Entrée to new markets? A competitor? Chapter 2 helps you answer this question.

- ✔ **What's the revenue range?** What revenue level does the target need to be worthwhile? How much is too much or too little?

- ✔ **What are your earnings requirements?** Does an acquisition need to be *accretive to* (increase) your company's earnings per share, or are you willing to acquire a money-losing company?

- ✔ **What are you willing to pay?** Are you prepared to pay a premium or are you strictly a bargain-basement Buyer?

- ✔ **What do you want ownership/management to do after the deal is done?** Do you want or need the target's higher-ups to stay on board and continue to run the business? Or do you prefer to replace them with your own team?

✔ **Where do you want or need the acquisition located?** Okay, this one isn't really a "what," but it's still an important consideration. Does the target's location matter to you? Do you intend to keep the acquisition at its current location or fold its operations into your existing locations?

None of these questions has a right answer. The right answer is whatever constitutes the right fit based on your specific needs as Buyer.

Accretive is mostly on the minds of public companies. If a public company has earnings per share of 25 cents, the acquiring company probably won't pay a price for an acquisition that erodes that earnings per share amount. For Sellers, pay attention to who is buying you. If you're asking a public company to pay a purchase price that isn't accretive (dilutive, in other words), the company probably won't be able to agree to your demands.

Seller: Knowing who's buying you

Seller's target list is a bit different than Buyer's target list due to one key aspect: Seller's main concern is Buyer's ability to close a deal. In other words, does Buyer have the dough?

That's not to say you as Seller should be blasé about who buys the company. Even though you're selling, you likely still have some sentimental or financial stake in the company's success. Here are a few points to consider when listing targets:

✔ **Can the new owner continue the company's successful operation?** If a selling owner plans to stick around for a period of time as an employee — especially if she plans to accept some kind of *contingent payment* (an earn-out, a note, or stock, for example), as part of the sale — she wants to make sure the company continues to be successful in order to increase the likelihood of collecting that contingent payment.

✔ **Does the target have a history of taking care of an acquisition's current employees?** Most Sellers (especially those who are retiring) want their companies to continue to be successful for the sake of the employees. Does your potential Buyer's record show a history of integrating existing staff into operations or canning everyone and starting over with its own people?

✔ **How will the new ownership affect the company's legacy?** Even if you aren't sticking around post-transaction, you probably want to see your company continue as a going concern.

If you're selling a company with losses, look for a *strategic Buyer* (a company seeking to fold another company into its operations). Financial Buyers (such as private equity firms) aren't likely to be interested in a money-losing enterprise.

Expanding and winnowing the list

Because contacting every company in this world and beyond doesn't make much sense (those interstellar telecom charges will kill you), you need to make sure you have the right type and number of targets on your list.

You do this by initially making the target list larger than it needs to be. To create the initial target list, take all the targets on your and your advisors' shortlists and then expand that list by applying your search criteria. Really dig in by dive-bombing online research sites (see the appendix for some site examples). If a company is obviously not a fit, discard it, but if you're not sure whether a company should be included in the initial target list, leave it in. The idea of this step is to err on the side of too wide a fit. If the company isn't a right fit, you weed it out in the next phase.

The initial target list will be larger than the final target list. Having 200 to 300 targets on the initial list isn't unheard of, nor is that a bad thing. Having an initial target list of that size increases the odds that you'll have a strong final list after you winnow it down.

After you've created your initial target list, you want to review that list with your team and reduce it to a reasonably sized final list. See the following section for more on determining what the length of this final list should be.

To prepare for this review, have someone who works for you print up as much information about the targets as possible, including pertinent reports found from online research sites. These reports contain contact info, URLs, financial info, employee counts, and brief descriptions of the companies. Next, you want to further torture the person by having him go through and print the Web sites of the target companies. If you want to save a forest and someone's sanity, use a projector and a computer to review the Web sites. However, and with apologies to environmentalists, printing copies of reports so everyone can have quick access to the financials is still probably the best bet.

Usually, a junior executive or some other low-level creature does the target list research because it's rather tedious and time-consuming work. Don't let this delegation make light of the importance of the research, though. Without a good target list of Buyers or Sellers, your M&A dreams stand a very good chance of being dashed. Take this duty very seriously; if you aren't doing it yourself, entrust the right person. Alternately, you can also hire an investment banking firm to take care of it.

During the review, the idea is to assess each company and talk about what it does, its financial situation, its history of doing deals, and whether it's a suitable target. This process is a pain. It's a bit like going to the dentist: It's no fun, but it's ultimately a good thing. Doing this review as a group is important. You need the feedback and the ability to rapidly bounce ideas off each other. I don't recommend conference calls for this rap session; get the group together in one room.

Reviewing the initial target list will likely take half a day. At the end of this process, you should have a manageable final target list that's shed of all the tweeners, borderline cases, or whatever term you want to use for "almost, but not quite."

Hold on to all those "rejected" targets. If your A-list targets don't yield what you're looking for, you can review the previously rejected targets and consider adding them into the mix.

Capping the list: How many (and which) companies to include

It takes only one. That's the phrase of the day. It takes only one Buyer or Seller to close your deal. That said, you need to consider the odds of successfully closing a deal when your target list amounts to a random sample of one. Those odds are poor.

The folly of seeking the perfect company to buy

Buyers need to take care not to overdefine their acquisition targets. As Buyer, don't match your search criteria to the absolute perfect company; you won't find it. Focus is important, of course, but being too narrow in your search criteria limits your ability to find suitable targets.

Years ago, I worked with a company whose executives were quite proud of their very thoughtful and narrow search criteria. They were seeking companies with revenues between $10 million and $20 million, revenue growth of at least 10 percent per year, EBITDA of at least 15 percent, and no customer concentrations. The targets' industry also needed to be highly fragmented with the potential for further acquisitions. Plus, Seller needed to be highly motivated and willing to sell for a low price, accept an asset deal, and stay on board to continue to run the business.

I pointed out that this hypothetical target sounded like a great company, and I asked them a simple question: Why would the owner of a perfect company be willing to accept a low price?

The odds of finding such a narrowly defined business are extremely low, so Buyers should temper their desire to narrow the search criteria with the reality that a search needs a large enough universe of targets to be successful.

Even if you do manage to develop a deal with that one suitor, the terms would likely be less than ideal, especially if you're the Seller. After all, how can you talk to other Buyers about a better deal if you're only talking to one prospective Buyer?

Because the odds of successfully closing a deal increase with a larger number of targets, you want a good-sized list. But how many make a good-sized target list?

- ✔ **Buyers:** For Buyers, I recommend a target list of 75 to 100 Sellers. Depending on the particularities of the industry and general market conditions, a suitable list may be 50, but I don't recommend going below that if you're serious about closing a deal. If you're seeking to make multiple acquisitions over a period of time, you're better off with a list of at least 100 targets. If this list doesn't result in a successful transaction, review your assumptions and perhaps change your search criteria.

- ✔ **Sellers:** For Sellers, I recommend a target list of at least 100 Buyers. A list of at least 100 qualified targets increases the likelihood of receiving multiple offers — the more targets you have the greater the odds you'll receive offers.

In both cases, I caution against the target list being much higher than 125; the larger the list, the more difficult managing that list is.

However, your target list may wind up with more than 125. As you make calls, you may discover a company on your list is actually a subsidiary of a parent, and you need to add the parent to the list. Or the parent is on your list but you end up dealing with someone at one of the subsidiaries, which you also have to add.

Should I include competitors?

The competitor issue is a tricky one. Companies are wary of divulging proprietary information to competitors for fear that a competitor will use the information against them in the competition for customers. And they're right for having a healthy amount of hesitation.

That disclaimer aside, contacting competitors usually doesn't create a problem for Buyers. Think about it. Letting your competitors know that you're so successful that you're poised to make acquisitions isn't likely to create any fallout.

For Sellers, on the other hand, letting the "we're selling" cat out of the bag can be disastrous, even if proprietary information doesn't change hands. Having a competitor find out your company is for sale (or even possibly for sale) can wreak havoc on your operations because that competitor may be able to scare customers away.

If you're selling, make sure you have a strong confidentiality agreement in place before proceeding with any discussion about selling your company. If an executive contacts a competitor with a message of "we're for sale, but we need you to sign a confidentiality agreement first," the damage is done. The competitor is under no obligation to sign anything and therefore isn't under any obligation to refrain from disclosing that the company is for sale. Chapter 7 gives you the lowdown on confidentiality considerations.

Although a confidentiality agreement is a key step before divulging proprietary information, the cat is out of the bag.

Hiring an intermediary is an absolute must if you're going to contact competitors with the message that your company is for sale. Because a nonemployee of the company (the intermediary) is making the contact, the competitor doesn't know the identity of the company until the confidentiality agreement is in place.

Should I acquire or sell to a vendor or customer?

The main question here is one of vertical integration. *Vertical integration* is your supply chain. That's it. If you do an M&A deal with an entity above or below you on that chain, you're integrating vertically.

For example, if your company is a paint distributor that sells paint to retail stores, the manufacturers are your vendors and the retail stores are your customers. If you want to sell your paint distributor, you may consider contacting your suppliers, the paint manufacturers, thinking they may be interested in doing their own distribution.

In most cases, however, the paint manufacturers probably don't want to get into the distribution business because distribution means carrying many different types of brands. The paint manufacturers would inherently have a conflict of interest: They would want to sell their own products and would have little or no incentive to sell a competitor's brand. Plus, the competitors would be less inclined to sell to the manufacturer-owned distributor, likely lowering revenue and profits.

Or maybe you think to target one of your customers, such as a retail store chain. Although the retail chain may be able to cut out some costs by acquiring a distributor, the reduction in costs to the retail stores would come at the cost of reduced profits to the distribution business, making acquiring that business less lucrative. And other retail stores may decide to find another paint distributor, thus further reducing the revenues and profits of the acquired distribution business.

Sellers on Your Mark: Contacting Buyers

Here's the skinny, the honest-to-Elvis truth, the bottom line: Some companies are sitting by their phones like a high-school girl waiting for an erstwhile date to call. But they aren't waiting to see whether Johnny wants to buy them a soda; they're hoping to hear from a company that's looking to sell.

These waiting-by-the-phone companies come in two types: *private equity* (PE) firms (which are basically pools of money seeking to buy companies) and strategic buyers.

Strategic Buyers can be a little more difficult to navigate, and the larger the firm, the more complex the hunt. But almost all buying companies will hear the sales pitch of another company that's for sale. The following sections show you how to get your foot in the door with the right person and what to say after you do.

Resist the urge to e-mail a target before calling. Most people consider e-mails from people they don't know spam and delete them sight unseen. And the recipient may not even be an employee of the company! For best results, have a phone call be your first contact with the organization. Have a conversation. Determine the appropriate person to speak to. Leave a voice mail if you have to. After you determine your target actually works for the company, and especially after you've left a message, a follow-up e-mail may not be a bad idea. But make the call first.

Speaking with the right person

Speaking with the right person seems like a basic tenet of making a sales call, but you'd be surprised how many people simply (and often nervously) plow through their script to whoever first picks up the phone. Bad idea; you just waste time. Instead, follow the lead in the following sections.

Phoning a PE firm

Finding the right person to speak with at a PE firm isn't difficult. Anyone will take your call. Despite managing hundreds of millions of dollars or even billions of dollars in capital, PE firms are often small (in terms of staffers), and everyone at a PE firm knows why he's there: to buy companies.

I recommend doing a little bit of homework prior to calling a PE firm. Look at the Web site, which often lists the firm's portfolio companies and/or its areas of interest, sometimes along with the specific partner who handles a specific area. If you can determine the correct person, call that person. If you're not sure, simply dial the main number at the PE firm and say

Hi, my name is [your name]; I have company for sale. I'm not sure who to talk to; can you help me?

Don't delve into your spiel right away. Most people have a limited attention span; the longer you speak, the less they listen.

The person on the other end will almost certainly be ready to help you and will ask a simple question:

Tell me about the company.

Here's where you need to be concise and to the point, which is why having a script with some talking points is important. (Flip to the later section "Following a script that works" for more on planning this document.) The main, if not only, facts you want to convey at this time are product/service, customer of that product/service, revenues, and EBITDA. That's it. That's all an employee of a PE firm needs to be able to route you to the correct person.

Don't go into hyperbolic hyper-drive when making calls! Some people, especially beginners, tend to gin up their company and attempt to add a mega sense of urgency to the call. That just makes you sound like a snake oil salesman. Keep your pitch objective. State the facts without offering subjective opinions (such as "This is the greatest company! You better act fast!").

Why you need to get to the point

As I cover in Chapter 3, M&A involves a generally accepted process that Buyer and Seller follow step by step. But that doesn't mean the process rockets in a straight path from start to finish. In reality, it can meander to and fro.

The reason is simple: People. People (even acquisitions-minded executives) have a lot of things going on in their minds. Yes, many Buyers are waiting to hear from potential sellers, but they're not literally staring at the phone for eight hours a day. They're probably not expecting your call at that exact moment, so their minds are elsewhere — on yesterday's missed putt, Junior's suspension from school, whatever.

When you get this person on the phone, get to the point. Give him the basics in an objective manner (see the nearby section "Phoning a PE firm" for more on this call). Providing more detail and color than necessary at this juncture simply reduces the odds that your phone buddy will be able to cut through the mental clutter in his brain and pick out the important facts of your rambling rant. Don't re-create history; your phone buddy doesn't need to hear a recantation about the invention of the Internet or how your specific industry developed. He needs to learn what he doesn't know: details about your company and the opportunity you're presenting.

After you establish the interest level of the potential Buyer, you can delve into detail and provide color, tell jokes, and you know, have a real conversation.

Navigating the phones when calling strategic Buyers

Finding the right person at a strategic firm can be a bit trickier than finding the right person at a PE firm (see the preceding section). After you find that person, your pitch is essentially the same as the one I lay out in the preceding section for contacting PE firm employees, so instead of reinventing the wheel, here I simply focus on getting to that right person at the strategic Buyer.

The first point to remember is that the larger the company, the more complex the process of simply finding the right person. This situation has something to do with the "the greater the number of people, the greater the chance you'll talk to someone who really doesn't care" theory. As a result, calling the general number on a company's Web site without knowing whom to talk to almost certainly gets you routed to a time-waster who can't help you. Check out the later section "Overcoming screener roadblocks" for help getting to the person you're contacting.

Search the company's Web site and/or use a fancy online research site if you have access to one (check out the appendix for some examples). You're looking for anyone with "corporate development" in their title. You can even do a general Web search by using the company name and "corporate development"; you may turn up someone quoted in a newspaper article or tagged as the author of a magazine column. If you can't find a corporate development person, go ahead and call the company's main number.

If you have to call the main number, don't ask for the CEO. CEOs make two or three decisions a year. Seriously. Now, those decisions are enormous and typically impact the direction of the entire company. But the CEO (the capable kind, that is) doesn't make a slew of small, nitty-gritty decisions. Those are for the CEO's lieutenants: VPs, directors, and all sort of sundry underlings. As far as acquisitions are concerned, the decisions the CEO makes are usually of the "go make acquisitions" variety.

Instead, ask for the office of the CFO. This line is great because you're not asking for the CFO. The CFO is a good bet, but depending on the size of the company, the CFO may fancy himself a quasi-CEO and therefore only make a handful of decisions each year. Most corporate phone-answerers are trained to be very careful about whom they route to those C-level executives. Every pesky Tom, Dick, and Harry salesperson in the world is calling up these people and asking them to get in on land deals or buy a hot penny stock, crap IT system, or insurance that no one really cares about.

Asking for the office of the CFO implies you aren't looking to speak to the CFO, which immediately becomes a point of relief for the person who answered the phone. Now, that person doesn't have to argue with you about how he's not allowed to connect you with the CFO.

After your call is being routed to the office of the CFO, you've got it made. Whether the CFO's assistant answers the phone or whether you get voice mail, you want to say the same thing:

> Hi, my name is Bill Snow, and I represent a company that is for sale. I think your firm might have an interest. I'm hoping to have a quick chat with the person who handles the initial screening of mergers and acquisitions opportunities to see if this opportunity might be a right fit. Can you help me out?

Piece. Of. Cake. The secretary may ask a couple clarifying questions about your company (product/service, size of company, that sort of thing), but because you have a script or talking points, that's a breeze. Most likely he'll tell you whom you need to speak with and what that person's number (and perhaps e-mail) is and then connect you.

If a seemingly earnest person says she'll find the right person for you and forward him an e-mail for you, realize that this exchange will most likely result in nothing. Don't expect someone else to do your job. Make sure you get the name and contact info of the person you want to speak to. This anonymous stuff never works! As a second choice, send an e-mail to that person's secretary with explicit understanding the e-mail will be forwarded to a specific person (as I discuss later in the chapter).

Following a script that works

When you get the right person on the phone, you need to be prepared. I always have a script in front of me. It quickly covers the basics: what the company does, its clients, the revenues and profits, and what the company is seeking to do. No hyperbole. No bragging. No subjective statements. I get to the facts quickly and I leave it at that.

Here's the standard script that I use when starting a conversation or leaving a voice mail for someone:

> [Individual's name], this is Bill Snow with [name of investment bank]. My number is 312-XXX-XXXX. I'm hoping to talk with you for a moment about a client of mine to explore whether this might be a suitable acquisition target for you.

> My client is a highly profitable marketing services company. It provides lists, list management, and data-aggregation services for companies that market to medical/healthcare providers. Customers include medical publishers, pharmaceutical companies, medical equipment/device suppliers, healthcare recruiters, and more.

The company represents a great add-on opportunity for a marketing services firm (especially one with a medical/healthcare focus), a publishing firm, or a data analytics company.

The company has grown at about 18 percent per year since inception in 2001; '07 revenues were about $19 million with $3.4 million in EBITDA.

[If leaving a message] Please call me at your convenience to discuss further, 312-XXX-XXXX.

Don't worry if the grammar isn't perfect! You're not reading the script as is. You simply want the salient points in front of you for quick and easy reference because you can easily skip or omit an otherwise important fact during a conversation.

Another benefit of the script is that, uh, having those, er,, main points in front of you helps you, you know, uh, cut down on those nasty verbal, uhhhh, stumbles. Those unfortunate syllables come because you know you need to add something else, but you just can't remember what. Having a concise script helps you avoid using those crutch words.

Practice your script a few times before making a call. You want to focus on getting the gist of the message across, not rereading the whole thing verbatim. Don't read it exactly the same time and time again, either. That just makes your pitch sound canned, and you want to sound conversational. The script is just there to help cue your memory about what to talk about.

The script's abbreviated cousin is the talking point document. If you feel a full written script may make you sound too rehearsed, you may find simply having the salient points in front of you helpful.

Here's an example from my past:

- ✔ $50 million manufacturer of food equipment
- ✔ Well-known brand names
- ✔ Biggest bang for buck for Buyer is someone who can move production to own facility, which would result in $15 million of contribution
- ✔ Company is profitable, roughly $3.5 million in EBITDA
- ✔ Owner is in his 80s, in the midst of estate planning, hence the interest in selling — would keep it otherwise

In this case, the basics of this deal were always in front of me and my specific words were based on the flow of conversation I had with potential Buyers.

Often Seller has one or a couple of top targets he believes will likely have the most interest. If you have top targets, don't call them right out of the chute. Work out the inevitable delivery kinks in your script on lower-ranking targets. After you smooth out your delivery, you can then call your top targets more confidently.

Just in case you get cut off when leaving a message, always start by stating your name and number at the beginning of your message. When leaving a message, speak slowly and clearly, especially when stating your name and leaving your number. This point is especially important if your name is unusual, has a strange spelling, or is simply difficult to pick up (see the nearby sidebar). Nothing's wrong with stating your name and number at the beginning of a message and again at the end.

Don't rattle off your phone number is a rapid fire, staccato fashion. I've heard many voice mails were the caller spoke at a nice, relaxed pace until he got to his phone number, which he sped through so fast I had to replay the message multiple times before I could decipher it. Make calling you back easy for the recipient of your message.

A problem of frequency

As you can see from the cover of this book, my name, Bill Snow, is simple and short. But that's often a problem when I'm leaving a voice mail. My name has only two syllables total, making it rather abrupt and quick (much like my personality, according to friends). Worse, the last sound is a vowel, which is often difficult to pick up because vowel sounds trail off while consonants have a hard stop.

Why does this issue matter? Early in my career, I was constantly puzzled and amused when people returning my call would ask for (or leave a voice mail for) someone named "Bill Stone" or "Bill Snell," or my favorite, "Mr. Sow." Sao, Snau, and Snoo also came up.

So what caused this problem? It was the telephone. Telephones have a far smaller frequency range than the human ear. The typical,

non-Pete Townshend human ear can hear a range of roughly 20 to 20,000 cycles per second. The average telephone only transmits frequencies between about 350 to 3,500 cycles per second. That means telephones eliminate the high and low ranges of sound, thus rendering an otherwise clear-speaking person slightly garbled and unclear.

To remedy this discrepancy, I simply began to spell my name (thankfully, it's short) and sometimes added the line, "Snow, like the white stuff in winter."

Most people immediately got it. "Oh! Snow! I thought you were saying Sow!" Well, except for one lady who, after I gave her my usual "like the white stuff in winter" line, paused for a couple of awkward seconds before sheepishly saying, "Sand?"

Sellers, avoid corporate purgatory

If you're calling on a publicly listed company, never, ever, upon pain of death utter the word *investment,* as in "I'm an investment banker" or "I have an investment opportunity." People hate investment bankers in the wake of the recent economic setback, but more to the point, if you say "investment" the person on the other end hears only "invest" and before you can finish your comment , the line is ringing. That means you've just been sent to corporate purgatory: the investor relations department.

These folks' jobs are to interact with investors. But an odd thing happens when your call descends into this dark corporate nether region: Nothing. Investor relation-types seem to be afraid of a ringing phone because they rarely answer it. They like to leave cheerful messages saying that your call is important and that they'll get back to you shortly, but that's usually a ruse. They don't return calls. Occasionally, you run across a chatty investor relations-type who answers the phone. He's probably new and doesn't know better.

Easy Does It: Contacting Sellers

Contacting Sellers is easy. You pick up the phone and call. What's tricky is having a meaningful conversation with a Seller.

When contacting a Seller, you want to speak with the owner, not an executive (even if it's the president). A high-ranking executive is only an influencer. You need to speak with the actual owner.

Sellers don't know they're Sellers. Sellers often don't even want to sell; you call them "Sellers" simply because you hope they'll take that role. What they currently are are business owners deluged by calls, e-mails, and letters offering to buy their companies. These communications all say the same thing:

> We have money, we have industry experience, we're different, and we want to buy your company.

The sad fact is that most would-be Buyers don't realize they say the same thing. In a typical week, I receive two or three phone calls and another three to five e-mails (often more) from Buyers. And I'm not even a business owner; I'm just an investment banker.

As Buyer, you have to understand that you're a commodity to Seller. And the more profitable the Seller, the more that statement is true. Sorry if that sounds harsh, but it's the truth. Those constant calls, e-mails, and letters simply become background noise to a business owner, so you have to know how to cut through the eardrum buzz.

Having a meaningful conversation with a business owner means grabbing that owner's attention and ingratiating yourself to that owner. The following sections give you some pointers on doing just that.

Sending an e-mail or a letter rarely helps you make solid contact with a Seller. Those communications are passive and easy for Sellers to throw in the recycle bin (virtual or otherwise). For best results, pick up the phone and have a conversation.

If a company that isn't for sale enters into a sale discussion as a result of an overture from a Buyer, that Seller may be in a strong-enough position to negotiate a deal with Buyer. After all, Seller can easily walk away because Seller wasn't planning to sell! Seller probably hasn't retained a full-service investment banker at this point — an offering document (see Chapter 8) isn't being compiled, research isn't being conducted — so the expense to Seller is relatively minimal.

Getting the call off on the right foot

Similar to *Fight Club,* the first rule of buying someone else's company is you don't talk about buying someone else's company! If you immediately come out and say, "We want to buy your firm," your approach is no different than the myriad other Buyers who have approached this owner.

But that's just the beginning. Here are a few more guidelines that can help you make the most of your call:

- ✔ **'Fess up.** Simply saying, "I know you get calls like this one all the time" is a great way to acknowledge that you understand and respect the Seller's situation.

- ✔ **Keep it conversational.** Be willing to steer away from business. Talk about sports, the owner's kids, your kids, your crazy neighbor, music, travel, anything. If you show genuine interest, you show you're a real person, not just someone reading a script and dialing for dollars.

   The key word here is *genuine.* You have to truly enjoy these conversations. If the talk eventually becomes a serious acquisition conversation that leads to a real deal (see the later section "You're having a serious conversation! What now?"), you need to have a rapport with that business owner during the process and perhaps after (if the owner is staying on board as an employee), and faked camaraderie is no way to achieve that. You and the owner have to play well together for real.

- ✔ **Get the other person to talk.** You don't want to have a one-sided conversation; you want the other side's input. A great technique is to simply tell the owner your *acquisition thesis* (your idea for combining the businesses) and ask whether it makes sense. Get her opinions on this thesis and let her showcase her expertise.

✔ **Be honest.** If an owner asks, "Are you looking to buy my company? I'm not interested in selling," simply reply with the truth: Yes, you're acquisition minded. You can add the caveat that specific talk of an acquisition is premature because you don't know her interest or even whether the company would be a right fit. All of that is true. That's why you have these conversations: to determine interest and fit.

✔ **Ask killer questions.** These big questions quite often start a deluge of information and sometimes end in an M&A transaction:

- What do you want to do?

- What are your goals?

- Where do you want to take the business?

These questions may seem simple, and they are, but if you pose them in the right way, they can get someone to go beyond her current day-in, day-out grind at the company and get talking about life after work. When you're trying to buy a company, understanding what the owner wants to do in retirement and when she is thinking of retiring are some of the most important bits of data you can collect.

If you can successfully engage an owner in a conversation, at a minimum you've made a solid business contact who will take your call in the future. At best, you have a viable acquisition target.

Not all calls go swimmingly. Despite your best intentions, some owners hang up on you (sometimes after telling you exactly what to do with your acquisition-minded company). Be prepared to handle rejection.

Using a successful script

The following is the basic script that I work from when I make acquisition search calls. As with the script I use when I'm selling a business (see "Following a script that works" earlier in the chapter), I rarely read this text verbatim. Instead, it sets up the flow of the basic information I want to convey during the initial call.

> [Owner's name], my name is Bill Snow. I'm with a business advisory and investment banking firm.

> One of my clients has asked me to help them grow their business. I know you probably get calls like this all time, but I was hoping to talk with you

for a minute, explain their vision and plan, where they want to go, opportunities that we see to create a lot of value, and see if anything holds water for you.

- My client is a profitable, midmarket telecommunications company.

- They're led by former top execs from leading telecommunications companies.

- They have deep industry knowledge, experience, and connections.

- Their company currently has strong customer relations with large companies, federal and state governments, universities, and midmarket companies.

- We believe there is a compelling story to combine with other well-run companies in a few seemingly unrelated industries, which include data centers, software, and alarm, fire, and security systems.

They'd like to build off of and leverage further their existing sales relationships and add other products to the mix. We believe the combination of my client's collective experience coupled with the management expertise of companies they merge with, or otherwise partner with, could build a billion-dollar revenue company, which would obviously create quite a bit of value for those who are involved. I'd like to talk with you to explore whether our notions might fit with your goals.

As I note earlier in the chapter, don't worry about your script being grammatically perfect. You're not going to read it verbatim. The goal is to pique someone's interest and have a conversation about the thesis, whether that thesis makes sense to the business, and eventually, whether the business owner is interested in exploring a deal.

Not every call results in a great conversation; that's why your target list (which I cover earlier in the chapter) needs to be large enough. But if you have enough conversations, are willing to immerse yourself in the calls and communicate, and are a genuine person with an approachable personality, you can find success with this technique. Believe me, it works much better than the usual "We have money . . . ." spiel.

You're having a serious conversation! What now?

If you segue into a conversation about doing a deal, start asking questions! Ask about the business: what it does, its history, the revenues, the EBITDA, how the company is incorporated. You can also inquire about customer mix, how the company goes to market, and who its vendors are. Of course, you've already researched this information to some extent; the idea here is to get the owner to start providing more detail to augment that research.

An owner eventually pulls back a bit as you ask her for more and more information. When that happens, suggest enacting a confidentiality agreement (CA) between your respective firms. (Check out Chapter 7 for details on confidentiality.) If you've planned ahead, you should have a CA ready that you can e-mail to the owner.

I'm also a big fan of managing the expectations of others, so lay out the next steps. Tell the owner that after the CA, you want to review the company's financials (income statement, balance sheet, and if handy, cash flow statement), and then set up a visit at his office/factory/facility if everything is "green light go." See Chapter 10 for more information about these early face-to-face meetings.

After the owner has sent you the financials, and if the company's numbers look like they meet your criteria, set up a meeting with the owner. If the owner asks for your intentions prior to setting a meeting, submit an indication of interest (which I cover in Chapter 9).

If you get into a serious conversation and find the Seller seems unusually reluctant, be wary. She may simply be seeking a free (or inexpensive) valuation on her business.

Additional Tips for Getting Past Screeners

Screeners. No, it isn't the latest horror flick by David Cronenberg, but it can be the name of your own personal horror when calling a potential Buyer or Seller. *Screeners* are the people who get in the way of you and your intended target. I discuss types of screeners in the following section and then tip you off to some common obstacles and how to best deal with them.

Recognizing who you're dealing with

Screeners usually come in two distinct flavors: those who are hopelessly clueless and the dedicated doer of evil. This section takes a look at both types.

The hopelessly clueless

At big companies, the person answering the general phone line is clueless about who you need to talk to. That person is either a receptionist at the front desk or (if it's a really huge company) a call center employee. They know nothing that can help you. You need to move on as quickly as possible.

Many times, these people go through the motions. They hate their mind-numbingly boring jobs and just want to get rid of you and your pesky questions as soon as possible. Of course, this description probably doesn't apply to all these employees, but I haven't yet spoken with the exception.

The dedicated doer of evil

Companies are full of personalities. You have the boss, you have the workers, and you have workers who think they're the boss. Speaking with the boss is ideal, although talking to an employee is acceptable if that person can route you to the appropriate decision-maker.

The problem arises when you fall in to the trap of a non-decision-maker who acts like a decision-maker. I politely call these people the *dedicated doers of evil.*

These people are usually lower-level employees such as associates and receptionists. Their intentions may be good — they're trying to do their jobs — but they're ultimately overreaching and making decisions when they have no authority to.

The dedicated doer is evil because he inhibits business and growth by throwing up roadblocks left and right. Trying to extricate yourself from the clutches of a dedicated doer is difficult because they can be so *exhausting!* They have little to do and worse, they're often so fearful of doing something wrong that everything they do to prevent doing something wrong turns out to be wrong!

How can you avoid getting stuck with a nondecision-maker who is suddenly acting like one? Do your homework. If you know exactly who you need to talk to, you can call that person directly. Worst-case scenario, you can tell the receptionist exactly who you need to talk to without requiring him to do any strenuous work.

Ultimately, if you get stuck in an endless loop of dedicated doers of evil, it's your own darn fault for not preparing more thoroughly.

Overcoming screener roadblocks

Getting past screeners is akin to fencing. No, I'm not talking about selling stolen goods, I'm talking about the verbal thrust-and-parry you need to master in order to improve your odds of getting past a roadblock.

If you find yourself in the grasp of a roadblock, level with the person. Tell him exactly what you're going to say to the person you're trying to reach. If your approach is level-headed, quick, and objective, most people relent and let you pass.

Don't get confrontational with a roadblock. Yelling and showing anger only make matters worse, so check your ego at the door. Kindness, a sense of humor, and honesty win the day.

Just send me an e-mail, and I'll find the right person for you

Back story: This person is confused and tired of talking to you. In an apparent attempt to appear earnest, he graciously offers to do your job: find the person with whom you need to speak. This approach never works. After the roadblock receives your carefully crafted e-mail, he realizes following through means doing work! The e-mail probably sits in his inbox for a few days or weeks before he simply deletes it.

Answer: "No, I appreciate your offer, but in my experience that never works."

Next steps: Explain one more time what you're trying to do; you can even recite exactly what you'd say to the person you're trying to contact. Bluntness, honesty, and patience are your best bets to get through this roadblock.

We don't do that kind of thing

Back story: I'm constantly amazed how often I hear this statement. I've even heard this roadblock recited by employees of companies that have a long list of recent acquisition activity on their Web sites! Anyone who makes this comment probably doesn't know what they're talking about. Instead of being stopped dead in your tracks, a simple little quip more often than not takes care of the issue.

Answer: "Oh, so you're the final decision-maker for acquisitions?"

Note: You may think this line sounds rude, but frankly, the person informing you that the company doesn't do that kind of thing is the rude one. I dealt with this roadblock so many times that I sat down and brainstormed a quick response; the next time I got the "we don't do that" line, this reply got me through to the right person's voice mail.

Next steps: After delivering the line, shut up. The first one who speaks loses. I've delivered this line many times, and it almost gets me past the roadblock, who quickly realizes the folly of his ways and almost immediately routes you to the right person.

What is this about?

Back story: This roadblock is heard most often by screeners at companies that are under constant barrage of callers trying to buy the company. The owner, tired of talking to these wannabe Buyers, instructs his receptionist to always quiz anyone who asks for the owner.

Answer: "I have private business that I need to discuss with your boss directly."

Next steps: If the boss isn't in the office, ask for voice mail. If the roadblock insists on taking a message, simply leave your name and number. If the roadblock presses you for a reason, reiterate your original answer. You may want to add, "I have a business opportunity I want to discuss."

You need to speak with Mr. So-and-so. I'm his secretary; send me an e-mail and I'll forward it to him

Back story: This scenario may sound similar to something I warn against earlier in the chapter, but it's slightly different. In this case, you're speaking with the person who has direct contact with the person you want to talk to. Although sending the e-mail isn't the best option, you've identified the specific person, and this solution can be an acceptable plan.

Answer: "Okay, I'll send you something shortly."

Next steps: Craft your e-mail and send it. If you're unable to get the contact info of your target, make sure you get the contact info of the secretary and then follow up with a call the next day. And the next day. And the next day. Always be professional and courteous. Your persistence will pay off, and the secretary will forward the message to the boss. And in many cases, you'll receive a direct reply from the boss.

If you're talking with the secretary or personal assistant to the boss, take steps to ingratiate yourself. Never be rude; always thank that person. A great way to get that person to help you is to simply ask, "I sure would appreciate your assistance — can you help me? I'm not going to waste your boss's time."

[nervous laugh] Like, I don't know what you're like talking about and stuff [nervous laugh]

Back story: You're interfering with this person's reading of his gossip rag. The best thing you can do is hang up the phone! Do not go back to this person, do not pass go, do not collect $200. The roadblock is clueless, isn't paying attention when you speak, and therefore is a consummate time-waster.

Answer: "Thank you, I'll talk with someone else."

Next steps: Do your homework. Redouble your efforts and check the Web site again. Find the right person.

Tracking Your Calls

Like any good salesperson, you want to keep track of your calls. I typically use a *customer relationship management (CRM) system* (a program that keeps track of contact info) coupled with a spreadsheet. The spreadsheet lists the company name, the contact name of the person I'm trying to reach, and a column for "last results." The last results column simply indicates where I am in the process with each target. Though I may tweak the specific wording of the entries in the last results column based on the specifics of a job, when I'm selling a company, the options for that column usually consist of the following:

- ✔ **No contact:** Before I start my calls, every target has a "no contact" in the last results column. My goal is to make sure every single target has something other than this initial "no contact" by the end of my calls.

- ✔ **Left message:** For inexplicable reasons, some people never return your call. Knowing who hasn't called you back allows you to try a different tack in trying to contact them. But if someone hasn't returned your call after five or eight messages, I think the old adage "My lack of response is my response" applies.

- ✔ **Sent e-mail:** If making calls fails to result in a live conversation, I may decide to send an e-mail, preferably to a specific person rather than a general "info@" address. I don't usually expect replies from "info@" addresses, but fortunately, very few of my targets end up in this category.

- ✔ **In contact with parent:** Sometimes the person I need to speak with works at the parent company, so I use this designation instead of simply deleting or writing over the name of the person at the subsidiary.

- ✔ **In contact with subsidiary:** This category is the flip side to "in contact with parent." Sometimes I speak with someone at the parent company, who informs me I need to speak with the subsidiary.

- ✔ **In contact with broker:** I use this note when a company has an M&A intermediary. This way, I have a record that I spoke with the actual company before shifting efforts to the broker (or investment banker).

- ✔ **Not a fit (no contact):** After I begin making calls, I discover some targets aren't suitable fits, in most cases because the target is out of business.

- ✔ **Conversations:** I end up speaking with most of my targets, so most last results columns have this entry at some point.

- ✔ **Teaser sent:** I usually end up e-mailing more than 50 teasers during a sale process.

- ✔ **Offering document sent:** When selling a company, I typically allow access to the offering document (or deal book) from anywhere between 25 to 50 targets.

- ✔ **Indication of interest:** After a target reviews the deal book, I record how many indications of interest I get; it's typically 5 to 15.

- ✔ **Management meeting:** I usually end up conducting five to ten meetings.

- ✔ **Letter of intent:** I like to have as many letters of intent as possible, hopefully at least five.

- ✔ **Purchase agreement:** This entry is the ultimate goal! One lucky target with whom you're hammering out a purchase agreement gets this designation.

At a glance I can tell where I am with each target. I can also very easily add up how many teasers I've sent, how many books are being reviewed, and how many targets are stuck at the left-message step.

I keep a similar spreadsheet when buying companies, with a few minor differences. For example, the teaser sent and offering document sent categories become teaser reviewed and offering document reviewed.

Reviewing a sample call-tracking system

When making my calls, I record every conversation and e-mail in our customer relationship management system (CRM). I also set up a spreadsheet such as the following so that I can keep quick tabs on the status of each target. Depending on your CRM system, you may or may not need to set up a spreadsheet.

Purchase Agreement	1
Letter of Intent	5
Management Meeting	6
Indication of Interest	8
Book Sent	33
Teaser Sent	57
Conversations	99
Left Message	11
Sent E-mail	5
No Contact	0
In Contact w/Parent	18
In Contact w/Broker	0
In Contact w/Subsidiary	4
Not a Fit (no contact)	8
Total	145

In the example shown nearby, I start the process with roughly 120 targets. As you see, the total number by the end of the process grows to 145. That number is a bit inflated because I add 18 new contacts as I make my calls and discover the decision-maker is at a parent company. At another four companies, I started with the parent company but ended up speaking with a subsidiary. These companies are essentially duplicates.

Eight of these companies prove to an inappropriate fit, and no calls are made. In five examples, I'm unable to get the decision-maker on the phone, so as a last gasp I send an e-mail to the general e-mail box of the company. Unsurprisingly, nothing comes of those five e-mails. In 11 cases I leave a voice mail (multiple voice mails, actually) and never receive a reply call.

For those of you scoring at home, that's 22 targets that are duplicates (granted, I add them as I make calls) and another 24 that aren't a right fit or don't respond to my overtures.

Of the 99 targets I speak to, 57 request a teaser, 33 review the offering document, and 8 submit offers. We accept six of those offers and conduct management meetings with those groups. Five of those companies submit LOIs, and from all of that, we close a deal with one Buyer.

As you can see, having a sizeable-enough targets list (which I cover earlier in the chapter) is vitally important. In this situation, relying on a random sample of one would be risky; we may not be able to close a deal.

Part III
Starting the Deal on the Right Foot

The 5th Wave   By Rich Tennant

"Get ready, I think they're starting to drift."

In this part . . .

Selling or buying a business involves numerous critical checkpoints, so this part covers the early milestones. Chief among these checkpoints is the *offering document,* otherwise known as the *deal book.* Also important is the issue of confidentiality: how to ensure it and what to do if someone breaches it. I discuss the documents and methods Buyers use to signal their interest to Sellers, and I provide insights and tips for meetings between Buyers and Sellers.

Chapter 7

Assuring Confidentiality

*E*lmer Fudd had the right idea; the wabbits surely would've scattered if he'd announced his intention to shoot up the forest. Similarly, broadcasting the details of an ongoing M&A deal can have disastrous effects (especially if you're the Seller). That's why confidentiality is so important in mergers and acquisitions. In this chapter, I introduce you to the methods Buyers and Sellers utilize to assure confidentiality.

Tempting Buyers with an Anonymous Teaser

A *teaser* is an aptly named document: Its intent is to give a Buyer just enough information (the product, the customers, the problem the company solves, and some high-level financials) to make him want to learn more. Another aspect of the teaser is that it's (usually) anonymous. Most often, a Seller's M&A advisor (investment banker or business broker, usually) is the person who forwards the teaser to a Buyer.

I don't recommend sending teasers to Buyers without initially phoning them to have a conversation to gauge whether they have any interest in the opportunity. This method keeps me from wasting my time and theirs. Also, speaking with Buyers means they'll be expecting your teaser and will most likely give it proper consideration instead of considering it unsolicited junk mail.

Of course, I sometimes make an exception if I have a long-standing business relationship with a particular Buyer who knows me well and will take a look at my e-mail because I've already established my credentials as a professional, serious business person. (Those who know me, stop rolling your eyes!)

If, after reviewing the teaser, the Buyer isn't interested in learning more about the company, the advisor hasn't disclosed the fact that a specific company is for sale. No names are divulged until the Buyer signs a confidentiality agreement (CA).

Teasers are obviously not anonymous if an employee of the selling company contacts Buyer. Using an intermediary (see Chapter 5) is imperative if Seller wants to maintain anonymity until a confidentiality agreement is in place. I cover confidentiality agreements later in this chapter.

Anonymity is another important facet of the teaser. If a competitor learns that a company is for sale, it may use that information to spook the common prospects and even steal existing clients of the selling company. Also, all things being equal, if you don't need to give up a bit of information, why should you?

Another important reason for the teaser is that a slow release of information is often better than dumping everything in Buyer's lap all at once. If Buyer is inundated with information, he may not be willing to dig in and find the reasons why he should pursue a deal. It's analysis paralysis. Releasing information slowly makes moving to the next step easy for Buyers.

Keeping it short and sweet

Brevity is the soul of a well-written teaser, so keep it to one page. The reader needs to quickly understand what the company does. The teaser doesn't need to delve into details; that's what the offering document is for (see Chapter 8). The teaser just needs to impart the basics.

Sellers, get to the point! The teaser should only provide enough information to spark the Buyer's interest. Don't waste time reconstructing the development of your industry or trying to impress the reader with your encyclopedic knowledge of this or that. Get to the salient points. Write it so that your mother can understand it.

Buyer isn't a "black box" that automatically and immediately processes a huge amount of data. Buyer is a person or a group of people who need time to process that data. Providing an overload of data will most likely result in Buyer not even bothering to wade through it; he has tasks he can do that require less effort!

Including high-level financial info only

In the spirit of brevity (see the preceding section), the only financials a teaser needs are revenue and EBITDA. (If a company has an excess of add backs — see Chapter 8 — the teaser should use adjusted EBITDA.) Some industries or situations may require slightly more financial information, such as gross profit of EBIT or other specific statistics (number of customers, units sold, and so on).

A teaser should have three to five years of historical financial recap plus three to five years of projections. For ease of use, the teaser's income statement should also show expenses as a percent of revenue.

Sellers, don't go overboard. Err on the side of keeping it simple. If the statistic doesn't add anything, don't put it in the teaser. Remember, Buyer may or may not be an expert in your specific industry, so give him only what he needs.

Touting key selling points

These selling points are the key strengths of the business. Companies have certain key discrete value propositions that differ from company to company and from industry to industry. Here are some examples:

- **Proprietary relationships with vendors:** If a company is the only company (or one of a limited few) that can buy from a certain vendor, that's a selling point you can trumpet in the teaser.

- **Nature of customer relationships:** For some Buyers, acquiring companies with Fortune 500 relationships is a main consideration. For others, selling to consumers or middle market companies is the key aspect.

- **Average sale size:** Some Buyers want to acquire companies that make large sales. The larger the average sale size, the faster/more easily the company can grow.

- **Recurring revenue:** Similar to average sale size, the holy grail of *recurring revenue* (revenue that occurs over and over again after making the initial sale; think of your cellphone bill) helps a company grow. A company doesn't need to have 100 percent recurring revenue; the more the better, of course, but any amount of recurring revenue is worth mentioning in the teaser.

- **Revenue growth:** A company with growing top-line revenue usually has growing bottom-line profits.

✓ **Profitability:** The only thing better than a highly profitable company is a highly profitable company that's growing.

✓ **Proprietary whatever:** If the company has proprietary software or processes — something that the competitors don't have — that becomes a potential selling point.

The items in the list are just some examples. The teaser should highlight whatever makes the company special and different. You can find an example teaser in this book's appendix.

Executing a Confidentiality Agreement

If a Buyer is interested in seeing more after reading the teaser (covered in the preceding section), the Seller should execute a confidentiality agreement with the Buyer.

A *confidentiality agreement,* or CA (also known as a *non-disclosure agreement* or *NDA*), is an arrangement where both parties agree to share information with each other but to refrain from sharing the information with outsiders.

They also promise not to divulge the fact that discussions are ongoing. In other words, if you sign a CA, you agree that you can't even talk about the talks!

The CA isn't just a piece of paper or some perfunctory step in the M&A process. It's a serious legal document, and you need to treat it as such. Signing a CA means you have a legal and ethical obligation to keep your mouth shut.

Perusing the CA's contents

Here are the key aspects of a confidentiality agreement:

✓ **Confidentiality:** This one seems like a given, but it's nice to get this agreement down on paper.

Make sure the agreement excepts information already known, such as public information or general information, from the confidentiality requirement.

✓ **Use of materials:** The CA specifies that any materials exchanged during the M&A process are for evaluation purposes only. In other words, don't use the evaluation materials to, say, write your own business plan or create a TV sitcom.

- ✔ **Disclosure of materials:** Despite a pledge of confidentiality, the CA also explicitly states who the parties are allowed to disclose information to, such as outside advisors. Each party agrees to be responsible for any breach that its advisors cause.

- ✔ **Who's covered:** A CA specifies the identity of Buyer and usually includes language stating that Buyer can inform employees and advisors (lawyers, accountants, investment bankers, and so on) of the transaction and share information with these advisors. Buyer agrees to inform these other employees or advisors about the CA and be held responsible for any breach of confidentiality by these employees and advisors. Check out the later "Keeping the Cat in the Bag: Advice for Buyers" section for more.

- ✔ **Destruction of materials:** The recipient of confidential material agrees, upon request, to either return the materials to the source or destroy them.

- ✔ **Chain of command:** The CA defines the chain of command all deal-related correspondence should go through.

- ✔ **Period of enforcement:** A good CA specifies the length of time the agreement is in force, usually one to two years. Don't sign an agreement that lacks an end date; you don't want your hands to be tied indefinitely.

Most confidentiality agreements are boilerplate legalese and don't differ that much from document to document. But you should read any CA before signing it to be on the lookout for language that differs from the norm. If something is out of sorts with the CA being offered, discuss it with the other side. As with everything in the M&A process, you don't have to accept a CA as is.

Figuring out which party sends the CA

Who sends the confidentiality agreement depends upon who initiated the contact. If a Seller is contacting a Buyer, she usually attaches the CA to the teaser, often with instructions (or polite reminders) for the Buyer to sign the CA if he wants to see the full book (or offering document, which I discuss in Chapter 8).

A Buyer contacting a Seller should have a CA at the ready. However, Buyer may want to offer Seller the option of using either her own CA (if she has one) or Buyer's CA, whichever makes Seller the most comfortable.

Determining who gets more value out of the CA

The confidentiality agreement is most helpful to Seller because she's giving up the most confidential information and is more at risk from others finding out that M&A discussions are ongoing. (Flip to the earlier section "Tempting Buyers with an Anonymous Teaser" for more on why these revelations are risky for Sellers.) The CA is so valuable to the Seller that any Seller contacted by a Buyer should execute a CA with the Buyer before any meaningful conversations occur.

On the other hand, the fact that Buyer is interested in making acquisitions has no negative impact on him. Seeking acquisitions essentially says that a company is so successful and profitable that it can afford to buy other companies. That's hardly a disclosure that can provide a competitor with an advantage.

Handling a Breach of Confidentiality

Breaching the confidentiality agreement means one party has not followed the conditions of the agreement, therefore violating the agreement. Breaches are serious occurrences and should be dealt with head on and immediately.

Here are some common types of breaches:

- ✔ **Speaking out of school:** Somebody privy to confidential information starts flapping his gums to his golf buddies or at Friday night cocktails or a lunch meeting.

- ✔ **Buyer making improper contact with Seller's employees:** Buyer contacts one of Seller's employees, specifically someone who isn't involved in the potential deal, without Seller's permission, alerting that employee that the company is for sale.

- ✔ **Involving a loose-cannon advisor:** An advisor who knows of the impending deal (usually someone who'll be brought in only if the deal moves forward) can't resist making comments to friends and strangers alike.

One of the signers of the confidentiality agreement may cause a breach, but in my experience that situation is very rare. The person signing the document is usually acutely aware he just signed a document! More than likely, the weak link occurs elsewhere in the chain.

The two most common weak points — the people most apt to cause a breach of confidentiality — are advisors and executives or other employees, both of whom can be further broken down into "active" and "I hope I get hired" categories. In fact, those employees or advisors who hope to get hired or retained if the deal closes often cause the most problems.

Confirming a breach

Although some breaches are easy to confirm (people who shouldn't know about the deal talk to you about it), others are more difficult to nail down if you don't receive direct knowledge of it. If you suspect a breach, immediately pick up the phone and have a conversation with the other side. (If you're a Seller represented by an intermediary, call him immediately and have him deal with the situation.)

A phone conversation is important because you can gauge the other side's tone and reaction to the news. Writing a lengthy, accusatory e-mail (or leaving a length, accusatory voice mail) may end up muddying the waters more than clearing them. You need to hear the other side's story.

 Only send an e-mail to recap your conversation about the breach of confidentiality. If you're unable to get the other side on the phone, leave a brief message and send a short e-mail. Simply say that you urgently need to speak with the other party as soon as possible; you have some concerns about confidentiality. Don't go into detail in the message or e-mail.

I've dealt with the occasional breach during my deal-making years. In each and every example, I contacted the other side and had a conversation. In some cases, the other side apologized and immediately took steps to fix the problem. In other cases, where the breach wasn't as clear, the phone call served to raise the other party's awareness to a potential problem, and the breaches magically stopped.

Thinking long and hard about legal action

Although your first instinct may be to sue the pants off the offending cause of the breach, remember that lawsuits can be expensive, lengthy, and time consuming and may end up hurting you more than helping.

In every breach I've encountered, we were able to eventually complete a transaction without getting the courts involved. Starting a lawsuit would have greatly compromised our ability to close a deal.

Talk to your lawyer and your intermediary about a breach or suspected breach. Although you want to avoid legal recourse if possible, doing more than talking to the other side may be the best course of action. It's a bullet you may have to bite.

In case of a dispute, the confidentiality agreement usually designates the state where the dispute is heard in court. The jurisdiction is often a sticking point, especially if Buyer and Seller are in different states. Each party may prefer to use its home state as the jurisdiction. In that case, a third state (most often Delaware, due to its standing as a business-friendly state) is usually the best option.

Keeping the Cat in the Bag: Advice for Buyers

As I note earlier in the chapter, a confidentiality agreement is a serious and real legal document, and a Buyer who signs a CA should take every precaution to speak only with those who need to know about the business and are covered by the CA. The following sections give you some guidelines on who you can talk to and how to discuss sensitive information without letting the whole county know.

Involving employees and advisors

Generally, a confidentiality agreement allows the signers to speak with employees and advisors about the transaction. The CA specifically delineates these people by job title or function (not by name).

In the CA, relevant employees are usually designated with a line such as

> "Employees who have a legitimate need to know in order to evaluate a possible transaction are permitted to review materials."

The language for advisors typically goes something like the following:

> "Independent accountants, investment bankers, or other professionals (collectively, 'Buyer's Advisors') may be retained for the sole purpose of assisting Buyer in determining the feasibility of entering into a transaction."

The Buyer must inform any employee or advisor that that person is bound by the terms of the confidentiality agreement.

Discussing the deal in public

I'm constantly amazed at what I overhear in restaurants, on airplanes, in elevators, and other places where people gather. I constantly overhear people talking about lawsuits, tax cases, criminal cases, health problems, their troubled kids, and of course, M&A transactions. More often than not, these conversations use the actual names of the individuals or the companies involved!

Of course, yapping about such sensitive information is a no-no. You never know who's sitting at the table next to you. That professional intently working the crossword puzzle (in ink, thank you) while awaiting his soup may be getting an earful of private, confidential, and sensitive conversation. It happens.

Instead of using specific names, I strongly suggest M&A deal-makers take a wiseguy approach to talking about sensitive material. Watch *Goodfellas* or *The Sopranos* for guidance. Here's an example of this cloak-and-dagger approach:

> Deal-maker 1: "Did you talk to that guy about that thing? You know, our friend in Columbus, did you take care of that thing with that guy?"

> Deal-maker 2: "Oh, yeah, don't worry, he won't be a problem anymore. I took care of it; we had a real nice chat the other day."

See how that works? Liberal use of "that guy," "our friend," and "that thing" goes a long way to help keep things under wraps. If you need to clarify, mention the city ("our friend in Seattle") or mention the type of business ("that guy in the apparel distribution business in Lexington").

Chapter 8

Creating and Reviewing an Offering Document

. . . .

In This Chapter

▶ Taking an overview of the offering document

▶ Relaying company info

▶ Noting financial numbers

. . . .

The *offering document,* also known as the confidential offering memorandum (COM), the information package (IP), and the deal book, is the main sales document in the mergers and acquisitions process. More commonly, it's simply called *the book.* Everything a Buyer needs to make an offer (not close a deal) is in the book.

In this chapter, I introduce you to the who, what, when, and how of the offering document. In case you're wondering about the where, that's up to you! Write it where you're most comfortable.

The Offering Document in a Nutshell

The offering document is the deal book, the almanac of fact, the atlas of numbers. The offering document is the bible of the company. As with any written document, it becomes dogma. In other words . . . it's kind of important. Take care to draft a complete, honest, and accurate offering document.

The Seller writes the offering document (or, as is often more accurate, the Seller's advisors do). Writing an offering document is a time-consuming process, so Sellers need to make sure the book-writing takes priority in their daily activities.

If advisors are handling the task, an employee (usually the CFO or some other high-ranking finance person) makes sure to provide the author(s) with all the necessary information. From the time all the necessary information is gathered, a well-written offering document should take 60 days to write.

Buyers don't need to write an offering document. However, unless the company is well known and/or has a very detailed Web site, Buyer may want to prepare a quick one- or two-page overview of his company and *investment thesis* (a description of the types of companies he wants to acquire as well as his rationale for why those acquisitions make sense).

A well-written offering document spells out the value proposition for the Buyer. It includes an in-depth review of the company's operations, finances, sales, marketing, customers, employees, facilities, and more. This collective information should be sufficient for an interested Buyer to make an offer for the company. (See Chapter 9 for more on how a Buyer makes that offer.)

I like to think of an offering document as a road map to value. Sure, Seller's intent is to maximize the price Buyer pays for the company, but Buyer is only going to pay a price that makes sense from his view. Seller has to show Buyer where Buyer can realize value. And of course, Buyer has to confirm that value proposition! (Chapter 12 offers more info on valuation.)

Don't include an asking price in the offering document. You want the other side to make the first move. If you as a Seller provide an asking price, you've merely set the maximum price. Buyers probably won't be willing to pay more. Worse, if you give one price to Buyer A and Buyer B ends up paying more, Buyer A will rightfully be upset because Seller provided information that turned out to be moot.

Despite the fact that Buyers do far less work regarding the offering document — they just have to read it — few Buyers do actually go through it. Some Buyers (and I mean decision-makers) do actually read it closely, but many others merely scan the document and have a junior team member do the actual reading and provide a synopsis, quite often verbally during a meeting.

So why write a document most people don't read?

First, writing an offering document often becomes an introspective journey for a Seller. The exercise reveals details about his company, the operations, what works, what can be done better, and what should not be tried again. In creating a roadmap of value for a Buyer, the Seller is able to understand his company, market, and industry.

In fact, during many of the sales processes that I've run, the Seller almost always remarks that although the exercise of compiling the book was a pain, it was ultimately worthwhile because he learned about his company. More than one has said, "If I knew then what I know now, this company would be bigger and better."

Second, even though Buyers often don't spend much time with the book prior to management meetings, they refer to it constantly as they craft offers. The offering document becomes a reference guide for the Buyer. The Buyer flips back and forth searching for specific bits of information as he contemplates what offer makes sense.

The following sections detail what goes into an offering document. The order that I list the offering document's contents in isn't set in stone. Don't worry about following my list exactly; instead, just make sure your offering document addresses each of these areas.

Compiling the Executive Summary

Put your brain in the way-back machine and think about what your high school English teacher told you about writing a theme paper: Start big, narrow your focus, introduce the thesis, prove the thesis, and conclude by widening narrative. Your offering document should begin with an executive summary that follows that same rhythm. The *executive summary* is the big picture overview of the offering document. It includes the thesis, Seller's rationale for seeking a deal, and some thoughts on the type of transaction Seller would find agreeable. The following sections delve into those parts.

The thesis

The *thesis* is your central argument — the value proposition for Buyer and the aspect of the deal you want to tout. When you're selling a business, you need to have a thesis; you can't maximize value in a transaction unless you provide Buyer with specific examples of the value she can gain. Seller's thesis should be Buyer's opportunity.

Highly profitable companies are often best sold based on multiples of EBITDA; the industry standard magic number is five times (5X) EBITDA.

(Head to Chapter 12 for more on multiples and valuation.) It's the easiest valuation technique for Buyer to understand (and obtain financing for).

In the following sections, you find some common examples of different possible theses. Take a look-see, think about your specific situation, and then consider what may be the best thesis to extract the most value for both you and Buyer.

You don't need to limit yourself to a single thesis; feel free to pick and choose more than one.

EBITDA thesis

EBITDA is probably the most common investment thesis. Actually, EBITDA is a de facto default setting in the brains for most business people; you can say it's hardwired into their brains, and for good reason.

EBITDA is a measure of profitability, and profits are the ultimate measure of a company. Bank loans are often based on EBITDA; maintaining a certain level of EBITDA is a condition of a loan. The business world is just plain mad for all things EBITDA, and therefore, EBITDA is simply a generally accepted business convention.

EBITDA theses come in a few flavors. They're all similar because they use EBITDA as a basis for valuation, but they differ in the timing for the measurement of EBITDA.

- ✔ **Most recent complete year:** In many cases, the valuation is based on the most recent year's EBITDA. This method produces a static number; because deals take months to complete, Buyer may want to obtain financial updates to make sure the company suddenly doesn't take a nose dive in terms of profits. However, the most recent complete year EBITDA can provide the basis for an offer.

- ✔ **Trailing 12 month (TTM):** This thesis is based on the EBITDA for the *trailing* (most recent) 12 months; the valuation isn't static like the most recent complete year figures, so it may fluctuate up or down depending on the continuing performance of the company.

- ✔ **Forward EBITDA:** In this case, all or part of the valuation is based on the future performance of the company. Forward EBITDA is a good thesis when an earn-out or some other form of contingent payment is part of the deal because if Seller is asking for a valuation based on the future performance of the company, he should be willing to put his mouth where his money is.

Contribution margin thesis

With the *contribution margin thesis,* Seller is essentially telling Buyer, "Pay no attention to the lack of profits behind that curtain." Instead of focusing on the bottom-line profitability, Buyer considers the effects (that is, benefits) of adding the Seller's "contribution" to the Buyer's existing operation.

What is contribution? Definitions vary, but essentially, *contribution* is sales minus direct costs for those sales. *Direct costs* include the cost of goods, as well as any sales or marketing costs in SG&A (selling, general, and administrative).

As an example, say a company has revenues of $40 million and is losing $2 million a year. Assume the direct costs associated with those revenues are $18 million. The gist of this thesis in this case is to say to Buyer,

> "Look, we know our company as-is is unprofitable, but instead of taking the entire company, what if you only take the client relationships and corresponding revenue and move operations to your facility? If you do that and subtract only those expenses directly related to those revenues, you pick up $40 million in revenue and realize a $12 million contribution before your costs. I know you'd have other expenses, but how you run the business is up to you. What is that $12 million of contribution worth to your company?"

The key to this approach is the realization Buyer is already spending money on operations, and adding the acquisition's contribution to the mix will have little or no impact on expenses.

Buyers are unlikely to pay the standard 5X multiple on a contribution margin, but 2X may be a reasonable amount.

Companies with thin profits (or losses!) are typically prime candidates for the contribution margin thesis because a company with thin profits or losses doesn't fetch much if the valuation is based on the bottom line. Contribution margin focuses on something other than the bottom line and asks Buyer to pay based on that alternative.

However, companies with a product that clients view as a commodity aren't suitable candidates for a contribution margin approach because their products aren't considered different or unique, a situation that makes a contribution margin approach difficult. Buyer is unlikely to pay a premium for a company that's a dime a dozen.

Gross profit thesis

Very simply, the *gross profit thesis* asks Buyer to value the business based on the *gross profit* (revenues minus the cost of sales). This thesis is similar to the contribution margin thesis in the preceding section and in some cases may be exactly the same. In this approach, a 5X multiple is probably out of the running, but a 1X or 2X multiple may be possible.

The gross profit thesis may be a suitable solution for another problem: structuring an earn-out. See Chapter 12 for more on earn-outs and other contingent payments.

Top line revenue thesis

As simple as it gets: This thesis is a valuation based on *top line revenue* (gross revenue). Similar to the contribution margin thesis, Buyers probably won't pay 5X EBITDA; a 1X multiple is usually a pretty strong valuation.

The top line sales thesis makes a great way to measure an earn-out.

Asset value thesis

Instead of basing the valuation on some sort of measure of cash flow, *asset value thesis* uses the value of assets. This type of valuation is another way to create value for a profit-challenged company.

When using asset value, do not use the depreciated value of assets, use the replacement cost of assets. Companies will have accumulated depreciation on their books. Add that back or do some research and determine the replacement value of those assets. Also, for those of you delving into cross-border deals, Chinese Buyers rarely look at cash flow as a valuation technique and instead prefer asset value.

Strong customer base thesis

This thesis moves out the realm of measureable accounting results and firmly places us in the touchy-feely, "gosh darn it, people like me" world of intangible valuation techniques. So burn some incense, put on your Ravi Shankar LPs, and dig it, man!

With this thesis, Seller is asking Buyer to consider the strength of the customers. *Strength* can mean both size/purchasing power of the customers as well as the point of entry to the customer — the higher up the corporate food chain, the more valuable the relationship. A Seller who has C-level contacts (folks with *C*s in their titles, such as CFOs) has more-valuable customer relationships than a Seller who sells to low-level associates.

Recurring revenue thesis

A company with *recurring revenue* (revenue that automatically generates, such as that from fees or subscriptions) is often a more-desirable buy than a company where the sales force has to make new sales every year, month, or week. Many Buyers are often willing to pay a premium for that consistent revenue stream.

Just an old fashioned growth story thesis

This thesis is the ol' venture capital, "we're going to take over the world" story. Sure, the growth story deal often results in a flameout, but certain investors are willing to pay a hefty premium for a company that touts an incredible ability to grow.

I don't recommend the growth story thesis for owners who want to retire or otherwise take some chips off the table. When an investor puts money into a growth story company, that means the money stays with the company to pay for growth! The ability for Seller to garner a premium by selling a growth story company *and* pocketing that money are extremely remote.

Synergies thesis

Otherwise known as the "You complete me!" thesis, the *synergies thesis* is a situation where 1 + 1 = 3. Two companies, perhaps in the same industry or closely related ones, have certain strengths and certain weaknesses that complement each other such that the result is greater than the sum of its parts.

For example, suppose two companies are in the auto parts distribution business. One company goes to market through a catalog, has a world-class distribution center, and a strong customer service department. However, competitors who are excellent Internet marketers are eating it alive. The second company is an ace at Internet marketing but lacks a customer service department and relies on a very expensive outsourced distribution center.

In this example, the second company may be willing to pay a premium to buy the first company to fill in its own weak spots. The two companies are stronger together than they are separately.

Deals with this thesis can be extremely tricky to negotiate. Most often, Seller needs to tailor a specific message to each potential Buyer; after all, not every Buyer needs the same weakness addressed. Don't make up a story; just realize that different Buyers may view different aspects as the most valuable.

Seller's rationale for seeking a deal

A well-written offering document should provide Buyers with information about Seller's reasons for selling (I discuss common motivations in Chapter 2).

As Seller, communicating your motivation is important because doing so helps Buyer determine whether pursuing a deal makes sense. A Buyer who needs the Seller to stay on board to run the business is unlikely to bid if the deal involves the owner's retirement.

When selling a business, don't sound desperate when listing your rationale. Doing so gives Buyer the upper hand in negotiations because he knows you need to unload.

Seller's deal guidance

The *transaction guidance* portion of the offering document indicates the type of deal that interests Seller — that is, how much structuring (notes, earn-outs, and so on) if any he's willing to accept, whether he strongly prefers cash at closing, whether he needs or prefers an asset deal or a stock deal, and so on.

I don't recommend providing a price in the book. Doing so places a ceiling on the valuation, and Seller runs the risk of leaving some money on the table. Also, providing a price may inadvertently provide Buyer with the wrong guidance. A Buyer who submits an offer by matching the listed price will be rightfully upset if the company is sold to someone who submitted a higher bid. The snubbed Buyer may have been willing to submit a higher bid but decided to follow the guidance of Seller.

Presenting the Company's Background

After the executive summary provides the rationale for seeking a deal and provides some rough ideas on what a deal would look like (see "Compiling the Executive Summary" earlier in the chapter), the next section of the offering document provides basic information about the company: past, present, and future.

I call this section the *B and B section:* the basics and the bragging. Learning the basics helps Buyer understand the company and whether it's a right fit. It's much like dating.

As for the bragging, Seller's touting the company's achievements gives Buyer something to brag about post-sale. Perhaps more importantly, the representative for Buyer may need to get final approval from someone higher up the food chain, and being able to brag about the great accomplishments of a target helps with that internal sales pitch.

When I say "bragging," I'm not suggesting you take license and devolve into full-blown Seller hyperbole! Subjective comments aren't readily provable and more often than not make you sound like a huckster. Instead, focus on making accurate and objective comments about your business. Quiet confidence and actual results go a long way toward getting Buyer to make a deal.

The company's past and present

An accurate assessment of the company's history (good, bad, or in between) is a necessary part of the offering document. Having a solid understanding of where a company came from and how it developed can help Buyer understand the company.

Consider the following questions as you write this section of the offering document:

- ✔ How was the company founded, and how did it grow? Is it still growing or has it run into some recent challenges?
- ✔ What are the great successes and the problems, and how did the company overcome those problems?
- ✔ What is the company's current situation?

Providing a timeline is a great visual tool and a quick way to point out key events in a company's history: new products, financial milestones, past acquisitions, and so on.

Ownership and legal entity

Who are the owners, what do they own, and how much does each owner own? Okay, that sounds like a tongue twister, but furnishing ownership information to Buyer is extremely important because most offers actually reference the ownership.

Another important consideration is what type of entity the company is. Is it an LLC, S-corp, or C-corp? Should any other affiliated or related entities be a part of an offer (or should they not)?

If Buyer is buying the stock of Seller's company, Buyer needs to understand what entity owns what assets. For varying (often tax-related) reasons, a company may be comprised of two or more related entities. Buyer needs to make sure the stock he is buying actually has title to the assets of Seller's business.

Employee info and benefits

A company with products and customers isn't a company unless it can sell, service, account for, and otherwise take care of those customers and run the business. Because droids and clones are still a few years away, most companies have to use this creature called people. Perhaps you've heard of it.

For many (if not most) companies, the largest, single expense is personnel, so not surprisingly, a discussion of people, pay, and job duties is mandatory in the book. A book should list the total number of employees, the headcount per department, and provide a salary and wage ranges per employee, department, or employee type. It should also include bios for the key employees, which typically includes the executives, key managers, and perhaps certain other employees (such as sales and product development).

Including an organization chart is often a good idea. Specific names don't need to be divulged in the offering document. Instead, listing the employee's title is sufficient.

An offering document should provide detail on the health plans, retirement plants (401k and the like), and vacation, sick day, and holiday policies. These plans may or may not match with Buyer's company, so Buyer needs time to plan accordingly and make adjustments if warranted.

Vacation can be a small but serious sticking point when buying a company. If Seller owes employees a certain amount of vacation time, Buyer may insist that the value of that vacation time be deducted from the sale price. The logic is if the employees used that vacation time prior to the close of the sale, Seller would have to pay for that time off. You can find the value of this vacation time lurking on the balance sheet in the liabilities section, most often called "accrued vacation" or something similar.

Locations of offices and facilities

The offering document needs to list all distribution and manufacturing facilities, including square footage as well as the number of employees at each location. Buyer may need this information as it considers how best to integrate the acquisition and the parent company.

Many salespeople work remotely. Seller should list any and all remote workers, the city where each person resides, and a description of the person's duties and/or sales territory.

Real estate

If Seller owns the real estate where the facility is located, she may be interested in selling the business but retaining the property and having the new owner pay rent. This situation is very common and in many cases is Buyer's preferred method. If Seller wants to sell the land as part of the deal, that sale is usually a separate deal.

Use a real estate agent to sell land or real estate; M&A intermediaries (investment bankers or business brokers) aren't usually licensed real estate agents.

Technology

Buyers need to know Seller's computer systems, software, phone systems, Web sites, domain names, and anything else technology related. After all, if Buyer is going to someday run Seller's business, Buyer needs to know how Seller runs it.

Legal disclosures

Major areas of legal disclosure include safety, environmental, and tax issues. The company should mention any lawsuits to which it's a party. Unless a company has specific issues to disclose (and it should disclose any and all issues), this section is a very quick read. Essentially, Seller says, "Ownership has no knowledge of any problems" or "Ownership believes it's in compliance with . . . ."

Sellers should speak with their legal advisors about proper wording of any legal disclosure.

Sharing the Go-to-Market Strategy

An offering document isn't just all numbers and accounting and EBITDA; a good deal book needs to describe the company's go-to-market strategy, commonly called *sales and marketing*. The following sections focus on some considerations to keep in mind when creating or reviewing the sales and marketing section of an offering document.

In addition to providing information about sales and marketing, a good offering document should provide the Buyer with information about the sales by product line and/or sales by customer, though it shouldn't use specific customer names at this juncture. See the later section "Customer names" for more on the to-name-or-not-to-name issue.

Description of market and products

A company exists to sell a product and/or offer a service, so the offering document should reflect careful attention to the explanation of the selling company's product/service, customers and suppliers, and sales and order processing. The following sections outline some basic questions Seller needs to answer regarding each of these categories.

Product/service

I doubt Sellers are shocked to find that Buyer is interested in buying the company because of its products or services. With that in mind, the offering document needs to provide plenty of information about products and services, including answering the following questions:

- **What is the product or service?** What does the company sell? The offering document should provide details about this most basic aspect of the company. You may think this information is something Buyer should already know, but remember that Buyer likely has multiple decision-makers, and some of the people reading the offering document may not have been involved in the early discussions and therefore may not know anything about the company.

- **What is fueling growth?** If sales are stagnant (or falling), what factors cause that? Providing Buyer with some insights as to market trends and challenges is important in helping Buyer understand the value drivers for a company.

✔ **Is any portion of the revenue recurring?** Recurring revenue is often the holy grail for acquirers. A company with high percentage of revenue that recurs month after month or year after year may be able to garner a higher valuation than a company that starts each month at zero.

You may also hear that a company scales very well. *Scale* can mean recurring revenue; in other words, after a salesperson has made a sale, she doesn't need to go back and sell that same customer again and can instead focus on winning new customers. Scale can also mean very large sale prices. For example, a company that sells $1 million pieces of equipment probably scales better than a company selling a $10 widget.

✔ **Does the company experience any seasonality?** In other words, are sales stronger during certain parts of the year and weaker in others? Buyer needs to know about seasonality so that it can plan accordingly. For example, companies with extreme seasonality may need a credit line. The company will tap the credit line during the slow season(s) and pay off the line during flush times.

✔ **How many product offerings does the company have?** If the company offers a physical product (as opposed to a service), how many stock keeping units (SKUs) does it sell? A *stock keeping unit* is simply a number assigned to a specific product; the more SKUs a company has, the more different products it can offer its customers.

A high number of SKUs can be a warning sign for Buyer because too many SKUs may mean the company is spread too thin or is stocking a lot of slow-moving inventory. Slow-moving inventory can be a waste of cash. Too many SKUs can also be an opportunity for Buyer because Buyer may be able to eliminate this slow-moving product and improve the efficiency and profitability of the company. What constitutes too many SKUs depends on each specific industry and each specific company.

Customers and suppliers

Having products and services without customers to buy them makes no sense, so as Seller, you want to give some information about customers in the offering document. Additionally, you need to provide some detail on your vendors and suppliers; you have to get those products or raw materials from somewhere! Here are some topics to consider in this section of the offering document:

✔ **Who buys the company's products/services?** Because a company is a pipe dream until it has actual paying customers, Seller needs to describe its customers to Buyer. Depending on its needs, Buyer may want access to new customers or to be familiar with the customers.

✔ **What is the demographic of the customer?** Are the customers businesses or consumers? Is this demographic growing or shrinking? What sort of macroeconomic factors affect these customers?

✔ **Where does Seller fit in its sales channel?** An offering document should describe a company's sales channel. Is it a supplier of raw materials, a manufacturer, a distributor, or a retailer? Does it offer a service to other companies or consumers? In other words, where does the company obtain the materials used to fabricate its end product? Who does the company buy from, who does it sell to, and who do those customers sell to?

✔ **Does the company have any customer concentration issues?** Flip to the section "Income statement basics," later in this chapter, for more on customer concentration.

If a customer that accounts for a big chunk of revenue is a large company (say, Fortune 500 size), you may be able break out the specific divisions and the corresponding sales to substantially lower the concentration issue.

Sales and order processing

Products and services are wonderful. Suppliers and vendors are great, too. But all of those products, services, and raw materials don't amount to a hill of beans without the ability to sell them. Buyers want some detail on sales information, so the offering document needs to cover the following:

✔ **How does the company go to market?** Does it utilize a direct sales force, e-mail, Internet, other social media, catalog, and/or word of mouth?

✔ **Who are the key salespeople?** What are their backgrounds and experience?

✔ **How are orders taken: phone, fax, e-mail, or in person?** Does the company have a dedicated customer service department?

✔ **What are the company's terms of sale?** How does the company get paid: credit card, cash, check, or wire transfer?

✔ **What is the average transaction size?**

Customer names

As Seller, should you provide customer names in the offering document? Yes and no. In other words: It depends. I provide both sides of the argument here; read both bullets and pick the option that best suits your situation:

✔ **No:** Customer names should not appear in the offering document because they're a highly sensitive bit of information, especially if Seller's direct competitors are reviewing the offering document.

> ✔ **Yes:** If Seller's Web site or existing materials list customers or if the names of certain customers are otherwise public information, specifically mentioning those customers doesn't hurt, especially if the customers are of the large and extremely well-known household names.

Whichever argument you follow, providing a full customer list in the offering document isn't a good idea because you should disclose detailed customer information (name, amount of annual purchases, and so on) only after you're reasonably certain Buyer will close a deal. For this reason, I always recommend Sellers wait until near the end of due diligence before providing the full, detailed customer list to Buyer.

Info about competitors

The offering document should also include information on Seller's competitors. Seller needs to demonstrate to Buyer that it understands the competitive landscape. Additionally, this information may help a Buyer who's new to Seller's specific industry get an overview of the main competitors and assess the competitive risks.

In addition to listing competitors, the offering document should provide some insight into each competitor's relative strengths and weaknesses, revenue size, and percentage stake (roughly) of the market.

Note: If one of the listed competitors is also reviewing the offering document, that competitor instinctively goes to the competitor section and corrects, contradicts, or otherwise chuckles about whatever the entry says. No matter what Seller writes, the competitor will take some sort of umbrage with it. Wouldn't you?

Doing the Numbers

Numbers don't necessarily speak for themselves, and Buyers don't want to have to translate them, so you as Seller should take care to present your financials in the offering document in the best light possible, as the following sections demonstrate.

You can't get around dealing with accounting and financials in the offering document, so make sure whoever is compiling this part of the offering document has strong accounting skills.

Historical financials

I recommend an offering document have at least three years of historical financial results; five years is much better.

An offering document with three to five years of financial results helps Buyer better understand the recent trends of the business. Some of the key historical financial aspects include

- ✔ Are sales increasing or decreasing? What about profits?
- ✔ Is the company maintaining its gross margin?
- ✔ Are any operating expenses getting out of control?
- ✔ How much working capital does the company have?
- ✔ Does the company collect accounts receivable in a timely fashion and pay its bills on time?
- ✔ Does the company have long-term debt, and will that debt get in the way of doing a deal?

Make sure you include a full set of financials: income statement, balance sheet, and cash flow statement.

When presenting financials, present the numbers down to an EBITDA calculation. If the company has substantial *add backs* (nonrecurring, one-time only, or owner-related expenses), include those add backs in the historical and current financials. Make sure you provide details of what exactly those add backs comprise.

The add back machine: What's legit and what's not

An *add back,* for the uninitiated, is an expense that is added back to the profits (most often EBITDA) of the business for the express purpose of improving the profit situation of the company. It's a bit of alchemy; when you toss in enough add backs to the profits of a company, you turn EBITDA into the mythical "adjusted EBITDA."

The theory behind these add backs is that these expenses are purported to be extraneous, one-time, and/or "owner's" expenses. In plain English, these add back expenses will either go away once the company is in the hands of the new owner or won't be incurred again.

Some legitimate add backs include the following:

- ✔ **Adjustments to owner's compensation:** Many owners of closely held companies, especially successful and highly profitable ones, give themselves outsized salaries and bonuses. Nothing is wrong with that, of course, but an acquirer is unlikely to pay that kind of compensation to the new president (and other execs). For example, if a reasonable salary for the president of a certain-sized company is $150,000 but the owner of such a company paid herself $500,000, a legitimate add back would be $350,000. This add back means EBITDA would improve by $350,000, thus improving the potential valuation for Seller and providing a roadmap of greater profitability for Buyer.

✔ **Taxes and benefits:** If making add backs for adjustments to owner's compensation, make sure to add back the corresponding taxes, too. If an owner and/or other employees are leaving the company post-acquisition, the benefits these people were paid may be appropriate add backs, too. The main benefit for most owners is insurance. If the owner won't be replaced, the full amount of insurance can be added back; if the owner will be replaced, the replacement insurance package may not have all the bells and whistles of Seller's plan.

✔ **Severance and lawsuit settlements:** Severance payments and lawsuit settlements may be cause for further due diligence on behalf of Buyer, but these payments can be another example of a legitimate add back, assuming these sorts of payments are truly rare and unusual for the company.

✔ **Personal expenses:** Running personal expenses through the company is a common occurrence in closely held companies. These companies often practice the so-called Family Accepted Accounting Principles, or FAAP (to use some slang), in addition to (or in replacement of) Generally Accepted Accounting Principles (GAAP). If an acquired company does utilize FAAP, these personal expenses are a legitimate add back because the new owner won't continue to incur these expenses.

Note: FAAP is firmly a gray area for taxation, so speak with your accountant as to the proper treatment of these expenses.

Disclaimer: Mergers & Acquisitions For Dummies doesn't suggest owners should engage in FAAP. Instead, the author realizes these expenses are often included in a closely held business's income statement.

Personal expenses may include the following:

✔ The clubs (hunting, country, health, and so on)

✔ Owner's car expenses (monthly payment, insurance, gas, and so on)

✔ Family members on the payroll

✔ Travel, meals, entertainment for personal use, not business purposes

✔ Any other expense that is personal in nature and not a business-related expense

So, what add backs aren't legit? This group is a little more difficult to quantify because types of expenses are virtually limitless. Instead, apply a simple two-part rule of thumb:

✔ If one-time-only expenses show up on a company's income statement year after year, they aren't one time; they're recurring and therefore not a legitimate add back expense.

✔ If the company will incur add back expenses post-acquisition, they aren't legitimate add backs.

Buyers, pay close attention to Seller's add backs. Don't be afraid to challenge Seller as to the legitimacy of the add back. And Sellers shouldn't try to add back expenses that will not go away post-closing. Add backs that aren't legitimate are expenses that the company will continue to incur, even after a sale transaction.

Financial projections

Ideally, an offering document should have five years of projections. I know that's a lot of work, especially when projections are taken with a grain of salt, but Buyer should be able to get a good sense of where you think the company is headed.

Your projections should include a narrative explaining the assumptions you used to create them. For example, explain your rationale for revenue increases and how expenses are related to those revenues. Achieving the projected numbers is imperative, so you're much better off to project low growth and beat that projection than to project rapid growth and fall short. You're sure to create problems for yourself if you pad your projections to an unobtainable level. Not achieving those higher projections often leads to a lower sale price. Plus, Buyers are on the lookout for overly rosy projections and may discount projections that the historical financials don't support. (See the preceding section for more on historical financials.)

Another important figure in the projections is CAPEX. CAPEX (short for *capital expenditures*) occur when a company makes some sort of investment in itself. Instead of immediately expensing the expenditure, thus reducing profits by the full amount of the investment, a company may be able to *capitalize* the expenditure and write off the expense over a period of time. Examples of CAPEX include anything that will be used for a long period of time: computers, software, furniture, improvements to the facilities, manufacturing equipment, and so on.

For example, say a company pays $1 million for a piece of equipment with an expected useful life of ten years. Writing off the full cost of the equipment in year one doesn't make sense because the equipment will be used for nine more years. Instead, the company writes off the amount of the equipment used each year, or $100,000 per year. This write-off is called *depreciation*.

Because annual capital expenditures are not captured in the venerable EBITDA calculation, Buyers should take a close look at a company's CAPEX needs to fully understand the true cash flow of the business.

Balance sheet basics

One of the most important figures from Seller's balance sheet is the company's working capital. For the purposes of M&A, *working capital* commonly means current assets minus current liabilities. Typically,

Current assets = accounts receivable + inventory + prepaid expenses

Current liabilities = accounts payable + short-term debt + current portion of long-term debt + accrued (*unpaid*) expenses

For the purposes of M&A, you don't include cash and equivalents in this calculation. However, for accounting purposes, you do include them.

Working capital is important because it represents the liquidity of the company. All current assets should be convertible into cash within 30 days, and all current liabilities should be able to be paid within 30 days.

Buyers, eye the balance sheet carefully to see whether the company you're looking to acquire is sufficiently undercapitalized, has a reasonable reserve against bad (uncollectable) accounts, and has its current liabilities all within terms. If any of these items are remiss, you may be taking over financial trouble.

Depending on the nature of the business, working capital may have some seasonality. For example, retailers typically have very strong fourth quarters as their sales are driven by the gift-giving season. Other companies experience peaks in late summer with the back-to-school season. As Seller, you want to spell out how this seasonality affects working capital so that Buyer gets a more accurate view of your company's situation.

Income statement basics

The selling company's income statement contains lots of important information for the offering document; check out the following sections for some notable income metrics.

Be sure to distinguish in the book which party gets any cash on the books. In most cases, cash belongs to Seller. If a company has $500,000 in cash and is selling for $5 million, Seller receives $5.5 million (before taxes, expenses, and advisor's fees, of course).

Recurring revenue and customer concentration

Recurring revenue is always a plus for a company, and Sellers are wise to mention the amount of recurring revenue in the offering document because it may increase Buyer interest and therefore the offer price.

Another metric, *customer concentration,* is the opposite of recurring revenue. If a company has highly concentrated sales (large amounts of sales with one customer or a small number of customers), Buyers may be less inclined to pursue a deal or offer a high price. Customer concentration is a bit of a slippery eel to grasp and define, but generally speaking, if a single customer accounts for more than 20 percent of revenue, or if a small number of customers (three to five) accounts for more than 50 percent of revenue, the company may have a customer concentration issue.

If Seller doesn't have a concentration issue, that's a key selling point definitely worth mentioning, if not touting, in the offering document. If Buyer cannot ascertain any customer concentration issues (after reading the offering document), Buyer should make a point to ask Seller about customer concentration during a follow-up phone call or e-mail.

If you do have a customer-concentration issue, try to mitigate that issue. For example, if a single customer accounts for 40 percent of revenues but is a large, multinational conglomerate with multiple decision-makers in multiple offices, point out this distinction to Buyer. In this example, you can argue that 40 percent of revenue is not under the control of a single decision-maker, thus mitigating some of the risk of the concentration.

Gross profit, gross margin, and SG&A

Gross profit is the amount of revenue that remains after the cost of producing sales is subtracted. For example, if sales are $100 million and the cost of goods sold is $40 million, the gross profit is $60 million. *Gross margin* is the percentage calculation of gross profit. In this example, the gross margin is 60 percent.

Contrary to popular usage, gross profit and gross margin aren't interchangeable. Any time you see the word *margin,* that means percentage. Far too many businesspeople refer to gross profit as gross margin, saying, "The company has $10 million in gross margin." Actually, the company has $10 million in gross profit. If revenues were $100 million, the company would have a 10 percent gross margin.

Gross profit is important because it's variable — it fluctuates based on revenue levels and pricing. Gross profit needs to be high enough to cover the other costs of the business, called SG&A. SG&A is comprised of salaries, rent, insurance, utilities, supplies, and so on. Although SG&A includes both fixed and variable costs, most companies have a good idea of their SG&A, and therefore know exactly how much it needs to generate in sales to create sufficient gross profit to cover SG&A.

When companies fail to generate enough gross profit to cover SG&A, that's a bad sign! If a company lowers its prices in order to generate higher sales, those lower prices may result in lower gross profit, and if gross profit dips below SG&A, the company is in trouble.

Other income and other expense

A good offering document should detail the nebulous "other income" and "other expense" categories. Essentially, these categories are revenues or expenses that aren't related to the underlying nature of the company. If a t-shirt manufacturer sells a piece of equipment for $50,000, it reports that income on the income statement as "other income." If that company also terminates an employee and pays that employee a $20,000 severance, it should report that expense in the "other expense" section. (Hopefully, firing employees and paying severance isn't a regular event.)

Although other income and other expenses should appear in the offering document, make sure you adjust the EBITDA for those other income or other expense items. Failure to clearly delineate other income and other expenses may blur the company's actual EBITDA (EBITDA generated as result of the company's normal operations and not as the result of one-time expenses or income).

Losses on the books

Companies with losses sometimes keep those losses on the books, applying those *net-operating losses* (NOLs) against future earnings and thus reducing a future tax liability. Be sure to mention any NOLs in your offering document. In years past, Buyers were able to acquire entities with NOLs and use those losses to reduce their tax burdens. However, Congress has greatly restricted that ability, so Buyers will want to know of any NOLs upfront.

If you're selling a business or attempting to buy a business with NOLs, speak with your tax advisor immediately.

Accounts receivable terms

An offering document should provide some guidance as to the selling company's terms with accounts receivable. Specifically, does the company expect payment within 30, 45, or 60 days (or some other amount of time)? Does the company provide a discount for early payments (and if so, what)? What is the reserve policy for uncollectible accounts? How much has been written off due to bad accounts?

Fixed assets (equipment)

Fixed assets are the assets a company uses to make its product. These items run the gamut from desks, phones, and computers to vans, trucks, and delivery vehicles to heavy machinery and production equipment.

The office stuff (desk, phone, computers, and so on) probably doesn't have much value to Buyer in terms of collateral for financing. Neither do the vehicles; they depreciate very quickly. However, the *hard assets* (the machinery and production equipment) often form the basis of assets that can serve as collateral to back a loan.

Inventory

Although not all companies have inventory (for example, consultancies and most business service firms), those that produce or distribute a product find that inventory is a key component for Buyer's financing and thus an important note in the book. Inventory is considered a *current asset,* which means (in theory) that it should be convertible to cash within a short period of time, usually a month or less.

If you're a Buyer, pay close attention to inventory. Is it all sellable? If the Seller has been building up inventory with unsellable or slow-moving stock, you may not be able to utilize 100 percent of the inventory to help with financing the acquisition.

Intangible assets

An offering document should have a listing of all intangible assets. *Intangible assets* include brand names, patents, trademarks, and Internet domain names — items whose value you can't easily measure. These assets don't usually help Buyer finance the deal, but they can still be valuable: Household names such as Apple, Exxon, and Walmart (and even smaller-market companies that are less widely known but still prestigious within their market segments) all have intangible value simply because their names are so well known.

If Seller doesn't want to include some of these intangibles in the deal (perhaps she wants to retain a certain domain name that isn't used), she needs to specify those carve-outs in the book.

Understanding a Seller's vulnerability

Going through an M&A sales process in general, and writing an offering document specifically, can leave Seller feeling extremely exposed. If you're a Seller or potential Seller, you aren't alone! And if you're on the buying side, take a moment to read this sidebar so you can sensitize yourself to the worries and fears of Sellers.

Sellers feel vulnerable because every decision they've made throughout their careers — good, bad, and everything in between — is fodder for discussion. Every problem, every wart, and every misstep that Sellers would rather forget get rehashed and brought to light. Sellers often have to explain and discuss embarrassing decisions and poor investments. It's the ultimate mea culpa for many business owners.

But Sellers can comfort themselves with the fact that they aren't the only ones to go through this process. Buyers are like doctors: They've seen it all or will at least pretend like they have.

Sellers afford themselves some level of safety by remembering the following tips:

✔ **Hire a capable intermediary:** As I discuss in Chapter 5, an intermediary often acts as hand-holder for the business owner and serves as a valuable buffer. An intermediary can make the initial overtures without tipping off the fact that a certain company is for sale until a confidentiality agreement is in place, whereas the mere act of a Seller approaching the Buyer sets off the alarms.

✔ **Keep your cards close to your vest.** Sellers can protect themselves through the slow, gradual release of information. Each divulgence has its time and a place.

✔ **Assume the position:** At some point, Sellers have to just get over their shyness and prepare themselves to feel as if they're being paraded naked through town, poked and prodded, and generally abased and abused. It isn't pretty, but it's what happens!

Buyers, be cognizant of these feelings, too. Be gentle! Buyers should only ask for documents and information needed to close the deal.

Chapter 9

Properly Expressing Interest in Doing a Deal

*T*he indication of interest (also known as the indication or IOI) is a key landmark in any business sale. This document provided by the Buyer suggests a valuation range that he is willing to pay for a company. Typically, a Seller receives indications from numerous Buyers. If the Buyer's indication is acceptable, the next step is for her to attend a management meeting (see Chapter 10) and submit a letter of intent (LOI — see Chapter 13).

Think of the indication as akin to a father asking his daughter's date, "What are your intentions with my daughter, young man?" The indication provides an overview of Buyer's intentions and sets the stage for what the final deal will (well, may) look like.

An indication may sound like a teaser (which I cover in Chapter 7), and in some ways it is. A teaser is compiled by a Seller (or a Seller's intermediary); an indication of interest is created by the Buyer. Essentially, the indication is the Buyer's teaser. The teaser is document (often anonymous) that explains the basics of the company for sale: products, customers, revenues, profits. The indication isn't anonymous; it's a specific Buyer's first volley, expressing the Buyer's interest in a written and therefore somewhat formal medium.

In this chapter, I introduce you to the ins and outs of indicating interest in doing a deal.

Understanding the Indication of Interest

As a rule, I don't allow a client to meet with a Buyer until I know that Buyer's intentions. An *indication of interest* is simply a quick way for the Buyer to say to the Seller, "We're interested in doing a deal." The document goes on to say, "Based on the information you've provided us, we're interested in buying your company and are willing to pay a price somewhere between X and Y." The key component of the indication is the valuation range. But other considerations lurk in this short and quick document.

Even though the indication isn't a binding offer and likely contains some legal-weasel words about it "not constituting an actual offer," the mere existence of the indication helps elevate the offer to something more substantial than a simple discussion. Putting words on paper is a powerful thing.

Putting your indication where your mouth is

Although an indication of interest isn't a binding offer, it's an important step that shows Buyer is willing to do something. Granted, that "something" is only typing out a page or two of mostly boilerplate text, signing that document, and e-mailing it to the other side, but it's still action.

An indication of interest is a way to separate the wheat from the chaff. Because people often take the path of least resistance, "doing something" means challenging the status quo, so given the choice between risking the wrath of their bosses by trying to break the boss's *stasis* (inaction), employees often elect to do nothing. It's easier that doing something and reduces the chances of getting fired by making an acquisition that fails.

When Buyer does take the time to submit an indication, Buyer is now signaling both his ability and his willingness to break through the chains of stasis. Someday, that may even involve real work, such as getting on an airplane, visiting a site, having meetings, and negotiating the final deal.

The other reason indications are so important is that for most businesspeople, saying you're going to do something, shaking someone's hand, or e-mailing an indication invokes the honor system where your word is your bond. You move from the purgatory of stasis into the arena of effort and work. You stir your own psyche into action.

Believe it not, many people in business are unwilling (or unable) to take concrete steps forward and make decisions. These are time-wasters. Although not the nominal intent of the document, the indication of interest can help cull the herd of timewasters and pretenders and provide the Seller with a concise group of Buyers willing (on paper, at least) to move forward.

Sellers prefer to get a quick "yes" or "no" answer from prospective Buyers. After contacting Buyer, Seller much prefers to either receive an indication of interest or a quick decline. The worst are the time-wasters who never respond (I call them zombies — the living dead). If you're a Buyer, have the common courtesy to always close the loop with any prospective Seller by giving a timely "yea" or " nay" answer.

Sellers want to receive as many indications of interest as possible. The actual number is a function of a few factors:

- ✔ The quality of the company/opportunity

- ✔ The thesis in the offering document (refer to Chapter 8)

- ✔ The quality of Seller's intermediary (that is, how good a job he does at generating interest)

- ✔ The strength of Seller's target list (see Chapter 6)

If a company is solid in all these categories, Seller should receive five to ten indications.

My recommendation is to get at least five indications. In most processes, that should give Seller enough potential Buyers to successfully close a deal with one. Sellers should not stop soliciting indications after they reach five, of course — the more the merrier!

Some Buyers simply paper the market with indications. As Seller, you want to obtain indications from more than one Buyer before moving on the management meeting phase (see Chapter 10).

Including Key Bits of Information in an Indication of Interest

The indication and its key piece of information, the valuation range, merely set up the next steps for the process: meetings, LOIs, due diligence, and (cross your fingers) the closing. But those aren't the only aspects of the indication. The following sections outline other important points in an indication of interest.

Preamble, platitudes, and Buyer background

The indication starts as most well-written letters start: with some introductory lauding. In this case, it's directed at Seller's company. Buyer almost always mentions how excited she is at the prospect of buying the company. It also states the obvious: "We are pleased to submit this indication of interest . . . ."

Most indications also include some boilerplate information about Buyer. This section lets Buyer do two things: brag and tout. Buyer can chirp about all the company's office locations, how much money it has made under management, its revenue size, its balance sheet strength — you get the idea. If Buyer thought slapping on some smelly cologne would impress Seller, she'd do that, too.

The intention of the background information section is to afford Seller with a modicum of security that Buyer is a stable, secure, and decisive outfit that can do what it says it'll do.

The proposed deal: Valuation range and other considerations

Here's the heart of the indication. Please rub your hands together in gleeful anticipation of learning the valuation range. Because the indication amounts to little more than a "dipping the toe in the water" exercise (Buyer isn't yet committed to the purchase), the valuation is estimated. Valuation usually appears as a range, largely to allow Buyer to hedge her bets. After Buyer gets more information in the management meetings (see Chapter 10), she can amend her offer and provide a specific valuation. In a practical sense, the Seller usually sees the higher number and focuses on that. Buyer has the wiggle room to offer the lower number.

For all intents and purposes, Seller should focus on the lower number in the valuation range because that's probably the valuation Buyer will end up using in the LOI. If Buyer comes back and uses a higher valuation, Seller will be pleasantly surprised.

The following sections give you the lowdown on the valuation range as well as how the indication lays out other parts of the proposed deal.

Finding the doggone valuation range

To help create a visual of the importance of the valuation range, imagine a dog. Specifically, a retrieving-mad Labrador retriever. Hold up a tennis ball in front of said retriever and shake your hand to generate enough movement to capture the dog's attention.

After the dog spies the tennis ball he wants only one thing in the world: THE BALL! If you throw the ball, the dog will chase it pell-mell, running through bushes and thorns and sniffing and snuffing until he finds it.

Sellers kind of have the same approach when it comes to the valuation range in indications of interest. In fact, you can say they're valuation-mad valuation seekers. They tear through the indication with total disregard for the rest of the information until they find that one prized nugget.

Bracing for the valuation

The truth of the matter is that most Sellers (or their investment bankers) immediately look for the valuation range. All of the work, including reading this book and going through the M&A process, boils down to one thing: the valuation. Because the valuation range is the first thing folks in-the-know look for after receiving an indication, Buyers sometimes put that bit in bold.

For first-time Sellers, seeing the valuation range is often anticlimactic. Even if the range is favorable, it's just a simple line that essentially says, "We offer to pay between $X million and $Y million."

This quick sentence can be a bit disconcerting because Seller immediately flashes back to all the hard work and toil she put in over the years and suddenly realizes that they've been distilled into a dispassionate range of numbers.

Evaluating the type of deal offered

After Seller gets over the disappointing shock of a low bid or anticlimactic relief of an acceptable range, the next step is to read the actual document. The indication should contain the other important elements of the offer, including the amount of the company Buyer proposes to buy and what kind of deal she's looking for.

The percentage of the company Buyer wants to buy can be divided in to two camps: control and non-control. Most (but not all) Buyers prefer to make *control* acquisitions, which means Buyer acquires enough of the company to have control over it (either by buying more than 50 percent of the company or by changing the company's operating agreement to give Buyer control over the entity). In this case, if Seller stays on board as president, the new owner has the ability to fire Seller.

The indication should also define whether Buyer wants a stock or asset deal. Most Sellers prefer asset deals due to preferential tax treatment; most Buyers prefer stock deals due to preferential treatment of successor liabilities.

The indication doesn't need detail on the structure of the deal: how much of the proceeds will be cash at closing, a note, an earn-out, and so on. However, a Buyer who expects to pay cash at closing and doesn't anticipate using an earn-out or Seller note should mention that in the indication.

Regardless of whether the offer is control or non-control or stock or asset, the most important question is whether it matches Seller's expectation as laid out in the offering document (which I cover in Chapter 8). If the Seller wants to sell 100 percent of the business, is Buyer offering to buy 100 percent? Are Buyer and Seller on the same page on deal structure?

Buyer should submit an indication based on what she can support. However, I recommend Buyer still submit an offer even if it doesn't appear to meet Seller's expectations. You never know; it may be close enough to what Seller is seeking.

Sellers should be on the watch for indications with a *financing contingency.* This phrase is legalese for "We don't have the money yet; we hope to find it after we strike a deal." Sellers should call the bluff and have the Buyer remove "financing contingency." Similarly, if you're selling to a private equity (PE) firm, the word to beware of is *committed* funds. The firm has to ask for these funds from investors. What you want to see instead is the phrase *under management,* which indicates the fund actually has possession of the funds. (Head to Chapter 6 for more on PE firms.)

Addressing Seller's debt and any other conditions

The indication of interest usually answers the question of "who gets the cash, who takes care of Seller's debt?" In most cases, Seller keeps all the cash in the company's bank account. Buyer usually assumes the current payables (defined by payables within terms; if Seller is late in paying her bills, she'll have to pay those debts at closing). If Seller has borrowed money, which shows up on the balance sheet as long-term debt, Seller is responsible for paying off that debt.

In some cases, however, Buyer may decide to assume Seller's long-term debt as part of the purchase price. When that happens, the amount of Seller's debt tacks on to the deal value. In other words, if Seller agrees to sell the business for $10 million in cash plus the assumption of $3 million in debt, the total deal value is $13 million.

Lastly, any special conditions, such as Seller maintaining or achieving some sort of financial metric such as EBITDA, appear in the indication.

The legalese

This part is usually just a quick sentence where Buyer states the offer is based on information provided by Seller or her intermediary (if she has one). This section gives Buyer an out if further due diligence uncovers issues or problems not disclosed or readily apparent in the materials provided.

In other words, if Buyer makes an offer to by a company with $5 million in EBITDA and due diligence shows the company actually has only $1 million in EBITDA, Buyer has recourse to amend that offer.

Toward the end of most indications, Buyer tosses in some more boilerplate legalese that reiterates the need to confirm everything in due diligence before the deal can close.

An enthusiastic send off

The indication will then conclude with enthusiastic, "Let's do a deal!" language. It's a call to action. When I take over the world, I'll mandate that every bit of correspondence conclude with an enthusiastic call to action.

Chapter 10

Ensuring Successful First Meetings between Buyer and Seller

· ·

In This Chapter

▶ Exploring the benefits of face-to-face meetings

▶ Organizing a management meeting

▶ Presenting the company to Buyers

▶ Getting ready for a facility tour

▶ Gauging the effectiveness of a meeting

· ·

*A*fter Buyer has reviewed the book (or *offering document* — see Chapter 8) and submitted an indication of interest (see Chapter 9), the next step is to meet with Seller's key management and/or ownership. The management meeting (run by Seller) provides a financial update (and any other pertinent updates) and allows a prospective Buyer to interact with Seller. It may even include a tour of the facility. Think of it as M&A dating.

In this chapter, I introduce you to meetings and more meetings all kinds of meetings.

Understanding the Importance of Meeting in Person

Over the years I have advised my clients that the management meetings effectively take the proceedings from black and white into Technicolor. A company described in a two-dimensional, black-and-white offering document suddenly becomes a living, breathing, three-dimensional entity when actual people meet face to face. The M&A process really comes alive.

Also, meeting in person rather than on a conference call, for example, gives you the chance to read the body language of the folks on the other side. Are they bored? Shifting in their seats? Playing with their smartphones? If you can't see someone, you can't observe body language.

Sellers shouldn't take a meeting with a potential Buyer until the Buyer indicates its interest in writing. Even a Seller who wasn't looking to sell and was contacted directly by a Buyer should refrain from meeting with the Buyer until the Buyer submits an indication of interest.

The following sections present a few reasons why personal meetings are so crucial.

The buyer gets to interact with key management

Not read about them, not talk to them on the phone, but meet face to face. Having a chance to engage in real-time interaction is far different from merely reading about people or processes. That's why people go on dates!

The "coming alive" aspect of the meeting phase manifests in the ability of one side to ask impromptu questions of the other side. Instead of merely reading a black-and-white book, Buyer gets the chance to engage in a discussion when a question or comment pops up.

Both sides perform due diligence on the other

Yes, Buyer does the vast majority of due diligence, but during the meeting phase Seller gets a chance to learn more about Buyer.

This step is keenly important if Seller is planning to stay involved with the business after closing. And even Sellers who plan to sell 100 percent of the business and retire often have a parental view of their employees: They want their people to continue to prosper and succeed.

Sellers (or their intermediaries) observe prospective Buyers at the management meetings and attempt to gauge which group has the best chance of continuing the business's success post-sale; who has the right skill sets to run the business; who has the ability to close a deal; and frankly, who they like. I know that criterion is subjective, and in most cases a high valuation trumps all other considerations, but sometimes doing a deal comes down to the more visceral "We didn't like them, let's go with the other guys." (See the following section for more on chemistry between parties.)

Buyers should remember that Seller is speaking with other Buyers in most cases. As Buyer, don't take it for granted that Seller will choose you. Put your best foot forward!

The parties gauge chemistry

In other words, do Buyer and Seller play well together? Chemistry is another subjective concept. Both sides either like each other or have some sort of tension.

Keep in mind that the actions of one side or the other can affect how chemistry develops (or dies) at a meeting. For example, a Buyer once told me he was bringing a "consultant" to the management meeting. The "consultant" turned out to be the CEO of my client's main competitor! The Buyer didn't inform of us of this fact; we didn't know the true identity of the "consultant" until we exchanged business cards at the start of the meeting. My client immediately said he wasn't going to continue until the offending "consultant" left the meeting.

This moment turned out to be the high point of the day; the discussions turned contentious and heated. Needless to say, the Buyer and Seller had no chemistry, and any chance of a deal between both sides was effectively DOA.

Ironing Out Management Meeting Logistics

Although the purpose of the management meeting is for Seller to impart information to Buyer, Seller shouldn't forget the goal of the meeting: to eventually obtain a letter of intent (LOI) from Buyer.

Before the Buyer and Seller can get to the LOI (see Chapter 13 for more details), they need to go through the song-and-dance routine of the management meeting.

Seller's team should run the management meeting; Buyer is Seller's guest. Seller does a lot of talking, explaining, and updating. Buyer takes notes, occasionally interjecting with clarifying questions.

Assembling key players

Some combination of Seller's ownership and management should attend. Of course, who exactly that entails varies from company to company, but basically the attendees should encompass people who can answer questions about day-to-day operations, the current and future financing needs of the company, and decisions made at the board level. In some cases, one person can address all these aspects, but more often than not these three broad areas require multiple people. Seller should also have her intermediary in attendance. In fact, that person will probably play the role of the emcee for the meeting.

Buyers should bring the people responsible for making the final decision. This group may include the president or CEO, the CFO, and sundry corporate development people. People who aren't decision-makers (or influencers to the decision-makers) shouldn't attend. They aren't needed at this juncture. If Buyer is utilizing outside financing, allowing the financing source to attend the management meeting may be permissible. Lastly, if Buyer has an intermediary, that intermediary will probably attend the meeting.

If occasional detailed information (say, the new marketing plan) needs discussing, bringing in a specific person (in this case, the VP of marketing) to cover just that issue is okay. But that's the only part of the meeting that person is involved in.

Lawyers and accountants shouldn't attend the management meeting! The meeting is for the businesspeople to discuss business issues, which are separate from legal/accounting issues. Although very important legal and accounting issues need to be settled or determined at some time, the management meeting isn't that time. Lawyers and accountants can later memorialize what the deal people create.

Agreeing on a venue

The meeting location largely depends on the type of company. Service firms probably don't hold the meetings their offices because the offices aren't that important; they don't have manufacturing equipment and inventory that a

Buyer may like to see. Instead, a service-firm Seller should utilize the office of her intermediary.

Traipsing a series of strangers through the office only tips off the employees. Most Sellers don't want employees to know the company is for sale, but employees figure out pretty quickly that the hush-hush and unannounced meetings with mysterious people probably means the company is for sale.

If Seller is a distributor or manufacturer, Buyer may want to see the facility. This desire makes sense and is a reasonable request. In this case, the meetings may be held at Seller's facility. Another option is to conduct the meetings off-site at a nearby hotel (if the intermediary's office isn't close). Seller can then take Buyer to the facility for a walk-though before returning to the hotel to continue the meeting.

As Seller, schedule a stealthy facilities tour if you're especially concerned about employees figuring out the company is for sale. Give the tour after hours or on a day the facility isn't in use.

Setting the meeting agenda

I recommend that Seller circulate a written agenda. Keep it simple: roughly five to eight items. Although specific agendas vary from deal to deal, a management meeting should generally include the following aspects:

- ✔ **Introductions:** The whole point is to get to know the other side, right?
- ✔ **Buyer's discussion:** Buyer introduces himself, talks about his company or fund, his investment strategy, and his reasons for pursuing this particular Seller.
- ✔ **Seller recap:** Seller provides a simple reminder of what she's seeking to do (sell 100 percent or some other amount of the company), whether she's amenable to structuring (including an earn-out, note, and so on), and whether she prefers cash at closing. If a selling owner is interested in staying on board after the sale, she should communicate that at this time as well.

  Seller-owned real estate isn't part of an offering document, so if Seller is open to selling the real estate, she should mention that at this juncture.

- ✔ **Opportunities for the buyer:** This section represents the thesis from Seller's offering document, updated if necessary or appropriate. Listing some of Seller's key strengths — recognizable brand name, revenues, profits — isn't a bad idea.

✔ **Recent improvements or changes:** Think of this section as Seller's brag-and-tout section, where she can discuss any pertinent updates, such as new systems that have improved margins, changes in the inventory techniques, new customers, better terms with vendors, or anything that's an improvement or change from the offering document.

✔ **Financial update and forecast:** In this part of the meeting, Seller provides Buyer with updated post-offering document financials and gives guidance on future financial results. In other words, are the projections in the offering document holding firm, does Seller think the company will actually be more profitable, or is the company failing to achieve the projected results? If the company isn't achieving its projections, Seller should be able to discuss why the company's financials are falling short of plan.

✔ **Additional opportunities for Buyer:** I call this part the "roadmap to value" section. Typically, these items are post-sale opportunities for Buyer. Although convincing Buyer to pay for improvements he'll bring to the company is difficult, showing him how the benefits that may accrue after closing helps him understand that the future prospects of the company are solid. After all, if Buyer believes the future is bleak, he probably won't proceed with a transaction.

✔ **Q and A:** A good meeting should allow at least two hours for a question and answer session. During the Q and A, Buyer usually takes the lead and asks Seller a lot of very difficult questions, although Seller can certainly return the favor as well.

Notice the flow of this agenda. The meeting starts with the basics, segues into the benefits Seller can offer Buyer, provides updated information and a forecast, and then addresses where Buyer will be able take the business. In other words, the meeting gets the basics out of the way first, thus clearing the table for where you want the discussion to go: doing a deal.

Seller should maintain strict control over the interaction between Seller's staff and Buyer. The employees may not know about the pending deal, and if Buyer starts calling employees to ask questions, the cat will be out of the bag. Also, Seller's employees don't work for Buyer yet, so Seller needs to guard against Buyer wasting the employees' time with question after question.

Perfecting the Seller's Presentation

The presentation deals with Seller: past, present, and future. Because many months (probably three to six) have transpired between finishing the offering document and sitting down with various Buyers in management meetings,

Seller should focus on providing Buyer with an update from when the offering document was written. But you're not just throwing some updated figures on the table and leaving; you're presenting the info to Buyer. The following sections give you some guidance on acing that presentation.

The goal of management meetings is to get Buyers to submit a letter of intent (LOI) and then choose one lucky Buyer to close a deal with.

Gathering the right material

First and foremost, a management meeting should provide a financial update as well as updated guidance for future performance. Discuss the sales pipeline; in fact, the *pipeline report* (a listing of upcoming potential sales) often makes a good handout during the meeting. Specific customer names do not need to be divulged at this point (using codes such as prospect A and prospect B is perfectly acceptable).

I note in Chapter 8 that Sellers should avoid overly optimistic financial projections in the offering document, and the management meeting is why. Eventually, Seller needs to defend those assumptions in the management meeting, and the best way to do so is to simply do what he said he'd do: achieve the projections.

You should also discuss any and all material changes. These items can include, but certainly aren't limited to, new key employees, new customers, new contracts, new competitors, changes in the industry, lawsuits, and so on.

Don't re-create the wheel! Although the presentation will undoubtedly cover some information from the offering document, the focus should be on providing Buyer with new information.

Making Seller's presentation shine

The greater the number of people who attend a meeting, the greater the odds someone hasn't actually read the offering document. At the beginning of a management meeting, ask, "Okay, so who has read the book?" If few people raise their hands, you may need to take a few moments recapping the basics of the business. Of course, you (or your intermediary) should be well versed in the offering document so that you can refer Buyer to the appropriate page or section if she asks a question that's already covered in the book.

Divide and conquer the parts of the presentation. In a general sense, the intermediary should provide the introductions and act as a navigator. Different members of your team should handle the various parts of the presentation based on their areas of expertise. If you don't have an intermediary, the employee or owner who's been the main point-person during communication with Buyers is probably the best bet to be the navigator.

A good old slideshow is a great way to give the presentation. Make sure the meeting room has a projector and a screen or a clean white wall. Yes, a slideshow. I know. You've sat through far too many painful presentations using the tiny fonts with enough text per page to make it seem as if the text was ripped from *Atlas Shrugged*. But your slideshow doesn't have to be that way. Here are a few pointers for effectively presenting your information to Buyer with slides:

- **Don't pack in tons of information per page.** Keep each slide to two to five bullets. Each bullet should be short and to the point: no more than five or ten words.

- **Make your font readable.** No 10-point fonts! Use big 30- or 40-point fonts. Also, avoid cutesy or hard-to-read lettering; you're in a business meeting, after all.

- **Use the bullets as a memory cue only.** The bullets aren't the presentation; they're just there to help with the flow. Read one bullet and elaborate on it, and then continue similarly through the rest of the bullets. Reading word for word from the slide makes the presentation sound boring and canned, and you want to come off as conversational.

Do a practice run of the presentation prior to the first Buyer's meeting. Inevitably, the presentation has some kinks that need smoothing out. Better to find those kinks in practice than during the first meeting. Furthermore, schedule the weakest Buyer as the first meeting if at all possible. If you're going to screw up a presentation on an early meeting, better it be on the weakest Buyer and not a favored Buyer.

Prepping Buyers for Management Meetings

As Buyer, you should prepare for management meetings by reading the offering document, reviewing the financials and Seller's Web site, and conducting research about Seller (to the extent that public information is available). Spending some time researching the industry and getting a handle on other companies and industry trends shows you're serious.

Come prepared by having read the materials provided; don't expect Seller to review information already discussed in the offering document. I always love seeing a Buyer come to a meeting with a dog-eared copy of the offering document with sticky notes jutting out from numerous pages. This situation tells me Buyer has done her homework and is ready to ask good questions.

If a facility tour is part of the day, take care to not inadvertently tip off otherwise-unsuspecting employees about the potential business sale. Asking a warehouse worker, "So, what would you think if I were your new boss?" is a big no-no! When in doubt, keep your mouth shut.

While walking through Seller's offices or facility, Buyer should pay close attention to the seemingly small things. Is the place clean and organized? Are the employees smiling and happy? Are lights burned out? Any water damage in the ceiling? How clean are the bathrooms? Although these aspects may seem to be rather small, a company that has issues in these areas often has employees (or management) who've simply given up and let things go to seed.

Plan ahead with Seller to determine whether a cover story is necessary. I've often asked Buyers to use the cover story of "We're investors, and we're thinking of investing in your company." This setup downplays the business-sale aspect but is still an accurate statement.

Buyers beware: Blowing a meeting

I once represented a Seller who had a meeting where more than ten people from Buyer showed up. Due to concerns about competition (the two companies were direct competitors), we conducted the meeting on neutral ground; allowing this direct competitor into my client's facility would almost certainly have set off alarm bells among the employees. The guy who organized the meeting spent most of our presentation alternately playing with his smartphone and getting up to leave the meeting for 20 or 30 minutes at a time. Needless to say, I knew that meeting wasn't going to be productive, and I advised my client after the meeting to find another Buyer. We ultimately closed a deal with a different group.

Reading the Tea Leaves: Did the Meeting Go Well?

Trying to determine whether a meeting went well is a difficult proposition. People are usually polite; regardless of whether they're interested in pursuing a deal, they usually end the meeting by saying something to the effect of, "Thanks for your time; my colleagues and I will confer over the next few days and get back to you with our thoughts."

Most Sellers will gladly accept an offer from just about any Buyer. If Seller set a meeting, most likely Seller is interested. Judging Buyer's interest level is the trickier job. Here are some clues you as Seller should look for during the meeting:

✔ **Was Buyer prepared?** Did she have a marked up copy of the offering document? If Buyer is genuinely interested, she'll come the meeting prepared.

✔ **Was Buyer actively engaged in discussions?** Did she ask a lot of questions, or was she otherwise preoccupied? Did she fidget with her phone or constantly shift in her seat? These signs indicate that someone is losing interest and would rather be elsewhere. Spend some time during each meeting looking at Buyers and paying attention to their facial expressions.

✔ **What was Buyer's mood and tone?** Was the conversation lively, animated, and frankly, fun? Or did the meeting take on a testy atmosphere? Personal chemistry is often a big part of getting a deal done.

✔ **Did the meeting end abruptly, or could you have talked all day?** Another sign of lack of interest is a meeting that ends sooner than you planned. Conversely, a meeting that could easily continue for a few more hours is often a good sign of interest by Buyer.

If you're Seller, the best sign of actual interest from Buyer is to get an LOI. And if you're Buyer, Seller's request for an LOI is a good sign of interest as well.

Part IV
Firming Up
the Deal

The 5th Wave   By Rich Tennant

"Is that your final response to our tender offer?"

In this part . . .

This part is where the M&A relationship starts to get more serious. I start by covering M&A negotiating and the ever-important issue of valuation. I also detail the Buyer's formal offer (the letter of intent, or LOI) and the due diligence process the Buyer undertakes after submitting that offer. Finally, I delve into some of the main issues of the final, binding purchase agreement.

Chapter 11

An Insider's Guide to M&A Negotiating

In This Chapter

▶ Preparing yourself to negotiate

▶ Knowing which negotiation techniques to use and avoid

▶ Staying on track when the negotiation falters

*N*egotiating is the name of the game. A Seller constantly jockeys for a higher price, and a Buyer constantly seeks ways to lower the price. Although these opposing points of view may seem to be at never-ending loggerheads, deals can come to fruition if both sides understand how to negotiate.

In this chapter I introduce you to some of the lessons and tricks I've observed from doing deals. This isn't your father's negotiating book!

Keys to Negotiating Success

Negotiating doesn't only happen during a tidily defined portion of the M&A process. Negotiations occur throughout the entire process, and M&A deal-makers should constantly remember that reality. Successful deal-making can be in the cards for you if you take a look at some key truths I've discovered from doing deals.

Know your position

As I note throughout the book, M&A deal-making is a lot like playing poker. For example, knowing whether you have a weak or strong hand is important because your hand's strength helps dictate how you negotiate the deal. Simply put, a weak hand means you have limited options. Time isn't your friend. Work as quickly as possible to wrap up a deal (but be wary to not appear too desperate because that tips off the other side to your situation.)

A strong hand means that you have more options; time is on your side. However, you still have to play that hand skillfully. Many novices overplay strong hands and end up chasing an otherwise-willing deal-maker on the other side away from the deal.

The worst thing you can do is to misplay a weak hand. I've seen people ruin their careers because they failed to understand the weakness of their position and pressed forward with a bad play.

You hand is weak or strong only in relation to the other hands. Don't just pay attention to your situation; assess the other side's position as well. A strong hand in one situation may be a weak hand in the next deal.

Remember the goal: Closing a deal

The process of buying or selling a business can be a messy affair. M&A insiders call it "making sausage" because it's an ugly process with a tasty end result. (Well, assuming you're not a vegetarian. In that case, think of a messily prepared falafel.)

As a result, those caught in the throes of a negotiation can lose sight of the end result: a closed deal. In fact, the experience of negotiating can be so frustrating that many people simply throw up their hands in frustration and scuttle the process.

But whether you're Buyer or Seller going through the M&A process, set your sights on that final, satisfying goal of closing the deal. Avoid getting testy and try to tamp down the irritability that almost always comes as the result of a heated negotiation.

If you're seemingly at an impasse, tell the folks on the other side that you're not trying to be punitive, capricious, or unreasonable. Tell them that you understand a deal will only get done when it's mutually beneficial to both sides. Ask them to sit down with you, face to face, to try again to hammer out a deal. Seemingly dead deals have been revived because of a willingness of both sides to continue talks toward a creative, mutually beneficial deal. If you need to, hire advisors who have structured deals before.

Negotiate with the decision-maker

The biggest, most important, and most basic negotiating rule is to make sure you negotiate with the actual decision-maker and not an influencer. Of course, speaking with an influencer isn't automatically bad. In many cases, the negotiations advance relatively smoothly.

But in some cases, an influencer who inserts himself into the proceedings may or may not have the authority to negotiate the transaction. These kinds of influencers tend to impede deals; in the best cases, they're overzealous underlings trying to make a splash with their bosses. In the worst cases, they're manipulative head cases following a personal agenda with little or no regard for the company's goals.

In other situations, the actual decision-maker may be hiding behind the influencer. In this example, the influencer is little more than the mouthpiece for the real decision-maker. Typical rants from this person include abrupt and curt ultimatums such as, "We don't think we will negotiate or find middle ground," or, "We're not going to contemplate your proposal."

What's going on here is that the decision-maker is using the influencer as a buffer. The decision-maker can easily bark unfiltered orders at the influencer, orders the decision-maker probably wouldn't make if she were speaking directly with you. In turn, the influencer simply parrots the decision-maker by delivering the same message without editing it or moderating its tone. This unfiltered communication, often the hallmark of passive-aggressive types or just someone who can't be bothered to deal with the situation at hand, is highly frustrating.

The best way, and perhaps the only way, to handle this situation is to try to set up a meeting or a conference call with the influencer and the decision-maker. You need to get the influencer out of the way and communicate directly with the decision-maker.

If you're speaking with an influencer and the negotiations are rocky, challenge the person. Simply ask if he is the final decision-maker. If not, ask to speak to that decision-maker. If you still get a block, suggest a meeting with the other side's full team.

Bend where you can

Flexibility wins the day. Know what you want. Rank the most important issues as must-haves. All the rest of the details of a deal are bargaining chips. Use the deal points you don't really need to obtain the concessions you need the most. Don't give away the house, but be willing to bend where you can bend in order to wrap up a deal. If a counteroffer cedes to your main wishes and asks for some concessions for the relatively minor issues, take the deal.

For example, Buyer and Seller invariably have a valuation gap (especially in today's market). If both sides are willing to be creative, structuring can provide a bridge to valuation gaps. Although cash at closing is great (and definitely preferred), Seller may be able to garner a higher price if he is amendable to earn-outs and/or accepting a Seller note. (Head to Chapter 4 for more on these topics).

Although some issues are more important to you than others, never throw away a seemingly unimportant issue. What's unimportant to you may be vitally important to another. That otherwise-worthless issue may end up being currency to help you win a concession you find important.

Take it one day at a time

I often refer to the M&A process as a big roller coaster ride. One day everything goes perfectly, and you leave the office on a high from a great day of high-level accomplishment. You think you're a deal-making genius! Nothing can go wrong. Then when you go to work the next day, everything that can go wrong does.

When I have those inevitable bad days, I always remind myself that the bad day isn't as bad as it seems. I also refrain from being overly excited and optimistic on those days where everything goes perfectly.

The biggest tip I can give to anyone involved in mergers and acquisitions or considering getting into the M&A industry is the following: Don't believe your press clippings. Don't let yourself get too high on the good days and too low on the bad days. You're going to have great days; you're going to have crushing days. Tomorrow may be completely different from today.

Remember your ABNs: Always be negotiating

Okay, so "always be negotiating" doesn't roll off the tongue like Alec Baldwin's immortal "always be closing" line in *Glengarry Glen Ross,* but you get the point.

For Sellers, negotiating starts with the teaser and the offering document (see Chapters 7 and 8 for more on these elements, respectively). Buyers are negotiating from the moment they place a phone call or send an e-mail to a business owner. A wise deal-maker is always looking for an angle. You're always under the microscope.

Throughout management meetings, due diligence, contract drafting, and right up until the day the deal closes, both sides should consider themselves in full-on negotiation mode.

Using Successful Negotiating Tactics

Negotiating is not about forcing your will on the other side. That's called unconditional surrender. If the other side has other options, they're not going to agree to your stringent and unbending demands. And if they don't have other options and instead reluctantly accept your offer, you're unlikely to find you have a loyal business partner.

To make you a negotiation mogul, I provide some thoughts and tips in this section on how to negotiate with the other side if you truly desire obtaining a closed deal.

Remember, negotiating is more art than science.

While you're spending so much time dealing with the other side, get to know those folks. Draw them close. If you know the other party, his habits, and his methods of doing business, you have a far better chance of successfully negotiating a mutually beneficial deal.

The following sections outline several helpful negotiating tricks.

Say "Here's the deal that gets it done"

This line is one of my favorites because it puts a closed deal on the other side's plate; all the others have to do is agree. It's usually best served toward the end of a negotiation, after some back-and-forth. Let a few issues get settled. Let both sides compromise. Then deliver the deal that gets it done.

Pick up the phone

Pick up the phone and have a conversation, especially if the subject is delicate. The flip side to "pick up the phone" is "avoid e-mail." E-mail is a wonderful tool, but it's a passive form of communication. A single five-minute phone call often resolves issues that otherwise would play out in five or ten (or more) e-mail exchanges.

I'm not opposed to using e-mail in M&A negotiations. In fact, e-mail can be an imperative tool because it allows you to memorialize a conversation. The trick is to know when to use e-mail. For example, I once represented a Seller in a negotiation where the Buyer wanted my client to pay for the cost of mailing catalogs (about $500,000) intended to support a marketing campaign. Those catalogs were to be mailed just before the scheduled closing. Typically in a business sale, Seller pays all expenses prior to close, and Buyer pays all expenses after.

I argued that the Buyer should pay for the catalogs because the resulting sales would benefit him, the new owner, and he finally agreed during an in-person management meeting that this solution was reasonable. I then sent him an e-mail reiterating that discussion.

A few weeks later, on the eve of closing, the Buyer suddenly informed us (rather coldly) that he refused to pay for the catalogs because expenses prior to closing are the responsibility of the Seller. The Seller would've otherwise delayed the release of the catalogs for a few days so that the expense would be incurred post-sale.

I don't know whether the Buyer forgot the conversation (and resulting e-mail) or whether he felt he had us over a barrel, but fortunately, I had the e-mail thread that showed he'd very clearly agreed to cover the cost of the catalogs. The Buyer, despite being rather irate, conceded the point and agreed to pay for the catalogs. We closed the deal a few days later.

Offer a conditional if-then agreement

I always refrain from offering up a concession without getting something else in return. As you try to work out a deal with the other side, don't simply offer a concession (or ask for one without expecting to give something back).

Instead, say, "If you can agree to A, B, C, and D, then we can agree to X, Y, and Z." If the other side balks at your idea, you've not conceded a point; you've simply offered an idea. Because the idea was rejected, any conceded points are therefore removed from the discussion. This bundle approach often works very well when coupled with saying, "Here's the deal that gets it done."

If the other side offers a concession without asking for anything in return, accept immediately and move on to the next point.

Understand that the first who speaks loses

Here's another insight I learned years ago at a long-forgotten job: The first person who speaks loses. Say your peace, make your point, and then shut up. We humans tend to have an innate need to fill the void of silence because it makes us uncomfortable. If you can fight against the need to fill that silent void, you may be surprised at what your negotiating opponent is willing to concede.

Don't be afraid to haggle

Haggling, or the incessant back-and-forth volleying of offer and counteroffer, is a typical negotiating tactic. You say 50, I say 30; let's agree to meet at 40. Is haggling permissible? Of course! It's a natural part of any negotiation.

Although you should pad offers to allow for some wiggle room, haggling can get tiring. In my opinion, it quickly becomes a waste of time. Padding an offer or counteroffer can help, but structuring a deal that you can support is the most important aspect of getting a deal done.

Although I don't recommend going overboard when structuring a deal or a counteroffer, don't be afraid to push the envelope. You never know whether the other side will accept your proposal unless you ask.

Don't negotiate against yourself. If you submit an offer or a counteroffer and the other side says, "Not good enough; please try again," hold firm and tell the other side, "This is our offer." But you can proceed to haggling if the other side gives you a counteroffer!

Beware of a bad bluff

Bluffing may be a bit Machiavellian, but it can be a useful negotiation tool. M&A negotiating often involves much of the same kind of bluffing (and knowing when the other side is bluffing) as is found in poker.

Bluffing most often happens when one side really wants to do a deal but feigns indifference in the hopes that the other side comes to the table with a better offer. I don't recommend this strategy. If you need to do a deal, you're better served if you're open and honest with the other side.

And in no way do I ever suggest that an M&A participant should lie to or deceive the other side in regards to material information. Saying you're not interested in a deal when you really are is one thing; falsifying financial records is another.

If you're going to bluff, keep the following points in mind:

- ✔ **Sell it!** Speak confidently, get to the point, don't oversell, and don't appear rushed or in need. The idea is to come across as nonchalant.

- ✔ **Be prepared for someone to call your bluff.** Know that if the other side reads your move correctly, you may be out of luck. Crawling back to the other side after a failed bluff may simply reduce your negotiating leverage.

If you suspect the other side is bluffing you on a subject, assess the strength of your position relative to the other side's position before you decide whether to call the bluff. If you're in a strong position — if you can ultimately walk away from the deal and you know that the other side needs to do a deal — you're in the driver's seat. Call the bluff. But if you're the one who needs to do a deal and the other side has a strong position, the bluff may not actually be a bluff. It may be the other side's actual position.

Avoiding Common M&A Negotiating Mistakes

The number one negotiating tactic to steer clear of is bullying. For some crazy reason, negotiating novices tend to think negotiating is about imposing their will on the other side with a take-no-prisoners approach. But M&A insiders simply laugh at negotiators whose main goal is being belligerent and tougher than the other side.

Bullying and cajoling don't work. A tyrannical or dictatorial style may suit you well if you're one of the bad Roman emperors, but for mere mortals, bullying simply gets in the way of getting a deal done. Someone experienced at negotiating M&A transactions either sidesteps the bullying, ignores it, or calls the bully out and flatly says, "I'm here to negotiate in good faith; I was hoping you'd do so as well."

Bullying puts the bully in a tough spot. It either kills the deal or yields nothing, thus rendering the bully an impotent blowhard. It also creates a situation where the recipient of the aggression may someday return the favor.

The only time you may be able to get away with a bullying approach is if the other side is completely desperate to do a deal. But even then, the belligerent approach may well backfire on you some day when you need a favor from the other side or if you need the other side to stay involved in the business.

But bullying is only the tip of the iceberg in terms of potential negotiating pitfalls. Here are some other tactics to avoid while negotiating:

- **Drawing a line in the sand:** This approach is a favorite of the belligerent bullying novices. Drawing a line in the sand merely places the line-drawer in a corner. If, and invariably when, the drawer needs to close a deal, that line can become a moot point. At that point, the line-in-the-sand approach actually backfires; if the line-drawer is willing to cede a point formerly ensconced behind the line, what else will she give up?

- **Resorting to "take it or leave it":** This tactic is the bratty cousin to the line-in-the-sand approach. Anyone who utters this line better be willing to have the other side leave it. If the other side simply walks away and the person who gave the ultimatum actually wants to do a deal, that person has simply exposed her position as weak and tenuous.

- **Yelling:** Yelling is the path of choice for the impatient and creatively bankrupt. Keep your temper under control. I know that can be difficult, especially when you find yourself in the midst of an inane argument with a silly, immature person, but blowing your top doesn't help advance the discussion. If calm, dispassionate logic and reason fail to win the day, histrionics do no better. And what's worse, yelling may simply poison the well and prevent future discussions.

  If discussions do devolve into frustration, illogic, and shouting, simply stop talking. Tell the other side that you want to table that particular point and revisit it down the line. Halting discussions for a short period of time allows the other side to reflect on its point of view and revisit discussions with a more reasonable approach.

- **Bogging down in minutiae:** Getting sidetracked by insignificant points and worthless detail at the expense of hammering out the main issues needlessly slows a negotiation and may kill your deal. Prioritize the issues and remember this phrase: "Let's table that for later."

- **Overselling:** In my first job out of college, a co-worker gave me a bit of advice that I've repeated ever since: When the other person says "yes," stop talking and take the offer. After you and the other side find agreement, stop selling your point. Say thanks and move on to the next order of business.

- **Devolving into personal attacks:** Separate the business issues from the personal issues. Don't allow a business negotiation to spiral into a personal insult slugfest. I know that can be difficult; as I write this section, I'm in the midst of a frustrating negotiation myself. Bite that tongue, stick to the business issues, and refrain from making the discussions personal.

The recipe for a successful negotiation

Based on my experience, successful M&A negotiating is the result of carefully mixing a few key ingredients:

1. **Slice and dice your strengths and weaknesses and then compare them to the other side's strengths and weaknesses.**

   Carefully strain out subjectivity and personal feelings, but make sure you reserve the objectivity.

2. **Add a dash of understanding of the other side's motivation.**

3. **Stir in a heaping helping of sincere desire to craft a mutually beneficial deal.**

Marinate through a careful combination of phone calls, e-mails, contracts, meetings, discussions, and more phone calls and let rise through due diligence and contract writing, and you too can have a successfully closed deal!

Be wary of lawyers, usually young and relatively inexperienced lawyers, out to make their bones — that is, to prove to their superiors that they're tough, hard-nosed lawyers. These lawyers tend to be a feisty sort and break many, if not all, of the nearby tips about negotiating. Their focus seems to be to prove they won't yield on a single point and therefore will beat the other side into submitting to every demand. This take-it-or-leave-it approach is a major impediment to getting a deal done because it usually results in the other side leaving.

Surviving Unforeseen Twists and Turns

Here's another key point for anyone who wants to get into M&A deal-making: The process isn't linear. Expect the unexpected.

Deal-makers need to have a plan, but they also have to be able to adjust and adapt to the curveballs the changing environment throws. The plan is important, even imperative, but you can't become a slave to it. As long as you always keep the end goal of closing a deal in your sights, you can successfully navigate the winding M&A road.

Getting a deal gone sideways back on track

A negotiation has a rhythm, a regular flow of information, phone calls, and e-mails where messages are returned in a timely fashion. If this rhythm is broken (extended periods of time elapse with no communication from the other side or communication is stilted, clipped, and forced), you may have a negotiating partner who is getting cold feet and a deal that's going *sideways* (off the rails).

"An extended period of time" is subjective; how much is too much depends on the situation. When you're not sure, trust your gut instinct.

If you find yourself in a situation where your negotiating partner has gone silent (or "radio silent," as some jokingly refer to the phenomenon), you have a couple options to try to get the discussions back on track.

First, you need to break the buzz — do something different from the usual deal-centric message. Constant professional communication can be stupefying. You need to do something to snap the other person out of the haze of kindly professional correspondence, which is so easy to ignore. Send an e-mail with a link to a relevant article or op-ed column. Offer to play golf or tennis or meet for a drink, invite the other guy to a professional event, or anything other than the usual "Please call me; we need to discuss something."

Keep your message succinct. Avoid leaving long voice mails. If someone isn't responding to your correspondence, that person probably isn't going to listen to a two-minute message. If all else fails, offer a mea culpa. Simply ask whether you've done anything wrong. Ask the person to contact you, even if they have bad news.

Bad news is better than no news. At least with bad news, you have a chance at crafting a solution, or if that fails, of moving on to the next prospect.

Negotiating in good faith

Negotiating in good faith is a term that you may hear bandied about during the M&A process. In my view, negotiating in good faith is a code of honor. It means you follow through on what you say you'll do, and that after you agree on an issue, you don't go back and try to renegotiate that point again.

When someone fails to negotiate in good faith, that person is poisoning the well. Backtracking on a settled issue only serves to throw all the other settled issues into question. That's akin to trying to reason with a child who agrees to one thing and then capriciously changes her mind if she senses she has a weak position somewhere else.

Thwarting backtrackers is why I'm a big fan of bundling negotiating points and using conditional concessions (see "Offer a conditional if-then agreement" earlier in this chapter). The conditional concession allows you to withdraw the concession if the other side refuses to accept their part of the bargain.

Of course, sometimes events occur during a negotiation that require one side or the other to go back on part of the deal. For a Seller, these events are typically called *material changes*. Material changes include losing a major client, being sued, coming under a federal investigation, and other changes that materially affect the business. If Seller's business takes a turn for the worse, especially if the change renders Buyer unable to close a deal, Buyer should let Seller know. In fact, both sides should immediately disclose any major bad news that may affect the closing of the deal.

All negotiators should hold themselves to a higher standard. Barring adverse material changes, you shouldn't ask for a change in a negotiated term after you've already agreed to it. Honor your commitments and don't allow the other side to renegotiate previously settled terms.

Chapter 12

Crunching the Numbers: Establishing Valuation and Selling Price

- -

- -

*U*nlocking the mysteries of how to know what to pay for a company was one of the reasons I became interested in entrepreneurship. Valuation is at the core of mergers and acquisitions. After all, if both sides can't agree to price, no deal happens.

In this chapter, I introduce you to the concept of valuation: how to determine it, why it's important, why Buyers pay what they pay, and how Sellers can create a more compelling valuation.

What's a Company Worth? Determining Valuation

Valuation (the price one party will pay another for a business) is based on what you can negotiate. That's why I include some negotiating thoughts in Chapter 11. And, as with most negotiations, valuation is more art than science. In fact, I call it alchemy because valuation is often subjectivity masquerading as science and logic.

Valuation is really the intersection of cash flow and time. In other words, how long will the Buyer take to recoup the cost of the investment? And how many years' worth of profits is the Seller willing to take today in exchange for giving up an infinite flow of profits from that business?

If you want extra credit for this valuation section, keep in mind that cash flow and time aren't the only contributors. You also need to factor in the following:

- ✔ **Future prospects of the business:** Is the business growing rapidly? Is growth stagnant and flat? This growth (or lack thereof) may affect how much Buyers are willing to spend.

- ✔ **The risk associated with the specific business:** For example, are the company's products high quality, or has quality slipped? Is the company able to recruit, train, and retain good employees, or does it have a problem with excessive employee turnover?

- ✔ **Systemic risk:** *Systemic risk* is risk affecting everything in the economy. The recent economic meltdown is a perfect example (unfortunately) of how the economy can affect everyone and every company. Plenty of well-run companies offering good products and services suffered due to a widespread downturn. Buyers feel a lot less generous in the valuation process when systemic risk is high.

- ✔ **Cost of capital:** *Cost of capital* is another name for "what else Buyer can do with that money." If Buyer has other options, he deploys that capital in those deals that offer higher returns and less cost.

And, on top of all that, valuation depends on negotiating prowess. In other words, are you a good poker player, or do you fold and collapse when someone puts a little pressure on you? (Chapter 11 offers you helpful negotiation strategies.)

You can craft all kinds of fancy algorithms and complex mathematical formulas, read every trendy business book and the writings of the ancients, and spend copious amounts of time searching for *comps* (comparable transactions) to see how other M&A deal-makers determined valuation. In my view, though, that's all overkill.

Most often, valuation boils down to a small, simple valuation range: four times to six times EBITDA (or 4X to 6X in M&A code). The magic number in the M&A deal-making world is smack-dab in the middle: 5X. These numbers are known as *multiples*, so when you hear someone say "a 5X multiple of EBITDA," that person means a company with EBITDA of $3 million would have a $15 million valuation.

Five times EBITDA is an industry standard, a convention of deal-making. Nobody knows where 5X came from, but all you need to know is that it's a de facto standard. In good or bad times, that multiple may be a bit higher or lower, which is why I give you the 4X to 6X range.

As Seller, you can get a valuation higher than 6X, but you need to have a strong negotiating position. The best negotiating position is to have a highly profitable company in a rapidly growing industry. For example, venture capital deals usually garner far higher multiples for Sellers than lower middle market and middle market deals do. In a venture deal, Buyer is willing to pay a higher price because he's expecting the company to grow rapidly; he's betting on the future prospects of the business. See the nearby sidebar "Other valuation techniques" for more on types of valuation.

Other valuation techniques

Although multiples of EBITDA is a typical valuation technique, it's not the only method to determine a company's valuation. Various industries may use different valuation conventions, including the following:

- **Asset value:** In this example, the Buyer pays a price based on the value of the assets on the company's balance sheet. This technique works best for companies with a lot of inventory and/or manufacturing equipment. Asset value is usually not a good idea for service businesses because they don't have inventory and manufacturing equipment.

- **Multiple of gross profit:** *Gross profit* (the difference between revenue and the cost of goods sold) can be a suitable method to determine valuation, especially if the company is losing money. Using gross profit can also be a suitable method to determine an earn-out (which I cover later in this chapter).

- **Multiple of revenue:** This simple valuation method is a good choice for a company that's losing money. Just apply a multiple to the revenue of the company. Top line revenue is also used in many earn-outs.

- **Discounted cash flow (DCF):** This technique is one of those fancy-pants MBA valuations

often used in the venture capital world. You estimate or project a business's cash flow (usually earnings minus capital expenditures) for a period of time, often five years. You then determine the *terminal value,* the expected future sale price of the business at the end of that period, and figure out the present value of this expected cash flow by *discounting,* or lowering, the future value of those cash flows. (Basically, you're figuring out the current equivalent of that future cash flow figure.) That becomes the price the Buyer is willing to pay. The higher the cash flows, the higher the price.

- **Multiple of contribution margin:** This advanced valuation method utilizes the *contribution margin,* the amount of cash flow a Buyer can expect after making changes to the business, such as eliminating some expenses by moving operations from the Seller's facility to the Buyer's facility. This approach isn't for beginners.

These sundry techniques often don't use the standard 4X to 6X multiple range I describe in the nearby section "What's a Company Worth? Determining Valuation." Multiples may be 2X, 1X, or even less than 1X. Revenue, gross profit, and contribution margin will all be larger than EBITDA.

Meeting in the Middle: Agreeing on a Price

Valuation is never a given. Valuation is not self-evident, nor is it obvious. Instead, valuation is an abstract concept open to interpretation. So how do a Seller, who wants a high price, and a Buyer, who wants a more reasonable price, find common ground?

During the valuation process, Sellers should signal strong valuation expectations, but fight against their own biases toward their companies. An owner who has spent years or a lifetime building a business is going to be rather subjective about the greatness of his company. But he must remember Buyers look at many potential deals every year and don't have the same emotional connection to his company that he does.

On the flip side, no matter what else they do during valuation, Buyers should be careful about bragging about how much money they have at their disposal. Sellers are liable to think a Buyer can liberally deploy that money on their deal and may develop unreasonable valuation expectations. In this section I offer suggestions for both Buyers and Sellers approaching valuation.

Testing the waters

Many Buyers ask me, "What does the Seller want?" This question is a test; I know that because when I'm buying companies, I always ask the same question! And I'm amazed at how many people (often other intermediaries) cough up a number.

As Buyer, asking for a valuation never hurts. If Seller demurs, though, be prepared to offer a valuation.

I don't recommend that Sellers offer up an *asking price* (the price they're hoping to garner). In fact, I don't provide an asking price in my deals for a simple reason: If I provide a Buyer with a certain price and she submits an offer with that price, she may be miffed if she later discovers another Buyer paid more. That first Buyer will, with good reason, say I provided bad information.

Instead, I ask the Buyer to review the information I provide in the offering document (see Chapter 8) and come up with a valuation that she can support based on that information.

I usually remind the Buyer that I am talking with other potential Buyers and try to point out certain key strengths of the business that this particular Buyer should consider as she formulates her valuation.

I also caution Sellers to have reasonable expectations. Reasonable expectations (no, that's not a mediocre Dickens novel) don't mean a Seller should undervalue his business. Instead, he should expect the Buyer's offer to be based on today's reality — financial performance, company and industry trends, market conditions, and so on — and not necessarily what that business may have been able to fetch a few years ago when sales and profits were higher and Buyers were paying higher multiples of earnings.

By the same token, though, Buyers should make an offer that is sufficient for the Seller to pay off the debts of the business. Study that balance sheet; if the offer doesn't provide the Seller with enough money to pay off debt, he probably won't be willing to essentially write a check in order to sell his business.

Buyers: Measure returns

Buyers utilize various measurements for their investments, or at least they should. A wise investor weighs the price of the investment against the expected return and then compares that expected return against other uses of that money. Simply put, the more money you pay to acquire a business, the lower the potential return. The following sections provide some common figures you can use as you measure returns.

Walking away is always an option. In addition to weighing several possible investments, you may decide that doing nothing is the best course of action, an option you may exercise with greater frequency as Sellers ask for higher and higher prices.

Internal rate of return (IRR)

Internal rate of return (IRR), or the percentage of return that causes the expected cash flows from an investment to be the same as the cost of the investment, is one of the favorite calculations for Buyers, particularly private equity (PE) firms. Buyers usually have a minimum target return they're seeking, and if an investment's expected IRR is greater than that minimum, they do the deal.

IRR is very important to PE firms because those firms raise money from investors by touting their stellar returns. Therefore, if the investments are too pricy and the resulting yields too low, a PE fund's returns are low, and that makes raising more funds from investors difficult. Investors simply choose to invest with funds that have returned higher rates of return.

For a *strategic Buyer* (a company looking to acquire another company for synergistic reasons), the same principle applies. If a deal is too costly, the strategic Buyer doesn't do the deal. The firm looks at its other options, which may include buying a different company, investing those funds in its own company, or doing nothing. A firm may decide investing some money in the market is a safer bet than the company purchase.

Return on investment (ROI)

Return on investment (ROI) is another favorite calculation of Buyers. You calculate ROI by dividing the company's earnings by the Buyer's purchase price. In other words, a company that generates $10 million in earnings and cost the Buyer $50 million has a 20 percent ROI.

Sellers: Create a compelling valuation

Seller should make the case for valuation and not expect Buyer to look for reasons to pay a higher price. Lucky for you Sellers, I have a four-pronged attack that, when executed properly, has fetched a figure higher than the usual upper limit of 6X. (See the earlier section "What's a Company Worth? Determining Valuation" for more on this common valuation multiple.)

But first, keep the following pointers in mind as you consider what you think your company is worth:

- **Take control of the process.** Sellers should be proactive in setting appointments and setting the tone for all discussions. Letting Buyer run the show doesn't usually result in Buyer willing to pay a premium.

- **Have reasonable expectations.** As I note earlier in the chapter, Buyers aren't as interested in how great your company was a few years ago as they are in its current financial performance, its future prospects, and the general state of the economy. Too many business owners hold on to peak year valuations, believing that those valuations should still apply.

- **Don't expect the Buyer to pay more for no good reason.** From my experience, one of the biggest mistakes Sellers make is falling prey to the "just because" fallacy — that is, expecting Buyer to pay more "just because." Here's how it manifests itself in the mind of Seller:

  - Just because Buyer has money, she should pay more.

  - Just because Seller has a great business, Buyer should pay more.

  - Just because Seller is asking for more, Buyer should pay more.

  - Just because the sun rises in the east, Buyer should pay more.

> Buyers don't pay more "just because." They pay prices they can support.
>
> ✔ **Don't assume Buyers have unlimited amounts of money.** Even if they did, they wouldn't be willing to pay unlimited prices for your company. A wise Buyer carefully measures the relative value of an investment, comparing it against other options, before proceeding with a deal.

Make sure the company is a noncommodity

First and foremost, if the company you're selling is going to garner a compelling valuation, it needs to have some sort of intangible quality, a super-special secret sauce. This quality that sets it apart may take the form of a recognizable brand name, outsized revenue and profits, great growth, a hot industry, or anything that differentiates the company from the drab and boring competition and provides something unique and different for Buyers. If a company is little more than a commodity — one of many faceless companies offering similar and interchangeable products — getting a favorable valuation can be a challenging proposition.

What also works is if your company has its very own Ahab, someone who has been pursuing it for years and is willing to do anything — and perhaps pay a high price — to obtain that elusive sperm whale of a company.

Gotta have competition: Shop around

If you're negotiating with one potential Buyer, you're at the mercy of that Buyer. Even a company that offers a unique and differentiating product (see the preceding section) will have a challenging time convincing a Buyer to pay a premium price if that Buyer is the only suitor.

Speak to as many Buyers as possible. The more the merrier. And if a Buyer balks at being part of a process that involves competition, don't view the loss of that potential suitor as a problem. That Buyer probably would not be willing to pay a premium price.

Provide a road map of value for Buyer

Seller needs to show Buyer where the value is, especially in down markets. Seller should clearly and explicitly point out the *value proposition* (how the company will create value for Buyer) and not expect Buyer to figure this out on his own.

Although it may be a bit of guesswork, Seller should make some assumptions as to how the deal can improve Buyer's bottom line and provide those assumptions to Buyer. Buyers may grumble that Seller has reverse engineered their financials, but this step helps signal that Seller has a grasp of the business's value to Buyer.

Make it easy to do a deal

Don't dwell on minor details. Counteroffers should be simple with a minimum of moving parts. If you want to get a deal done, refrain from introducing new elements into an offer. Instead, work from a Buyer's offer, making adjustments to that offer rather than making wholesale changes.

Focus on the main deal issues and avoid getting tripped up by minor and inconsequential details. Don't let nonissues get in the way of getting a deal done.

When Buyer and Seller Disagree: Bridging a Valuation Gap

Disagreements about the price of the company are sure to pop up in any sale process. In fact, I can't think of a single deal I've worked on where valuation wasn't the central issue of disagreement. But you have a few options for reaching a valuation agreement, including structuring an earn-out, using a note, accepting stock, and selling only part of the company. The following sections explore these alternatives in more detail.

If you're a Seller thinking about agreeing to any or all of these arrangements, I still heartily recommend getting some cash at closing. Sellers who agree to put 100 percent of the sale proceeds in contingent payments (earn-out, note, stock) are effectively agreeing to put 100 percent of the sale price at risk. Get some dough at closing!

Using an earn-out to prove valuation

In my estimation, the venerable earn-out is probably the most common method of bridging a valuation gap between Buyer and Seller.

The *earn-out* allows Seller to prove the company is worth a higher valuation by agreeing to get paid a higher price only if the company achieves certain agreed-to goals. Buyer pays that higher price only if the company achieves financial results that warrant a higher price, thus providing him some protection. Essentially, Buyer tells Seller, "Okay, if you really think the future prospects of the business are as rosy as you say, put your money where your mouth is."

The earn-out is especially useful for Sellers who want be paid for the future performance of the company. You can structure earn-outs in an almost unlimited manner. See Chapter 21 in the Part of Tens for some examples of earn-outs.

Settling a valuation disagreement with a Seller note

As I discuss elsewhere in this book, Sellers can help Buyers with the financing by agreeing to take part or all of the proceeds in the form of a note that Buyer pays off at some future date. In addition to helping Buyer acquire the company with less money down, the note provides Buyer with the benefit of the time value of money. In other words, $5 million in three years is worth less than $5 million today. A Seller willing to wait for payment is providing a benefit to Buyer.

Paying for a company with stock

In certain circumstances, Buyer may want to use stock to pay for all or part of an acquisition. And in certain circumstances, Seller may be wise to accept that stock, though she should speak with her tax advisor about the tax ramifications of that arrangement.

Issuing stock allows Buyer to make an acquisition without using cash or borrowing money (or by using less cash and borrowing less money). The downside for Seller is that the stock obviously isn't the same as cash. Seller has to convert that stock into cash by finding a Buyer for it.

Although Buyers may be tempted to issue more stock as a way of financing an acquisition, they should carefully consider the effects of diluting their stock in that way. Is issuing more stock really the best course of action, or does borrowing money to finance the acquisition make more sense?

The pluses and minuses of accepting stock as a form of consideration really boil down to the issue of liquidity: How easily can Seller sell that stock? Here are a few issues Sellers should consider when thinking about accepting Buyer's stock:

- ✔ Is the stock traded on a public exchange, and if so, which exchange? If stock isn't publicly traded, the owner of that stock may be severely limited in his ability to convert that stock into cash. If Seller doesn't anticipate needing that cash anytime in the foreseeable future, perhaps she can risk owning illiquid stock. But accepting illiquid stock doesn't make sense if Seller needs the cash soon.

  Sellers looking at accepting nonpublicly traded stock should consider Buyer's prospects of eventually going public. If those prospects are limited, Seller may be in for a long-term ownership position in a private company.

If Buyer's stock is publically traded, the next thing to remember is that not all stock is equal. Accepting stock traded on a major exchange (NYSE or NASDAQ) is far more desirable than accepting stock traded over-the-counter (OTC) or on the Pink Sheets because the major exchanges have far stricter listing requirements.

✔ What is the average daily volume? *Average daily volume* (the average number of shares traded per day over a period of time) is an important consideration, too. If a stock is *thinly traded* (has a low average daily volume), the Seller who accepted it may be limited in her ability to sell that stock. For example, say Seller receives 10 million shares of stock as part of the consideration for selling her business. If the stock trades at $1 per share, Seller has $10 million worth of stock.

However, if the average daily trading volume is, say, 10,000 shares, she essentially has an illiquid stock. Putting in a trade for all 10 million shares results in crashing the share price. If only 10,000 shares (on average) trade hands per day, the odds that she can sell 10 million shares in a short period of time are virtually nil. On the other hand, a stock with a higher trading volume is usually easier to sell.

In general, the average daily volume is higher for stocks listed on NYSE and NASDAQ than for stocks listed OTC or on the Pink Sheets.

✔ Stock (public or nonpublic) received as a result of a business sale is usually *restricted,* meaning that the owner of that stock can't sell the stock for some period of time. That length of time depends on securities regulations. In order to help prevent a crash of the stock price, Buyer may ask Seller to agree to a restricted period longer than current securities laws.

Even if securities law restrictions no longer restrict a stock, a thinly traded stock is effectively a restricted stock (it's pretty hard to sell a stock that no one's buying).

Selling less than 100 percent of the company

If Buyer and Seller disagree about valuation, another possible solution is for Buyer to acquire less than 100 percent of the business. Selling a piece of the company allows Seller to take some chips off the table and create some liquidity right away while allowing her to participate in the future upside of the company.

Most Buyers want to have a *control stake* in the business, meaning they want to acquire at least 50 percent of the company. In rare situations a *minority stake* (less than 50 percent) may be palatable to Buyer.

Taxation of entities

Taxing corporations is complicated because you have two basic types of entities (C-corps and S-corps/LLCs), two types of business sales (asset or stock), and three types of taxes (corporate, individual, capital gains). A C-corp's profits are taxed at the corporate tax rate, and then any distributions to ownership are taxed again, this time at either the owner's marginal tax rate or at the capital gains rate.

The S-corp offers the benefit of removing a layer of tax and avoiding double taxation. The profits of the entity flow to the owners. The owners must pay tax on the income, usually at their marginal income tax rate. One of the limitations of S-corps, though, is that they're limited to 100 shareholders while C-corps have no limits to the number of shareholders. LLC's are similar to S-corps (with some different terminology) for taxation purposes; I lump them in with S-corps here, but check with your tax advisor about some subtle differences.

But the tax issues don't stop there; selling a business opens another can of tax worms. The following table helps break down how a business sale affects the business's taxation:

Taxation of entities		
	Asset deal	**Stock deal**
C-corp	2 layers of tax (corporate tax and then capital gains tax)	1 layer of tax (capital gains tax)
S-corp/LLC	1 layer of tax (individual or capital gains tax)	1 layer of tax (capital gains tax)

I cannot stress this enough: Sellers need to plan ahead and speak with their tax advisors. Your specific tax situation depends on your company's specific situation.

Warning: An owner who converts a C-corp to an S-corp shortly before a sales transaction may be in for another nasty little tax surprise: In some cases the conversion from a C-corp to an S-corp may take ten years before the owner is able to realize the full tax benefit. Ideally, conversion to an S-corp should take place years before the owner sells the company.

A Seller agreeing to sell less than 100 percent of the company is wise to include a put option as part of the sale. A *put option* allows Seller to sell her remaining shares to Buyer at some future date and at some future price. Most often, that price is an agreed-upon formula based on some sort of financial performance of the company.

Dealing with Renegotiation

Yes, valuation can change during the sale process. In fact, that occurrence even has a name: renegotiation. Or, as disappointed Sellers may call it, the dreaded renegotiation.

Theoretically, when Buyer and Seller negotiate a valuation, both sides want to see the deal close with that valuation. In practice, however, one side or the other may try to change the sale price before the closing.

If Buyer is trying to change the valuation, you can bet that he's trying to lower the valuation.

Buyer may have a case to ask for a lower valuation if the company has experienced some sort of material changes, such as the following:

✔ Decline in profits

✔ Loss of major customers

✔ Loss of key executives

✔ Lawsuits

✔ Change in regulations

✔ Change (downturn) in the economy

However, if Buyer doesn't have a solid reason for asking for a lower price, that Buyer may be exhibiting a little bit of gamesmanship and a lot of negotiating in bad faith, so I don't recommend that Buyers unnecessarily try to lower the valuation. Check out Chapter 11 for more on negotiating in good faith. Similarly, if the business improves (especially profit-wise), Seller may feel that renegotiating for a higher valuation is warranted.

This proposition is tricky, and in most cases I don't recommend it. Focus on getting the deal done. During the time Seller spends convincing Buyer to pay more, the business may take a step backward, reducing profits and thus causing Buyer to ask for a lower valuation. In this situation, the only winners are the lawyers and anyone else billing for time as the process drags on.

Chapter 13

LOI and Behold: Making or Receiving an Offer

In This Chapter

▶ Understanding the LOI's purpose

▶ Looking at the LOI's inner workings

▶ Considering extending exclusivity

▶ Moving forward after the letter is signed

*A*lthough many things — an indication of interest (see Chapter 9), a term sheet, a phone call where Buyer says, "We're interested and we're willing to pay $10 million" — can be an offer in the M&A world, not all offers are created equal. In the world of offers, the letter of intent (LOI) is in a class of its own; it's the gold standard of offers. This chapter gives you the lowdown on this document, including its important parts and some considerations to keep in mind while reviewing it.

Signaling Sincerity with a Letter of Intent

An LOI is basically a marriage proposal from Buyer. Both parties promise to stop seeing others and signal to each other that they're very serious about wrapping up the deal. In dating, that deal is wrapped up at the wedding; in M&A, it happens at the closing.

As the name implies, the LOI lays out the intent of both parties: Seller states she is willing to sell for the proposed terms, and Buyer states what he is willing to pay. They are both agreeing to move forward to close a deal based on the terms in the document. It's not binding, which means it's not enforceable in court (well, except for the parts about confidentiality) and it doesn't bind Buyer to the deal. In fact, either side can still walk away for any reason.

Buyer submits the LOI to Seller. If Buyer is working with an investment banker or other M&A advisor, that advisor will most likely submit the LOI to Seller (or to Seller's advisor, if she has one). Buyer's lawyer may be the one to actually craft the LOI, although the lawyer works under the direction of Buyer's advisor to make sure the business terms are what Buyer wants. After the LOI is ready to be submitted, sending it via e-mail is perfectly permissible (I don't recommend sending a marriage proposal that way, though).

The LOI is an important step because it lays out the basics of the final deal: the purchase price and terms, closing date, length of exclusivity, approvals, and much, much more. (See the nearby section "Understanding the Salient Issues in the LOI" for more detail.) However, the LOI isn't necessarily the final deal. Rather, it's the framework or roadmap for that final deal. Based on what each side discovers during due diligence, and/or whether the profits of the company decline, the deal may change.

For most people, the transaction to buy or sell a business will be the biggest deal of their lives and careers. It usually involves lots of money and even more risk. When you buy or sell a pack of gum or a bottle of wine, for example, you don't need to issue an LOI. You simply buy or sell the object. If you sell some bad gum or wine, you may have to refund some money, but neither example will ruin you. Given the size and complexity of a company, on the other hand, one bad merger or acquisition may well ruin you. Because of the risk of buying or selling a company, you need to take gradual steps.

Think about buying a house. Most people don't wake up one morning, decide to go out and buy a home, and expect to own one an hour later. Instead, they talk to a real estate agent, look at a bunch of houses, find one they like, and make an offer. If the seller accepts that offer, the buyer signs an agreement that sets the terms of closing the deal and usually allows the buyer to inspect the house; if the house meets the buyer's satisfaction and the buyer can obtain the financing, the house is sold.

In M&A, the LOI acts as an important step in closing that deal. It defines the terms and the timing, and Seller agrees to stop talking to other potential Buyers. And assuming the company passes the inspection (see Chapter 14 for more info on due diligence) and assuming Buyer has (or can get) the dough, the deal closes.

Although they're similar in some ways, an LOI is different from an indication of interest (IOI). Both documents are part of the process of buying or selling a company; however, the LOI lays out more specific terms. An IOI typically has a valuation range; an LOI has a specific valuation. An IOI doesn't ask for exclusivity, but an LOI usually does ask for exclusivity from Seller. Think of it this way: An IOI is asking for a date, while an LOI is a marriage proposal.

The LOI's more specific terms provide protection for Buyer. The LOI allows Buyer to get serious about closing a deal without having to worry about another Buyer swooping in at the last minute and stealing it. The LOI also allows Buyer to get a close look at the company without having to lay out the money to buy the company.

Exclusivity is a key consideration. An LOI usually includes a lock-up period where Seller is out of the market — that is, unable to speak with other Buyers about doing a deal. Sellers should grant exclusivity very carefully and should do everything possible to limit the amount of time they're prevented from speaking to other Buyers. I cover exclusivity in more depth later in the chapter.

Understanding the Salient Issues in the LOI

Although no one-size-fits-all approach applies to writing an LOI, the basics include some boilerplate legalese and some detail about the specific deal at hand. In the following sections, I lay out some of the main areas of coverage you're likely to see in an LOI. Check out the appendix for an example LOI.

As with all these specific legal documents, speak to your advisors. I highly recommend that Buyers and Sellers speak to their intermediaries about the business issues (price, timing, and so on) and to their attorneys about the legal aspects.

You may notice that I don't include a section for a *break up fee* (a fee Buyer pays Seller if Buyer walks away from the deal). The truth is that most Buyers don't care to include those clauses for obvious reasons, so the odds of getting one in an LOI are slim. Sellers can ask for them, but they shouldn't get their hopes up.

Buyer and Seller should both guard against negotiating every single last detail of the purchase agreement in the LOI. You want to hammer out the main issues, absolutely, but certain advisors (ahem, lawyers) are wont to settle every single minor issue at the LOI stage. Focus on the salient issues in the following sections.

Salutation and preamble

The LOI starts with basics, like any other business letter. After a flowery greeting, Buyer usually provides a lengthy preamble with some comments about how excited he is to submit the LOI and how beautifully Seller and Buyer will fit together after a deal is done. This section is simply cosmetic politeness: nice, but not important.

Valuation and deal structure

Valuation (which I cover in Chapter 12) is the key number everyone looks for. Usually the valuation appears in the third or fourth paragraph of the LOI. Buyers often load up their LOIs with a bunch of boilerplate in hopes of differentiating themselves from other Buyers, but this boilerplate isn't what's important; the valuation is. The valuation in the LOI should be a static number (as opposed to the range typically seen in the IOI).

The structure of the deal is also very important, and frankly, many first-time Sellers overlook it. The valuation may provide an eye-popping number, but the devil is in the details. Here are some deal-structure questions to consider:

- **How much of that valuation does Buyer pay in cash at closing?** Cash at closing (I'm repeating myself here for dramatic effect) is the most important detail for any Seller because Seller can't spend a note, an earn-out, or stock. Cash is king, and a wise Seller places a premium on getting actual cash as opposed to a promise to maybe get some cash at some point in the future.

- **How much of the valuation is in the form of a contingent payment?** *Contingent payments* include earn-outs, notes, and even stock in Buyer's company (see Chapter 12 for more). I consider these forms of payment contingent because Seller may or may not eventually receive that money.

  If the LOI includes contingent payments, what are the details?

  - **How much money is in the form of a note?** What is the interest rate, and when does Seller receive that money? Does the interest *accrue* (all the interest is paid when the principal is paid)? Is the note *amortized* (Seller receives interest and principal payments)? Or is the note *interest only* (Seller receives regular interest payments and a balloon payment at the end), and if so, how often are the interest payments due?

- **What are the specifics of any proposed earn-out?** Seller should be most concerned with one thing: how she gets her money! You can structure earn-outs in virtually limitless ways, but in my strongly held opinion, the earn-out should be simple and easy to understand. The more complex the deal, the less likely Seller ever sees any money from the earn-out. Check out Chapter 21 for some earn-out ideas.

- **How easily can Seller convert any stock to cash?** If the stock is *thinly traded* (doesn't trade many shares daily) and is on a lesser exchange (OTC or Pink Sheets), Seller has a lower probability of converting that stock to cash than if the stock were a high-volume stock on NYSE or NASDAQ.

No single contingent payment structure is right or wrong for any given deal. Each deal is different. Seller needs to confer with her advisors and weigh the merits of a particular offer.

Buyers, if a Seller rejects your offer after reviewing it, provide that reluctant Seller with a detailed calculation of the deal. Many Sellers simply look at the cash at closing and they may miss the true value of the deal. Calculate the proceeds over time. Add in earn-outs, notes, stock, and so on.

Holdback and escrow

Most deals delineated in an LOI include a *holdback*, an amount Buyer withholds from Seller for a period of time just in case the company has some sort of problem (usually a breach of a representation or warranty, which is covered in Chapter 15) after the deal closes. The holdback goes into a third-party account called *escrow*. This escrowed money is released to Seller, assuming Buyer doesn't make claims to the money.

Escrow should be 10 percent (or less) of the purchase price, and that money should be paid to Seller within 12 months of close. However, a deal involving a Seller with a history of problems or challenged earnings may warrant a higher holdback amount and a longer period of time.

Some Sellers view the escrow as money they're not receiving, but Sellers should remember that Buyers need to come to the closing meeting with that money. Just because Seller doesn't immediately receive that money doesn't mean Buyer isn't providing it. If the purchase price is $10 million with $1 million to be placed in escrow, Buyer needs to come to the closing with $10 million!

Representations and warranties

Buyer and Seller agree to a slew of representations and warranties (sometimes abbreviated *reps and warranties* or *R&W*). *Representations and warranties* are legal promises regarding past and future events, and you should take them very seriously. I provide more detail about reps and warranties in Chapter 15.

Sellers can and often should provide Buyers with R&Ws for past events such as the previous year's financial statements. But providing R&Ws for future events is a mistake because the future has no guarantees. Asking Seller to provide R&Ws that, say, the company's top customer will still be the top customer in one year is an unreasonable request.

The R&Ws tend to be biased against the Seller, and so Sellers usually provide far more R&Ws than Buyers do because Buyers have many more worries about the deal than Sellers.

The biggest concern for Seller is that Buyer shows up at closing with the money; Seller isn't too preoccupied with getting Buyer's R&Ws. After the deal closes, Seller doesn't have financial responsibility for the company; Buyer does. That's why Buyer is so keen on Seller providing some reps and warranties.

For Buyer to have the ability to claim some of the escrow money against Seller, a problem usually needs be the result of Seller's failure to disclose something to Buyer, or worse, of some sort of fraud or malfeasance by Seller. If the problem is the result of Buyer making a mistake post-close, it's Buyer's problem, and Buyer can't claim a breach of a rep or warranty.

If the business takes a nose dive due to a general economic decline, that's not the fault of Seller, and Buyer will not be able to claim a breach of a rep or warranty.

Financing

Most LOIs contain some info about where Buyer proposes to obtain the dough needed to effect the transaction. I heartily recommend Sellers pay very careful attention to this part of the LOI. The phrase you're on the lookout for is *financing contingency*.

A financing contingency is a hedge for Buyer. He's saying he may not have the money right now and hopes to obtain it before closing, but he wants a way out of the deal in the event that he can't get the necessary money.

As a Seller, tread carefully if a Buyer is asking for a financing contingency, especially if the Buyer is a large company or a private equity (PE) firm (see Chapter 6). I'm not saying a financing contingency is inherently bad — deals can still get done if a Buyer wants to include one — but Sellers should try to move forward with an LOI that doesn't include a financing contingency if at all possible. If Buyer decides not to do the deal, all he has to do is claim he can't get the money. The inability to get the money contradicts his claims to be a big PE firm or another sizable company: If Buyer is using his strong financial position to entice Seller, then why would that Buyer need a financing contingency?

Due diligence and timing

Due diligence (which I explore further in Chapter 14) is the inspection period for Buyer. It comprises a short section, perhaps just a single sentence, in the LOI where Buyer indicates how long he needs to complete it. After Buyer successfully concludes due diligence, he can close the deal.

Sellers should pay close attention to the length of time Buyer seeks; if it's too long, Seller shouldn't proceed until Buyer agrees to conduct due diligence and close the deal in a shorter, more reasonable amount of time. As a guideline, Buyer should be able to conduct due diligence and close within 60 days of signing the LOI.

Approvals and conditions

This section is usually more boilerplate where the Buyer may reference certain executives who need to sign off on the deal before it can close. Buyer may also ask Seller to make sure her ducks are in a row, so to speak, so that whoever needs to approve the transaction on her side is willing to do so.

As with a financing contingency (see the earlier "Financing" section), Sellers shouldn't move forward with an LOI if a Buyer is including what amounts to an approval contingency — that is, a hedge for the Buyer to back out of the deal simply by claiming some executive won't agree to the deal. Make sure closing the deal isn't contingent upon the Buyer gaining approval of some yet-unseen executive.

Role of management

An LOI may define the expected role of the company's management after the deal closes, including Buyer's intent to retain certain employees in the current roles and at their current compensation levels.

Sellers should be on guard against an LOI that includes a well-meaning but potentially destructive clause where Buyer won't move forward unless he can sign certain employees to employment contracts and noncompete agreements. This practice can become tricky because if an employee realizes she can hold up the deal and prevent it from closing, she may dig in her heels and make outsized demands. Don't let an employee hold up the process of closing a deal.

Access to information

Seller agrees to furnish Buyer with all information necessary for Buyer to conduct due diligence and close the deal.

Just because Seller agrees to give Buyer access to the company doesn't mean Buyer has permission to simply waltz into the office, speak to any employee, and dig into any file he chooses. Instead, Sellers should carefully and tightly control the process. Buyer shouldn't be able to speak with employees unless Seller agrees to the communication. Communication should follow the chain of command at all times; if Buyer desires a certain piece of information, he should route that request through Seller's intermediary, of if Seller doesn't have an intermediary, through a previously defined point person. If Seller doesn't tell Buyer who the point person is, Buyer should ask.

Expenses

This section is an important bit of boilerplate. The LOI usually stipulates that the expenses incurred by Buyer are Buyer's responsibility and the expenses incurred by Seller are Seller's responsibility.

Because this problem does often arise, Sellers should make sure Buyers don't try to have them pay for Buyers' deal-related expenses; those, too, should be the responsibility of the Buyers.

Exclusivity

Exclusivity (also known as *no shop*) is one of the main differences between an IOI and an LOI. It's the clause where Seller agrees to halt all other conversations with other potential Buyers. The length of exclusivity should coincide with the amount of time Buyer requires to conduct due diligence (see the earlier "Due diligence and timing" section). From my experience, 60 days should be sufficient; I wouldn't agree to an LOI that had more than 60 days, but in practice the due diligence and contract-writing sometimes take longer than 60 days. Check out the later section "Agreeing to and Extending Exclusivity" for more on exclusivity issues.

Non-disclosure and publicity

More boilerplate. Both sides simply agree to not tell anyone (outside of those in their respective inner circles) about the proposed deal. This provision is especially important for Seller because premature release of news about the pending sale may harm Seller's business by spooking customers, employees, and/or vendors. Flip to Chapter 7 for more on confidentiality.

Nonbinding agreement

Just in case the nonbinding nature of the LOI isn't clear, the letter includes language that indicates the document isn't binding in a court of law. This text is usually boilerplate, but it's important boilerplate for Buyer because it gives him a clear out should he want to walk away.

Governing law or jurisdiction

In the case of a dispute that needs to be adjudicated in a court of law, both parties agree to the state where that adjudication will take place. If Buyer and Seller are in the same state, that decision is pretty easy because they typically agree to use their mutual home state.

However, if Buyer and Seller are in different states, each party will naturally want to use its own home state. In these examples, most Buyers simply list their home state in the LOI. Therefore, Seller has to pay close attention to the designation in this section of the letter and suggest a change of venue. Buyer may agree to use Seller's state, but in most cases, a neutral state is the best option.

If you and the other party can't agree on whose state to use for jurisdiction, remember that many deal-makers choose Delaware, mainly because Delaware has a separate court system for business issues.

Agreeing to and Extending Exclusivity

Buyers often prefer to negotiate deals without the nuisance of competition. Strike that; Buyers *always* prefer to negotiate deals without the nuisance of competition. Who can blame them? Removing competition puts Buyer in a stronger position. That's why Buyers often want to lock Sellers down with an exclusivity clause (which I discuss in the earlier section "Exclusivity"). In the following sections, I give you the skinny on giving your exclusivity away appropriately and deciding whether to extend expiring exclusivity.

Considering exclusivity in pre-emptive bids

An exclusivity clause prevents you as a Seller from engaging in M&A talks with other Buyers, so I recommend Sellers wait until the IOI stage before agreeing to exclusivity. Competition is a boon to any Seller; as a Seller, the odds of closing a deal are lower when you have only one potential Buyer. Play the field until you have multiple offers.

Granting exclusivity is a form of capital; don't give it up without getting something in return.

Buyers sometimes ask to make a *pre-emptive bid* (an offer made before the due date for offers from other Buyers), which usually includes exclusivity. I'm all for reviewing and considering any offer, but I recommend pursuing a pre-emptive bid only if Buyer is willing to forgo exclusivity. This way, you have protection if the pre-emptive Buyer backs out (the process has been continuing, so you don't lose any time). Otherwise, you can lose momentum and essentially end up back at square one. Remind such Buyers that if they're genuinely interested in making a pre-emptive bid, that bid ought to reflect your potential lost opportunity cost. In other words, that pre-emptive bid ought to have some sort of premium in the price.

Asking for a *breakup fee* (a fee Buyer pays you if he ultimately walks away without closing a deal), may not be a bad idea. Note that most Buyers are reluctant to include a breakup fee (in both pre-emptive bids and regular bids) in a deal, though, so the odds of getting one are rather low.

If you require a quick close, perhaps due to an eroding business situation, a pre-emptive bid may make sense. You may not get the best deal possible, but given the time constraints, it may be the last and best option. Holding out for a slightly better deal may backfire if you run out of time before that better deal materializes.

Running out of time: Prolonging exclusivity

If Buyer is unable to close the deal in the time the LOI allots, you as Seller should confer with your advisors to determine whether Buyer is having problems that may compromise the deal. For example, Buyer may be stalling for time because she doesn't yet have the money lined up. If you and your advisors believe Buyer isn't able to close the deal, you may be better off refusing to grant her continued exclusivity. If you think Buyer is stalling, informing her that you'll begin to talk with the other interested parties is often a good technique to get her to wrap up the deal and close.

However, before refusing to extend exclusivity, consider whether your own actions caused or contributed to the delay. Have you released information in a timely manner? If you've been slow in providing Buyer with needed due diligence information, you're partially responsible for her slow pace and should take that into account when evaluating the situation.

If you do decline to grant Buyer an extension of exclusivity, I don't recommend actually telling her that you don't want to do a deal. Never shut a door and walk away. If the situation is seemingly untenable, let the other side be the one to close that door. You never know whether that other side will eventually see your point of view and come around to your position, so give yourself a chance at closing a deal.

Buyers, do your work quickly and push as hard as possible to close the deal within 60 days. Based on the situation, Seller may not decide to extend exclusivity if you need more time and may instead reengage conversation with other interested parties.

You Have a Signed LOI — Now What?

Signing an LOI doesn't mean you have a deal. In many ways, the LOI is simply the beginning of the process. As Seller, the deal isn't done until the money hits your account! As Buyer, the deal is done when everyone has signed all the documents at closing day (see Chapter 16) and the money has been wired to Seller.

In the meantime, Sellers should continue to run the business as though they haven't made a deal, focusing on profitability and controlling costs as they normally would. Buyers should place the escrow with a third party, usually a bank, and give an escrow agent a set of instructions detailing when to release the money to Seller. Sometimes all the money is released at one time, but in some cases, the escrow may be released over a period of time. The staggered release can be a good way to satisfy both Seller, who undoubtedly wants the money as soon as possible, and Buyer, who may want to keep money in escrow for a longer period of time. See the earlier section "Holdback and escrow" for more on escrow.

Chapter 14

Confirming Everything!
Doing Due Diligence

. . . .

In This Chapter

▶ Understanding due diligence

▶ Conveying important due diligence information

▶ Evaluating whether to provide extra information

. . . .

*T*he Buyer conducts *due diligence* (a thorough review of the Seller's books, records, inventory, contracts, and more) concurrent with the drafting of the purchase agreement (see Chapter 15). Due diligence is the "open the kimono" time when the Seller reveals intimate details of the business, including (but not limited to) financials, customer information, pricing detail, sales pipeline, contracts, and employee compensation.

In this chapter, I introduce you to the ins and outs of due diligence, what to expect, what needs to be done, and perhaps just as importantly, what doesn't need to be done. Please refer to the appendix for a full list of information provided in a typical due diligence process.

As you conduct due diligence it's a good idea to begin thinking ahead to the integration phase. You'll need a dedicated team in place to help make the transition smooth, so I recommend getting a head start on that important step. Chapter 18 talks more about assembling your transition team and what pre-integration considerations a Buyer should make.

Digging into the Due Diligence Process

The goal of due diligence is for Buyer to confirm Seller's financials, contracts, customers, and all other pertinent information. In other words, the goal is to make Buyer comfortable enough that he goes through with the deal and closes.

Buyers often have other partners (usually banks or private equity firms) who are providing some of the financing and have stricter requirements than the Buyer does. In other words, Seller may have to overcome both Buyer's demands and Buyer's financial partner's demands.

The following sections look at some considerations for the overall due diligence process.

Getting the process underway

Due diligence commences the moment the letter of intent (LOI — see Chapter 13) is signed, or at least it theoretically should. But frankly, many Sellers are wholly unprepared at this moment; they often don't realize the vast amount of data they have to provide during due diligence. (To get an idea of just how much data due diligence requires, check out the later section "Providing Appropriate Information" and the appendix.)

All due diligence information should be ready and available for Buyer the moment both parties have signed the LOI. Because compiling due diligence information takes time, I recommend that Seller begin to gather this information when she starts marketing the business to Buyers.

How long compiling this data takes is largely contingent upon how quickly Seller works, but I recommend planning on one full month, assuming Seller is highly motivated and works quickly. Given the inevitable delays due to the demands of running a business, she may discover that she takes two or three months to fully compile all the due diligence info.

Allowing enough time for the due diligence phase

In theory, due diligence should take no longer than 60 days. When buying or selling a business, I never submit or agree to an LOI of more than 60 days. In both cases, I want to close a deal as soon as possible

In reality, however, the due diligence phase can take longer than 60 days. In most cases, the delay is the fault of the Seller, who's often slow in getting information out. As I note in the preceding section, Seller needs to have all the due diligence materials prepared and ready to provide to Buyer as soon as both sides sign the LOI.

Regardless of whether you're buying or selling, push hard for a 60-day due diligence period. Stay proactive with the process: Push and prod for information, and don't be reluctant to pick up the phone and be a pain in someone's side. However, other people don't always work as fast as you'd like, so mentally prepare yourself for 90 days.

Sellers can't be afraid to remind Buyers that due diligence is confirmatory in nature, meaning Buyer should spend the time confirming Seller's information and not planning, creating, and combining the two entities. The Buyer should take care of post-closing activities after closing! Otherwise, due diligence will drag on longer than necessary.

The length of time for due diligence should coincide with the length of exclusivity laid out in the LOI because Buyer wants to avoid Seller being able to negotiate with other Buyers while due diligence is still under way. See Chapter 13 for more on LOIs and exclusivity.

Covering the expense

Each side pays its own expenses. Buyer hires his own lawyers, accountants, investment banker, and other sundry consultants, and Seller retains her own similar set of advisors. Each side is responsible for paying only its own set of advisors.

However, Buyers may be able to negotiate with their advisors to accept payment after the deal closes, meaning a Buyer can pay the bills by either using Seller's cash flow or perhaps by adding the cost of the advisors to the amount of money the Buyer borrows from other sources.

Due diligence means that you as a Buyer are spending a lot of money on auditors, lawyers, and other consultants, so refusing to move forward with those expenses until you know the Seller isn't continuing negotiations with other Buyers makes perfect sense. You don't want to show up on closing day only to discover that the Seller has picked a different Buyer!

Conveying the due diligence info to Buyer

In days of yore, back when the slide rule and rotary-dial phone ruled, M&A deal-makers conducting due diligence would sit in a room, informally called a data room, with a stack of financial statements, contracts, and all manner of information, and slowly but surely confirm what they needed to confirm.

This task wasn't fun, so Al Gore took it upon himself to invent the Internet. Okay, I'm joking, but thanks to that non-Gore invention, the insanity of the physical data room ended. The M&A deal-makers of today use an online data room (sometimes called a virtual data room).

An online data room has numerous advantages over the old fashioned "a bunch of documents dumped in a cold, impersonal room" approach, including the following:

- **Seller can control who sees what information and when.**

- **Buyer can conduct due diligence from the comfort of his cold and impersonal office instead of traveling to Seller's facility and sitting in her cold and impersonal office.**

- **Multiple people from Buyer's side can access the data room.** Seller only needs to grant them access (user name and password).

- **The online data room acts as a central depository.** This function cuts down on multiple people from Buyer's team making the same request over and over.

- **Seller can monitor who from Buyer's team has accessed the online data room and which documents those people have reviewed.** This helps Seller gauge Buyer's seriousness. Is he looking at all the information or just certain bits — say, the customer list?

- **Seller gets a level of security.** Documents loaded to most online data rooms have a watermark displaying the name of the user, the date of access, and the IP address. If Buyer breaches confidentiality and gives the due diligence materials to someone not approved by Seller, the documents clearly point out the person responsible for the breach.

Business as usual: Running the company during due diligence

Seller should continue to run the business as if she weren't in the process of selling it. The company should buy supplies, pay bills, and make sales calls as before.

However, if Seller is thinking about making big business decisions, such as substantially increasing overhead or hiring new salespeople or executives, she should probably confer with Buyer first because huge changes to the business may affect the company, notably the profits.

Selling a business is a highly sensitive process, and Sellers need to tell their employees of the sale (or pending sale) at the right time. Furthermore, Sellers need to control that right time. Unless an employee needs to know (usually executives and certain financial personnel need to know), Seller should wait until the deal is closed before making an announcement to the employees.

Keeping the cards close to one's vest is important for a couple of reasons. If Seller informs the employees of a potential sale that ends up falling through, Seller loses face. Worse, employees may start to wonder why the deal didn't close. They may assume that the company is facing some sort of problem and start a mass exodus. Additionally, employees who hear about the pending deal may assume they'll get fired after the deal closes and begin to jump ship as they look for new jobs.

If the news of a pending sale is released prematurely, the company may suffer major losses. For this reason, Sellers shouldn't give Buyers carte blanche to contact Seller's employees at will. Buyer shouldn't call or contact any of Seller's employees without Seller's explicit approval. Seller needs to carefully control this release of information and the timing of when Buyer speaks with employees.

As Seller, if someone on Buyer's team has caused a breach by making unapproved contact with one of your employees, immediately pick up the phone and call the other side. Don't rely on e-mail. You need to have a conversation. Remind Buyer he's not to make contact without your approval and ask him to adhere to protocol and the terms of the confidentiality agreement (see Chapter 7). Most Buyers immediately understand the gravity of the situation and take steps to fix the problem. In other words, someone on that team is about to get an earful!

After making such a phone call, send an e-mail memorializing your conversation and ask the other side to confirm receipt and understanding of the e-mail. This way, if the problem occurs again, you have a written record of the first breach.

Providing Appropriate Information

The expanse of due diligence information is far deeper and wider than the information that the offering document, or deal book, provides. The offering document (see Chapter 8) provides enough information for a Buyer to make an offer. Due diligence provides enough information for that Buyer to be able to close the deal. Another difference is that the offering document is intended for laypeople. It's relatively easy to read and comprehend, and its focus is high level; that is, it contains fewer nitty-gritty details. The due diligence material is for experts and can be mind-numbingly boring!

Please review the appendix for a very, very detailed listing of due diligence items. The due diligence items I list in the following sections are only a recap of typical due diligence items and are intended to give both Buyer and Seller an idea of the depth of materials needed to conduct due diligence.

Corporate info

Buyers want to pay close attention to a bevy of legal paperwork to make sure Seller actually has the legal right to sell the business to Buyer. Not having the legal right to sell something poses a wee bit of a problem in selling a business!

Here are some of the items Sellers should provide for the review of corporate information:

- The company's articles of incorporation, bylaws, and minutes from board meetings
- Annual reports
- Names and contact info of shareholders and number of shares held by each
- Names and contact info of directors and officers
- Listing of the jurisdictions where the company is incorporated or qualified to do business
- Listing of any assumed names or DBAs (doing business as) of the company
- Listing of all federal, state, local, and foreign governmental permits, licenses, and approvals
- Listing of all law firms, accounting firms, consulting firms, and similar professionals engaged by the company

As you may be able to tell from reviewing this list, Seller's lawyer be involved with this part of due diligence. Many Sellers, when faced with some of the items on this list, respond with a blank expression and mumble, "Huh?" Sellers should check with the lawyer who incorporated the business if they're unable to locate these documents.

Operations

A company's operations are highly important. That should go without saying. But what does "operations" mean, and more specifically, how does a Buyer conduct due diligence on operations?

In a typical due diligence process, most Buyers seek the following information for evaluating operations:

- ✔ Listing of all existing products or services, all products or services under development, any major operations discontinued or expected to be discontinued, and copies of all complaints and warranty claims
- ✔ Correspondence related to any product or services regulatory approval (or disapproval)
- ✔ Detail on any rebate programs or other special deals with customers (discounts, terms, and so on)
- ✔ Contracts or agreements with customers, whether formal or informal
- ✔ Customer quality awards, plant qualification/certification distinctions, quality certifications, or other awards or certificates
- ✔ Listing of all business application software, vendor and version, number of licenses, and approximate acquisition date

In addition to reviewing a slew of operations-oriented documents, Buyers often want to see Seller's facility, especially if Seller is a manufacturing or distribution company — in other words, a business with inventory and/or involved with fabrication. Flip to Chapter 10 for more thoughts on meetings between Buyer and Seller.

Financials

I hope no one is surprised to hear that financial information is the cornerstone of M&A deals. As you can probably guess, Buyers conduct a thorough review of Seller's financial information. In all likelihood, the financial review will be the most intensive and important of the due diligence process.

Buyers also want to analyze Seller's accounting policies for various procedures, including, but not limited to, capitalizing assets, depreciation and amortization methods, and adjustments to EBITDA, as well as reviewing any changes in accounting methods.

The following list is simply an abridged list of typical financial due diligence, but it gives you an idea of the amount of data typically required to close a deal.

- ✔ The usual trio of financial statements (income statement, balance sheet, and cash flow statement), preferably prepared by an outside accountant
- ✔ Accounts receivable and accounts payable information, including aging schedules and details on bad accounts

- ✔ The general ledger

- ✔ Projections, capital budgets, and business/strategic plans

- ✔ Listing of all bank accounts and safety deposit boxes, including authorized signatories

- ✔ Schedule of prepaid expenses with backup documentation and accumulated amortization

- ✔ Schedule of deferred income at most recent year-end and month-end

- ✔ Schedule of security deposits at most recent year-end and month-end

- ✔ Schedule of all indebtedness and contingent liabilities

- ✔ Detail of accrued expenses as of the most recent year-end and month-end

- ✔ Detail of any customer advances, deposits, and credit balances as of the most recent year-end and month-end

Accrued vacation is often the one lurking problem Sellers don't think about. If employees are due vacation time but haven't yet taken that time prior to the closing, Buyer will demand a reduction in the purchase price equal to the value of that vacation time.

Sales and marketing info

Who are Seller's customers, and how does she market to them? Who are her competitors? The following are some of the sales and marketing basics any Buyer wants to determine during due diligence:

- ✔ Complete customer list, including name, address, telephone number and contact name

- ✔ Listing of any major customers lost

- ✔ Listing of open orders and copies of all supply or service agreements

- ✔ Surveys and market research reports

- ✔ Schedule of the company's current advertising programs, marketing plans, budgets, and physical marketing materials

- ✔ Listing of the company's major competitors

Sellers should provide customer data by major product line and by percentage of sales. A customer with sales that represent more than 5 percent of the gross sales should be considered major.

One of the most sensitive bits of information for any company is its customer list. Most companies would give their corporate eyeteeth to learn their competitors' intimate customer details. If you're a business owner, I'm sure I don't have to do much to convince you that your customer list is highly confidential.

Due to the sensitivity surrounding the customer list, I recommend Sellers release customer information on a staggered basis, especially if Buyer is a direct competitor at the beginning of due diligence.

Initially, Seller should provide Buyer with an anonymous list (using a code such as "customer 1," "customer 2," and so on). Only if and when Seller believes Buyer will close the deal should Seller release specific customer names. For convenience, that list should match the anonymous list (that is, customer 1 should be the first customer on the list, and so on). Release of the specific names of customers should occur as late as possible in the due diligence session, ideally as close to closing as possible, to minimize any potential problems.

If Buyer is asking to speak with some customers prior to close, Seller should only grant that request as a last and final step before closing. In other words, all other due diligence should be finished and the purchase agreement should be completed.

Real estate and facilities info

A business isn't a business unless it has a place to operate from. Providing Buyer with the following details on the business locations and the nature of those locations is another key responsibility of Seller during due diligence:

- Listing of all business locations
- Listing of all owned or leased real estate, including locations
- Copies of all real estate appraisals, leases, deeds, mortgages, title policies, surveys, zoning approvals, variances, or use permits
- Lease terms, including date signed, termination dates and rights, renewal rights, rent amount, and unusual provisions (such as purchase option), as well as any defaults or breaches
- Listing of current and pending construction in progress, including date commenced, expected completion date, and any additional financial commitment necessary to complete the project(s)

Who owns the facility, and is it part of the deal? Is Buyer also buying the facility, or will she be leasing it from Seller? In most cases, the parties need to conduct any real estate transaction outside the business sale.

Fixed assets

Fixed assets can play an enormous role in financing an acquisition and helping an owner to obtain a loan. For this reason, Sellers need to spell out any and all of the company's fixed assets to Buyer during due diligence. This information includes the following:

- ✔ Listing of all fixed assets, with separate lists for owned assets and leased assets

- ✔ Information on the assets, including a basic description of the asset, date acquired, original purchase price, depreciation years, accumulated depreciation, net book value, and asset location

- ✔ All Uniform Commercial Code (UCC) filings (any time a lender makes a loan secured by the assets of a business, that lender files a document stating it has a claim against the business's assets)

- ✔ Listing of sales and purchases of major capital equipment

- ✔ Listing of unpaid balances and open purchase commitments for any capital equipment

- ✔ Listing of any surplus or idle equipment and the equipment's dollar value

- ✔ Vehicle registrations

Consulting and service businesses likely don't have much in the way of fixed assets (desks and computers are about it). Buyers of these types of companies shouldn't expect much in the way of fixed assets.

Inventory

Inventory is another key component of a company's assets and therefore impacts the ability of an owner to obtain financing for the company. Buyers need the following information:

- ✔ Listing of all items in inventory listing (by location, if applicable), including item description, item number, acquisition date, number of units, and acquisition cost

- ✔ Description of practices regarding inventory aging, valuation, and obsolescence, and any methodology changes

- ✔ Details of inventory reserves and/or write-offs

- ✔ Details of any consigned inventory arrangements

Companies with inventory likely need the Buyer to inspect the inventory in person. In fact, the Buyer may require the Seller to conduct an inventory prior the closing of the deal.

Supplier info

If a company has inventory (see the preceding section), that inventory must come from somewhere. Therefore, Buyer needs to know all about a company's suppliers and how that company makes purchases. Required information includes

- ✔ Listing of major suppliers and dollar volume of purchases from each supplier

- ✔ Listing of open purchase orders

- ✔ Summary of the company's purchasing policies

- ✔ Contracts with suppliers or descriptions of any significant supplier agreements

Buyer may want to contact certain suppliers, but as with making contact with customers, I recommend waiting until the end of the due diligence process before Seller grants this request.

Intellectual property

Intellectual property is an area that many skip over when thinking about due diligence. But make no mistake: a company's intangible assets may be among its most valuable. The following list covers the pertinent due diligence info:

- ✔ Listing of all patents (including title, registration/application number, date of registration/application, initial expiration, and country of registration), patent registrations, trademarks, trade names, and copyrights

- ✔ Listing of Internet domain name registrations

- ✔ Summary of any claims made or threatened by or against the company over intellectual property

Human resources

A company's most valuable assets, especially for consulting and service firms, are the assets that enter and leave the building each day: the employees. A Buyer is wise to understand during due diligence how the company hires, compensates, and accounts for employees. This information can include

- Organizational chart for the entire company
- Listing of employees with details of hire date, position, job description, and current pay rate.
- All agreements with employees and consultants (typically these include employment or consulting agreements as well as non-disclosure, non-solicitation, and noncompete agreements)
- Key employees' résumés
- Copies of executive compensation plans, including salaries, bonuses, commissions, vacations, club memberships, and so on
- The company's employee handbook, including all employee benefits and holiday, vacation, and paid time off policies
- Documentation for retirement plans
- Listing of employee benefits programs and insurance policies
- Listing of all employee problems, including alleged wrongful termination, harassment, discrimination, and labor disputes
- Listing of worker's compensation claim history and unemployment insurance claim history

Debt and financial dealings

A wise Buyer needs to fully understand the Seller's financial dealings for two basic reasons. First, Buyer wants to know what she's getting herself into. In other words, are any hidden or unforeseen problems with a creditor on the horizon? Second, she wants to understand the company's ability to garner financing. Required information may include

- The rundown of all promissory notes, commercial paper, loan or credit agreements, letters of credit, and financial surety/performance bonds or similar credit support devices
- Listing of all security agreements, pledge agreements, mortgages, and other agreements where another company has a claim to Seller's assets

✔ Listing of any compliance certificates, including borrowing base certificates and covenant compliance calculations

✔ Schedule and details of any existing defaults under credit arrangements and any events that, with the giving of notice or the passage of time, will become such a default

Buyers should retain a capable and experienced accounting and auditing firm to conduct a thorough investigation of Seller's financial dealings.

Environmental concerns

Environmental concerns are an increasingly important part of due diligence. A consulting firm or other business service company probably doesn't have an environmental issue. Important environmental due diligence info may include the following:

✔ Copies of any environmental reviews or inspection reports relating to any of the company's owned or leased properties

✔ Copies of any notices, complaints, suits, or similar documents sent to, received by, or served upon the company by the U.S. Environmental Protection Agency or other local or state regulatory body

✔ Copies of outside reports concerning compliance with waste disposal regulations (hazardous or otherwise)

✔ Listing of hazardous substances, including (but not limited to) asbestos, PCBs (polychlorinated biphenyl), petroleum products, herbicides, pesticides, or radioactive materials used in the company's operations

✔ Listing of permits, licenses, and agreements of the company relating to air or water use or quality, solid or liquid wastes, hazardous waste storage or disposal or other environmental matters.

✔ Listing and description of any environmental lawsuits or investigations

✔ Copies of the workplace safety and health programs currently in place, with particular emphasis on chemical handling practices

A Seller concerned about possible environmental issues should hire a qualified environmental firm to conduct appropriate tests on the real estate or facility in question *before* beginning the process of selling the business.

Taxes

Not surprisingly, taxes are a major concern for any Buyer. Taxes run the gamut from income taxes to payroll taxes to sales taxes. Paying taxes drives everyone mad; not paying taxes may send you to jail! The following list outlines tax information Buyers should review during due diligence:

- ✔ All federal, state, local, and foreign tax returns
- ✔ State sales tax returns
- ✔ All employment tax filings
- ✔ Real estate and property tax filings
- ✔ Copies of any tax liens
- ✔ Listing and description of any pending or threatened disputes regarding tax matters

Nonpayment of any kind of tax is serious, of course, but Buyers should be especially on guard for a Seller who has not made FICA payments. Nonpayment of payroll taxes is a major warning sign for any Buyer: When a company stops making FICA payments, the owners or executives can face jail time.

Contract information

Contracts, in other words, the written and oral obligations of the company, are hugely important for any Buyer; she needs to have a clear idea before closing of what contractual commitments her new company has. This information may include

- ✔ Written description of any oral agreements or arrangements
- ✔ All contracts or agreements pertaining to any subsidiary, partnership, or joint venture relationship
- ✔ All contracts between the company and any officers, directors, 5 percent shareholders or any of their respective families or affiliates
- ✔ License, sublicense, royalty and franchise agreements, or equipment leases
- ✔ All distribution, agency, manufacturer representative, marketing, and supply relationships and obligations with copies of all related agreements
- ✔ Letters of intent, contracts, and closing transcripts from any merger, acquisition, or divestiture
- ✔ Options and stock purchase agreements involving interests in other companies

- ✔ All non-disclosure or noncompetition agreements the company is a party to

- ✔ Any agreements a change in control of the company affects in any manner

- ✔ All management contracts

- ✔ Any brokers or finders agreements applicable to the company

- ✔ Contracts relating to other material business relationships, including, but not limited to, any current service, operation, or maintenance contracts and any current contracts for purchase of fixed assets

Insurance

Insurance — that is to say, risk management — is another important factor for any Buyer. Understanding the costs of insuring Seller's business is important, of course, but so is understanding the underlying risks associated with the business. Insurance info for due diligence may include the following:

- ✔ The company's insurance policies, which may include general liability, personal and real property, product liability, errors and omissions, directors and officers, and worker's compensation.

- ✔ Schedule of insurance claims

- ✔ Listing of areas of self-insurance

- ✔ Listing and description of any outstanding premium adjustments

Buyers may be able to get better insurance rates after the deal closes; larger companies are often able to warrant preferred pricing from insurance carriers.

Litigation history

Understanding Seller's history with lawsuits, both as a defendant and plaintiff, is another must-know due diligence area for any Buyer. The following list lays out some important litigation info:

- ✔ All litigation, arbitration, and other proceedings to which the company is a party

- ✔ Listing of all pending or threatened claims, lawsuits, arbitrations, or investigations (including investigations by any governmental authority)

- Description of settlements of litigation, arbitration, and other proceedings

- Bankruptcy proceedings in which the company is a creditor or otherwise interested

- All orders, injunctions, judgments, or decrees of any court or regulatory body applicable to the company

- All agreements in which the company agrees to indemnify or hold harmless another person or entity for claims against that person or entity

- Schedule of any litigation involving an officer or director of the company concerning bankruptcy, crimes, securities law, or business

Watch the advisors closely; they make mistakes

Advisors are very important to the M&A process, and while most advisors do a fine job, you may run into one who isn't doing his best. As an example, a few years ago I was representing a Seller during a particularly difficult due diligence process. One of the Buyer's executives contacted me to berate me about a problem his plethora of expensive accountants had uncovered with my client's financials.

According to the accountants, the earnings we provided in our materials didn't jive with what they uncovered during their very intensive and extensive exploratory exam of my client's finances.

This executive from the Buyer was convinced we were "hiding something" (those were his words). I asked to review the Buyer's work, and after much delay, the other side finally e-mailed me its spreadsheet.

Sure enough, the accountants were showing a $500,000 hole in my client's earnings. Their analysis clearly showed that we overstated

earnings by that amount. I also knew they were positioning themselves to renegotiate the deal and demand a lower price.

But the devil is in the details. I pored through their work, literally cell by cell, until I found the one blatant and obvious mistake: Someone incorrectly (and probably carelessly) transcribed the audited numbers. The raw data the accountants were using to calculate earnings was inputted incorrectly. The mistake was a case of user error. When I popped in the correct numbers, guess what? The earnings as calculated by the Buyer's accountants suddenly fell in line with how the Seller represented earnings.

I calmly reported this information to the executive and e-mailed my findings. I knew the issue was resolved because the other side dropped it and never mentioned it again.

To this day, I wish I had been a fly on the wall of the accountants' office when they received the call from that executive.

Governmental filings

Depending on the industry and the nature of Seller's business, a slew of government filings and paperwork are a part of due diligence. These documents include

- ✔ Any governmental licenses, permits, and authorizations

- ✔ All filings to any national, state, or local governmental agency or authority, including the SEC, the IRS, the FDA, and the INS, to name just a very few

- ✔ Any complaints, investigations, or other informal or formal proceeding by or before a governmental agency or authority and involving the company

Considering Requests for Additional Information

Instead of simply responding to request after request from a Buyer when I sell a company, I always provide a detailed list of due diligence items and tell the Buyer that we'll consider adding requests on a case-by-case basis.

Due diligence should focus on confirming material facts: the numbers, the ownership, the customers, the contracts, and so on. But what falls outside "material facts" can be a complicated matter. Each deal is different, of course, and although the due diligence list provided in the appendix is a comprehensive list, a particular Buyer in a particular industry may require additional items. Sellers should consider those requests from the Buyer. However, asking for sales and marketing materials from years ago is probably useless to the Buyer. Asking the Seller to construct a financial model or write a sales and marketing plan isn't appropriate. Seller should not do Buyer's work. If Buyer wants a financial model or sales and marketing plan, it's the responsibility of Buyer to create those documents.

To help gauge whether a request is appropriate and covers material facts, Sellers should ask a simple question: "How does this information help close the deal?"

If there's no clear answer to how the extra info helps close the deal, the request is likely busywork. Well-meaning busywork, perhaps, but busywork nonetheless. In this case, Sellers shouldn't be afraid to challenge the Buyer's request.

Buyers, make sure your advisors have all prior information from the offering document and any management meetings. Sellers quickly get ticked off if advisors ask for information previously provided.

Chapter 15

Documenting the Final Deal: The Purchase Agreement

In This Chapter

▶ Putting the final purchase agreement together

▶ Examining the parts of a purchase agreement

▶ Looking at important representations, schedules, and exhibits

Concurrent with conducting due diligence (see Chapter 14), Buyer and Seller draft a purchase agreement to memorialize the deal. Although most documents during the M&A process are nonbinding (that is, generally unenforceable in a court of law), the purchase agreement is a final, binding document.

Exciting, isn't it?

In this chapter, I introduce you to the purchase agreement, what to watch for while writing and reviewing it, and what you should leave to your lawyer.

In most cases, the purchase agreement passes the baton from the investment banker, who negotiated the business deal, to the lawyer, who settles all the nits and gnats of the legal issues. Find a good attorney; you're going to have to trust that person!

Drafting the Deal

The purchase agreement is the final, binding contract between Buyer and Seller. In layman's terms: This is the deal. In written correspondence, the purchase agreement is often referred to as the SPA (stock purchase agreement) or the APA (asset purchase agreement).

The purchase agreement can seem like a large, cumbersome document, but most of the document is boilerplate legalese that's in most agreements. The following sections give you an overview of the writing and refining process.

Purchase agreements like verbs. For example, you don't simply write *sell* or *buy*. You write *sell, convey, assign, transfer and deliver* or *purchase, acquire and accept*. Be prepared for some very long and exacting sentences!

Writing the first draft

Purchase agreements don't float in the ether, alighting to terra firma after being summoned to memorialize a deal between Buyer and Seller. Instead, someone has to write the darn things! Although both sides contribute to writing the document, someone has to provide the first draft; conventionally, that's the Buyer, but in reality, either side can write the first draft of the purchase agreement.

In other words, Sellers shouldn't feel compelled to wait for Buyers to provide a draft of the purchase agreement. As with most legal documents, the side that writes the agreement usually has a leg up on the other side. In fact, you may want to have a draft of a purchase agreement written well in advance of signing a letter of intent (LOI — see Chapter 13). That way, your side can quickly claim the high ground by submitting the initial draft, and you cut down on how much you have to wade through someone else's work.

See, the side who writes the first draft sometimes (but not always) writes an incredibly one-sided document that the other side needs to spend an inordinate amount of time fixing, tweaking, and adjusting. That is, lawyers spend that time fixing, tweaking, and adjusting, and lawyers don't work for free (or even cheap). Submitting a draft that's fair and reasonable can help cut down on how long the refining process takes (see the following section) and reduce the associated legal fees.

Although I encourage Sellers to submit a draft, a highly motivated Seller may be wise to agree to use the Buyer's draft if the Buyer balks at the Seller's draft. In this case, the Seller needs to get the deal done and isn't in much of a position to try to force the Buyer's hand.

Redlining the initial draft

No matter who provides the initial draft, the next step in the writing process is something I call *redline ping pong,* where both sides send marked up (or *redlined*) versions of the purchase agreement back and forth as the lawyers work through as many issues as possible.

Keep an ear out for the term *turns,* which also describes the process of sending a redlined draft to the other side. You may hear something like "When will we see your turn of the purchase agreement?" in conversation with the other side.

Amazingly enough, redline ping pong often allows the lawyers to settle many of the legal issues in a purchase agreement. However, the lawyers invariably end up at loggerheads on certain issues, usually of the business variety; at this point, the deal-makers (investment bankers) need to reconnect to settle those remaining issues.

Don't let the lawyers play redline ping pong too much. Stay on top of their process; after you clearly see that they're unable to settle an issue, make sure the deal-makers speak or meet to settle the remaining open issues.

Navigating the Final Purchase Agreement

Purchase agreements are lengthy, detailed documents that can make your eyes bleed if you don't know how to read one properly. Seriously. They're dreadful.

Joking aside, knowing how to read a purchase agreement is as important as what's in the purchase agreement. It's a two-step process:

1. **Review the document to make sure it accurately represents the main (and major) facets of the deal.**

2. **Take a deeper dive into the minutiae of the document.**

   For that in-depth review, you may want to rely on your attorney.

Defer to your lawyer for matters concerning legal issues. Most purchase agreements contain legal boilerplate that doesn't differ much from one document to the next. You need to pay attention to this legalese, of course, but leave it to your lawyer to deal with it.

When first reviewing the document, deal-makers should focus on the key, very specific areas in the agreement. Because you've already negotiated these aspects, you're making sure the agreement conforms to those negotiations. These main points are

> ✔ **Purchase price:** This point includes any conditions to the Seller getting the full purchase price. Does the Seller have to jump through any hoops

to get her dough — in other words, does the deal include contingent payments such as a note, earn-out, and so on? Check out Chapter 12 for more on these structuring options.

✔ **What's being sold:** Confirm that the purchase agreement adheres to the deal type (stock or asset) that you've negotiated. I explain these deal types more in the later section "Determine what's being sold, for how much, and when."

✔ **Escrow:** The agreement lays out the amount of escrow, how long that money stays in escrow, and what the Seller needs to do (or not have happen) to obtain that money.

✔ **Cash at closing:** This figure is the actual amount the Seller receives in cash after escrow, debt, advisor fees, and taxes come out of the purchase price.

✔ **Post-closing adjustments:** Post-closing adjustments (see Chapter 17) are usually relatively straightforward. However, the mechanisms for delivering a post-closing balance sheet (in order to calculate those adjustments), the ability to dispute, and what happens if Buyer fails to deliver necessary information to Seller after close can take multiple paragraphs or even pages, so be sure to review them carefully. If you're a Seller, consult with your attorney!

That's it! Those are the main issues you should be initially concerned with as you make your first review of the purchase agreement. These are the big issues, but they aren't the only issues.

Some M&A deals involve transactions outside the scope the purchase agreement. If the Buyer is assuming some or all of the Seller's debt, is also buying real estate the Seller owns, or is taking over leases from the Seller, those transactions involve other agreements. However, the purchase agreement itself may mention or refer to them.

The following sections outline the highlights of a typical purchase agreement. These agreements often run 50 to 100 pages and up; I'm covering them in a far shorter span than that, so buckle up!

Confirm the name, rank, and serial number of the deal

I call this part, which is usually toward the beginning of the document, the "whereas" section because most paragraphs start with the word *whereas*. This preamble sets the tone for the rest of the document. Here are a few items to verify:

✔ Legal names and addresses of the entities (Buyer and Seller) are correct.

✔ Deal is either clearly defined as an asset sale or a stock sale.

    If it's a stock sale, make sure the share information (number of shares issued, outstanding, and authorized) is correct.

✔ Definition of the business is accurate.

✔ Intents of Buyer and Seller are clearly stated — Buyer desires to buy, and Seller desires to sell.

Determine what's being sold, for how much, and when

The purchase agreement also very clearly defines what is being sold: the company's stock or the company's assets. Sellers usually prefer stock deals because of tax reasons. Buyers typically prefer to buy assets because assets can help reduce the worries of *successor liabilities*, or problems caused by the Seller (such as wrongful termination lawsuits) that may pop up after the deal closes. The agreement should also specify the purchase price, the structure of that price (cash, notes, stock, earn-out, and so on), and the amount that goes into escrow.

This section also details the anticipated closing date and location. Usually, the closing occurs in the lawyers' offices. In the old days, the closing took place in a specific office, but because of today's technology, most closings are virtual closings conducted via e-mail, fax, and phone. See Chapter 16 for more on closing.

Know what to bring to the closing

The purchase agreement defines certain items the Buyer and Seller may need to physically bring to the closing (or deliver ahead of time, if the closing is virtual as I describe in the preceding section).

Seller's deliveries may include

✔ Stock certificates or other documents providing evidence Seller actually owns what she's selling

✔ Resignations of any or all officers or board members, if Buyer requires that info

✔ Stock books, ledgers, minute books, other corporate records, and corporate seals

✔ Documentation that Seller has complied with all conditions required by the purchase agreement

✔ The company's articles of incorporation and bylaws

✔ Written documentation that all outstanding options, warrants, or other instruments that can claim ownership in Seller have been extinguished or exercised prior to closing

✔ Written opinions from Seller's lawyers that all the necessary legal documents are in order

✔ Signatures from both parties for the escrow agreement, confidentiality agreements, noncompetition and non-solicitation agreements, and employment agreements

✔ A closing financial statement (generally as of the close of business from the previous day)

Buyer's deliveries may involve the following:

✔ The money! This delivery is the single most important one (at least in the eyes of Seller). Buyer brings the money in the form of a wire transfer, not a check.

✔ Some sort of documentation, signed by an authorized officer, that Buyer has performed all necessary due diligence

✔ Approvals by Buyer's board of directors

✔ Legal opinion by Buyer's attorney

✔ Signed counterparts to various agreements, including the escrow agreement, noncompetition and non-solicitation agreements, employment agreements, confidentiality agreements, leases, and any other agreement between Buyer and Seller

Review the representations and warranties

The purchase agreement spends an inordinate amount of space dealing with the issue of representations and warranties, or reps and warranties for short. *Reps and warranties* are basically promises and fall into three camps: promises the Seller makes, promises the Buyer makes, and promises both sides make. These guarantees tend to be pretty similarly worded from deal to deal; in fact, many lawyers simply use the language from an earlier agreement they worked on!

In most deals, the reps and warranties are far more onerous for the Seller than for the Buyer. Seller, prepare thyself for a slew of schedules and tables and a huge amount of work!

You can provide representations and warranties on the past (in other words, on known events). Don't provide reps and warranties on the future (unknown events). For example, a Seller can provide a representation that the books are accurate but shouldn't offer a representation that her largest customer will still be the largest customer in one year.

Seller's reps and warranties

The Seller typically provides the Buyer with a bevy of representations and warranties to proclaim that everything that she says (or represents) about the company in the purchase agreement is true to the best of her knowledge.

The gist of all these promises is that Seller has run the company in the *normal course* of business (that is, a clothing distributor suddenly hasn't entered the music business), that she has the right to sell the business, that the company hasn't experienced any adverse material changes since the LOI was signed, and that she's being completely truthful — Buyer won't discover any unpleasant surprises after the deal closes.

Representations and warranties, although full of legalese, should be taken very seriously. These representations will come back and haunt Seller if she lied or misrepresented any of them. In that case, Buyer has recourse to be reimbursed from the money in escrow and possibly through a lawsuit against Seller.

In an actual purchase agreement, each bullet consists of a lengthy paragraph chock-full of legalese. In brief, these promises can include

- ✔ Seller is the owner of the shares or assets and that those shares or assets are free from liens.

- ✔ Seller has the authority to legally sell those shares or assets.

- ✔ The sale of the assets or stock doesn't violate or conflict with any laws, rules, or regulations of any governmental authority.

- ✔ The company is a corporation duly organized, validly existing, and in good standing.

- ✔ The company has full corporate power, legal right, and corporate authority to execute and deliver this agreement.

- Change of control will not trigger some sort of material change, such as an agreement with a major customer that allows the customer to cancel an important contract.

- Seller represents the *capitalization* of the company — that is, how many shares are authorized, issued, and outstanding and any other specific details about that stock. Details on the capitalization may be included on a schedule.

- No options, warrants, or other agreements pertaining to a claim of the company's ownership are outstanding.

- The company has filed all required tax returns, and no taxing authority has any liens against the assets of the company.

- Seller has made all corporate documentations (articles of incorporation, bylaws, and so on) available to Buyer.

- The company has full corporate power, legal right, and corporate authority to operate its business.

- Seller has provided a complete list of all arrangements, contracts, and agreements between the company and other parties to the Buyer. This information is usually in the form a schedule.

- Seller doesn't need the approval of a domestic or foreign governmental authority to execute the transaction. If Seller does need any approvals, she lists them in a schedule.

- Seller actually owns all of the property and assets being sold.

- Any property involved in the deal has no pending condemnation proceedings, lawsuits, or administrative actions relating to it.

- The company has filed all required tax returns under applicable laws and regulations.

- Seller has withheld or paid all taxes.

- No tax problems with any governmental entity exist. Details of any issues that do exist appear in a schedule.

- Seller represents that financial statements (balance sheet, income statement, and cash flow statement) from the most recent year-end, often audited by an accounting firm, are accurate.

- Seller has provided the closing date balance sheet, and that document fairly presents in all material respects the financial condition of the company as of the closing date.

- The company has performed appropriate procedures to ensure the year-to-date financials are accurate and correct.

✔ Seller has presented Buyer with a list of all material contracts, including credit and loan agreements, mortgages, leases, collective bargaining agreements, employment agreements, severance plans, employee benefit plans, and supplier and vendor agreements.

✔ Seller has provided Buyer with a listing of all bank accounts, certificates of deposit, safe deposit boxes, and credit cards issued to employees.

✔ Seller doesn't know of any litigation or pending litigation involving the company.

✔ Seller has presented Buyer with a schedule containing each employee plan, including, but not limited to, bonus; deferred compensation; incentive compensation; stock purchase; stock option; severance pay; medical, life, or other insurance; profit-sharing; and 401(k), pension, or retirement plans.

✔ All employee benefit plans have been operated and administered in accordance with the plans' terms.

✔ Seller knows of no labor problems (strikes, slowdowns, lockouts, work stoppages, and so on).

✔ The company is in compliance with the requirements of the Worker Adjustment and Retraining Notification Act (WARN) and is in compliance with the Occupational Safety and Health Act of 1970 (OSHA).

✔ Seller has provided all patents, patent applications, trademarks, trademark applications, trade names, service marks, service mark applications, customer lists, copyrights, and copyright applications to Buyer.

✔ The company owns all intellectual property it's selling to Buyer.

✔ All computer software and proprietary databases owned or licensed by the company are paid for or owned by the company.

✔ The company takes reasonable measures to protect the confidentiality of trade secrets and proprietary data (including any customer lists and record of financial information constituting a trade secret).

✔ Seller has provided all environmental reports and permits to Buyer.

✔ The company is in compliance with environmental laws.

✔ The company hasn't received written notice that the company is in violation of the requirements of any environmental law or the subject of any lawsuit arising from any environmental law.

✔ The company hasn't transported, stored, or disposed of any hazardous material.

✔ Seller has given a listing of all insurance policies to Buyer.

✔ All insurance policies are legal, valid, binding, and enforceable.

✔ Inventory is usable and saleable.

✔ The company isn't in possession of any inventory it doesn't own.

✔ Seller is responsible for paying any intermediaries she hires during the sale.

✔ Seller has provided Buyer with a complete list of all accounts receivable.

✔ The company doesn't have any prepayments or deposits from customers for products to be shipped or services to be performed after the closing date.

✔ No officer or director of the company (while in the employ of the company) has filed bankruptcy or been convicted of a crime.

✔ Seller has given Buyer a purchase order list (the commitments the company has made to buy from suppliers and vendors).

✔ Seller doesn't know of any customer who is requesting to buy less than previous levels.

✔ Seller has provided a list of customers and vendors to Buyer.

Buyer's reps and warranties

Although the Buyer provides far fewer reps and warranties than the Seller, he does still make a few promises:

✔ Buyer represents that his company is a duly organized entity, validly exists, and is in good standing. In other words, Buyer promises that his company is a going-concern.

✔ Buyer has authority and legal right to execute the purchase agreement.

✔ Buyer pays the fees for any intermediary he utilizes during the sale.

Mutual promises between Buyer and Seller

Most purchase agreements have at least a couple of mutual representations and warranties that both sides agree to. These may include

✔ Buyer and Seller agree to refrain from making any public announcement of the deal until after the deal closes.

✔ Buyer and Seller agree on the method to calculate taxes for the pre-closing period.

✔ Both sides take reasonable best efforts to fulfill their obligations of the agreement.

Secure against loss with indemnifications

All the representations and warranties (see the earlier section "Review the representations and warranties") are meaningless unless one side has some sort of recourse against the other. *Indemnification* means one side is providing security against a loss for the other side. The term you see in legal documents is *hold harmless.* One side agrees to hold the other side harmless in the event something happens (or doesn't happen).

As with the representations and warranties, Seller generally provides Buyer with many more indemnifications than Buyer provides to Seller.

Indemnification is why the Seller usually places some of the proceeds from the sale in an escrow account. In case of a breach of a rep or warranty, the Buyer has recourse to recover damages by obtaining money from escrow.

The purchase agreement defines how long the representations and warranties are in effect. Generally, this period ranges from one to two years.

In addition to time limits, the purchase agreement also spells out the limits on the amount of damages from indemnity. This figure depends on the specifics of your deal, of course. A good rule of thumb is to limit the damages to the amount of money in escrow, but as with all legal issues, speak to your attorney to determine damage limits (as well as indemnity periods) for your deal.

Instead of nickel-and-diming each other with relatively small damage claims, M&A parties often agree not to seek money from each other until the net damages reach a certain amount, called a *basket.* In other words, if the basket is $100,000, Buyer won't ask for reimbursement if he suffers $500 in damages from some sort of breach of representation. However, if the net damages reach that $100,000 threshold, Buyer can seek reimbursement from Seller (usually from the escrow money).

Whether you're buying or selling, don't agree to a limitless indemnity because you may be on the hook for a limitless amount of money.

Agree on how to handle a rep and warranty breach

The purchase agreement defines the process for one party to pursue a claim against the other. Usually, the process involves submitting a written complaint and trying to settle the issue with the other party. If the parties can't settle the issue, the agreement lays out how to settle a dispute, often through mediation or the courts. As with most agreements, the specifics depend of the deal, so talk to your legal advisor.

The purchase agreement defines which state's laws govern the agreement. If the parties fail to agree on which side's home state to use, Delaware is a good compromise because it's considered a business-friendly state and even has a separate court system for business issues.

Get acquainted with the exhibits and schedules

As I note earlier in the chapter, purchase agreements are long, and that doesn't even address the exhibits and schedules. For any given agreement, you may see 50 to 100 exhibits and schedules that run the gamut from the escrow agreement to legal and accounting opinions to employment contacts and a lot more!

Many of these exhibits and schedules are part of Seller's representations and warranties. The burden of producing these schedules falls on the shoulders of Seller. Flip to the earlier section "Review the representations and warranties" for more detail on those promises.

The following list gives you a partial view only. Depending of the specifics of a deal, a purchase agreement may have more or different schedules than those I list here. Check with your lawyer to see which documents your deal requires; I can't provide a one-size-fits-all approach.

- ✔ Escrow agreement
- ✔ Flow of funds at closing
- ✔ Adjusted EBITDA calculation table
- ✔ Real estate leases and deeds
- ✔ Confidentiality agreements
- ✔ Noncompetition agreements
- ✔ Non-solicitation agreements
- ✔ Employment agreements
- ✔ Calculation of net working capital
- ✔ Products in development

- Shareholder list
- Liens
- Owned properties
- Rights of use or occupancy arrangements
- Real estate options/rights of first refusal
- Leased properties
- Capital leases
- Annual financial statements
- Interim financial statements
- Closing date balance sheet
- Material contracts
- Bank accounts
- Litigation
- Employee benefit plan
- Labor relations and employees
- Intellectual property lists
- Computer software and proprietary databases
- Environmental reports, disclosures, and notifications
- Storage of hazardous materials
- Material changes
- Compliance with laws
- Insurance policies
- Inventory list
- Open purchase orders
- Brokers and finders agreements
- Accounts receivable
- Product design
- Prepayments and deposits
- Change of control obligations
- Reimbursable expenses

- Open sales orders
- Customer order changes
- Customers and vendors
- Buyer consents and approvals

Part V
Closing the Deal ...
and Beyond!

"I assume everyone on your team is on board with the proposed changes to the office layout."

In this part . . .

In this part, I dig into what happens after all the work is complete and it's time for closing. I discuss what occurs on that day and how to prevent last-minute issues that can blow up a deal. Lastly, I discuss some post-closing challenges that companies face as they integrate and combine.

Chapter 16

Knowing What to Expect on Closing Day

In This Chapter

▶ Rounding up the closing's participants

▶ Executing the actual closing

▶ Considering working capital adjustments

*A*fter the due diligence is completed and the purchase agreement finalized, closing time is nigh. Closing the deal occurs on a day called, ingeniously enough, closing day, where both parties sign the agreements and the money changes hands.

Although this setup seems simple and pretty straightforward, failure to be prepared can cause unexpected problems. When you've gotten this far, the last thing you want is to have the deal fall apart at the last minute because of a lack of planning.

In this chapter I introduce you to a day in the life of a closing: what happens, what to expect, and how to successfully close a deal.

Gathering the Necessary Parties

In the olden days (you know, before the advent of the Internet), closing day meant lots of people gathering in an office, signing a boatload of documents, perhaps haggling over last-minute details, and exchanging the money.

Today, most if not all closings are virtual, meaning they occur by fax and e-mail. Each party gathers in its respective lawyer's offices, signs what it needs to sign, and faxes/e-mails the signature pages (not the full documents) to the other side. The lawyers assemble the documents, confirm everything is in order, and make the instructions to wire the money.

Then it's done. The deal is closed.

Representatives from Buyer and Seller (that is, the owners and executives of both companies) are present at a closing, along with lawyers for both sides. Accountants, investment bankers, financing sources may also be present — they should at least be available by phone in case anything goes wrong.

Being prepared before closing is imperative; being unprepared increases the odds of tempers flaring, problems arising, and delays occurring. You don't want hiccups. The longer the closing takes, the greater the odds something goes wrong and the closing falls through. To increase the odds of a successful closing, the deal-makers (investment bankers) and lawyers should have all the business and legal aspects of the deal worked out. The lawyers should be prepared by having all the necessary documents laid out and ready to be signed.

Believe it or not, closing an M&A transaction is actually highly anticlimactic. No bells and whistles, no soaring music, no quick cut to a celebration in a tony watering hole. When the deal is done and the money has exchanged hands electronically, you simply go back to work or head home. It's just another day.

Walking Through the Closing Process

A closing should occur like a well-oiled machine, with steps that are well laid out and planned in advance. As a general rule, a closing should take less than two hours. Essentially, a closing should involve the considerations in the following sections, although variations to the following may exist.

Reviewing the flow of funds statement

The *flow of funds* is a very detailed list of the sources and uses of money — where the money comes from and where it goes. It's typically created in the days right before the closing and is among the last steps of the process. Usually Buyer is responsible for compiling this document (usually a spreadsheet). The statement lists everyone and every entity that is either providing money for the acquisition or getting money as a result of the closed deal, the amount of money being contributed or collected, all necessary contact information (company name, contact name, maybe a phone number), and wire instructions (bank, account number, and routing number).

Typical entities that show up on the flow of funds include the Buyer's and Seller's advisors (investment bankers, accountants, lawyers, and any other consultants), any bank or entity holding a debt that's being paid off at closing, and any vendors Seller has been slow to pay who are owed money. After all entities have received their cut, whatever is left over flows to Seller. After Buyer has compiled the flow of funds, he circulates it to Seller and any other advisors who may need to review the document for accuracy. Seller (and her advisors) should carefully check and double-check the document for accuracy and immediately contact Buyer with any corrections.

Advisors should be included in the flow of funds statement. Advisors who wait until after the deal closes to submit a bill will find their chances of being paid greatly diminished.

Take a look at the flow of funds statement in Figure 16-1. Buyer is contributing $13.3 million and obtaining $4 million from a bank, plus another $2.5 million from a mezzanine fund. The mezzanine fund is also known as *subordinated debt,* meaning it's subordinate (or second in line) behind the bank loan (also called *senior debt*). In addition, some executives from Buyer are contributing an aggregate amount of $700,000.

The purchase price of the business is $20 million. However, based on the purchase agreement, a working capital adjustment of $200,000 in Seller's favor needs to be added to the price. (See "Making a working capital adjustment" later in the chapter for more info on this adjustment.) Buyer owes his advisors a total of $300,000, to be paid at closing. So in this example, Buyer needs to bring $20.5 million to the closing in order to make a $20 million acquisition.

The flow of funds statement in Figure 16-1 is severely simplified from the flow of funds statement you're likely to see in a real deal. In an actual flow of funds, you may see many more sources of funds; many more uses, such as fees the funding sources earn for providing the funding; and notations referring to Buyer assuming Seller's debt.

Buying or selling a business doesn't simply involve transferring money from Buyer to Seller. In other words, Seller doesn't walk away from the closing with a pile of money and a pile of bills. Instead, the Seller pays off her debts, including debts to lending sources, vendors, taxing authorities, consultants, and any other creditor, at closing. In addition to debts, money for the escrow account is deducted from the sale price.

Sources	
Buyer	13,300,000
ABC Bank	4,000,000
Mezzanine fund	2,500,000
Executives	700,000
Total sources	**20,500,000**
Uses	
Purchase price	20,000,000
Working capital adjustment	200,000
Buyer fees and expenses	300,000
Total uses	**20,500,000**
Funded to Seller	
Purchase Price	20,000,000
Plus: Working capital adjustment	200,000
Less: Seller expenses	(660,000)
Less: Bank loan	(3,250,000)
Less: Note payable	(2,500,000)
Less: Funding of escrow account	(2,000,000)
Net Amount Funded to Seller	**11,790,000**
Buyer expenses	
Lawyers	200,000
Accountants	50,000
Marketing consultant	25,000
Environmental consultant	25,000
Total Buyer expenses	**300,000**
Seller expenses	
Lawyers	125,000
Accountants	35,000
Investment banker	500,000
Total Seller expenses	**660,000**

Figure 16-1:
A sample
flow of
funds
statement.

In Figure 16-1, Buyer brings $20.5 million to closing. However, because Seller owes the bank and her advisors money and needs to put money needs in escrow, she actually receives only $11.79 million. Buyer wires that amount to Seller and also wires money to every other party that is due money at closing.

Buyers, make sure the Seller pays off all debt, especially any and all outstanding tax bills. In fact, Buyers should not close until every outstanding Seller debt is extinguished. If you assume control of a company and Seller hasn't paid off a debt, that creditor is liable to come after the company — in other words, the new owner: You. That's why Sellers usually are the ones who remit those payments (using Buyer's money) at closing.

Also, Sellers may want to make estimated payments to taxing authorities (for income taxes or capital gains taxes as result of the transaction) at the time of the closing. These authorities may or may not be represented in the flow of funds, but paying them off along with the other debts may be beneficial simply because Seller gets those payments out of the way and thus reduces the odds she'll forget to make the payments or she'll spend the money before making required payments to the sundry taxing authorities. Speak to your tax advisor for the best way to handle your specific tax situation.

Make sure wire instructions are correct, and make sure each entry has an entity name and a contact person. Making an error or omitting this information may cause a delay in a party receiving its money.

Signing the final purchase agreement and other documents

After both sides have approved the flow of funds statement (see the preceding section), the closing proper begins. This time is when both sides sign the final purchase agreement and sometimes other agreements, such as employment contracts, noncompete agreements, non-solicitation agreements, leases, and so on. The documents pass back and forth as I describe in the earlier section "Gathering the Necessary Parties," and then all that's left is paying out the money.

Generally speaking, both sides agree that the deal isn't final until both parties sign all documents. In other words, being the first to sign a document doesn't put you in some sort of danger that the other side will balk at signing the documents and thus leave you on the hook.

Distributing the funds: Show me the money!

After all the necessary agreements have been signed, Buyer *funds* the deal by obtaining money from his sources and distributing that money to Seller and any other party that appears on the flow of funds statement.

A typical funding occurs as follows:

1. Money from Buyer and any other funding source (such as a bank) comes into a Buyer-controlled account.

2. Seller's debt, including bank loans, notes payable, promissory notes, loans by shareholders, and so on, is paid off with Seller's money.

3. Seller's advisor fees, including legal, accounting, investment banking, and so on, are paid off. These expenses come out of Seller's money.

4. Money is wired to the escrow account.

5. Money is wired to Seller's account.

6. Buyer's advisor fees are paid off. Buyer usually pays these expenses.

Although wire transfers are highly recommended for most deals, cashier checks may be a suitable alternative for smaller deals where the total proceeds are less than $1 million. Speak to your advisors about the recommended course of action for your specific deal.

Schedule your closing at an appropriate time of day so that you can complete the transfer. You can't close a deal at 11 p.m. because you can't wire money that late! Most closings begin in the morning with the goal of closing by 2 or 3 p.m. Eastern Time because that's the nominal cut off time for banks. So even though wiring money after that time isn't unheard of, plan on closing by 3 p.m. Eastern.

Popping the champagne

After the wires are sent, both sides should contact any advisors or team members not present at the closing and inform them of the happy news. Your advisors can then constantly check their bank accounts waiting for news of their wire transfer.

And you're done with the deal. Pop some champagne, celebrate a bit, and start spreading the news, 'cause the deal is closed.

It's not a deal until the wires clear. Make sure you've received your money before you celebrate a successfully closed deal.

Tying Up Loose Ends Shortly after Closing

Closing a deal really doesn't mean the deal is completely closed on closing day. That's not a version of "how much wood would a woodchuck chuck," it is a reality of M&A. In most deals, Buyer and Seller have little bit of work to conduct after the deal closes.

Allowing time to fully close the books

Although the deal is closed as of the closing date, a company can't produce an accurate balance sheet on that very day. Depending on the business, 30 to 90 days are necessary to fully close the books. For that reason, the closing uses an estimated balance sheet.

At some agreed upon post-closing date, the parties make adjustments to that closing day balance sheet based on the fully closed books. In some cases, Buyer pays more, and in other cases Seller receives less. Often, this adjustment is made to the money in escrow.

Making a working capital adjustment

Most purchase agreements include an adjustment for working capital. Prior to closing the deal, Buyer and Seller agree to the amount of working capital that Buyer is purchasing.

Working capital is the difference between assets that can quickly be converted into cash (accounts receivable, inventory, and prepaid expenses) and the bills that are due immediately (accounts payable, wages payable, interest accrued, and unpaid liabilities). Think of working capital as being the same thing as cash.

At closing day, the parties adjust the purchase price based on the amount of the company's working capital. Working capital adjustments help prevent a Seller from simply not paying bills prior to closing; cash belongs to the Seller, so he may be inclined to sell off inventory and accounts receivable and stop paying bills in order to generate cash. In that scenario, the Buyer assumes a business with huge debts at closing. For example, if both sides agree working capital should be $1 million at the closing date but the closing day balance sheet shows $1.2 million in working capital, the Buyer pays the seller an extra $200,000 at closing.

If the Buyer has to pay more at closing, it's because she's purchasing more cash. Say you agree to buy a car for $5,000. Would you be willing to pay $5,100 if that car also included a $100 bill on the dashboard? The net expense to you is the same, $5,000. The same principle applies to a working capital adjustment.

Chapter 17

Handling Post-Closing Announcements and Adjustments

In This Chapter
▶ Disclosing a sale to employees and the media
▶ Tackling post-closing adjustments and contingent payments
▶ Covering breaches and escrow claims

*J*ust because the deal is closed doesn't mean all the work is done. You need to announce the deal to employees and to the rest of the world. And in most cases, both Buyer and Seller have to continue to interact with each other on some level for some period of time after the close.

In this chapter, I introduce you to the wonderful world of post-closing issues, including informing employees about the deal, making media announcements, taking care of the post-closing adjustments, addressing any contingent payment, working through breaches, and handling escrow.

Start Spreading the News

Following the close of the deal, the first order of business for many deal-makers is to announce the deal. Make the announcement to employees and the media as soon as possible after confidentiality no longer prevents you from talking about the deal.

Despite the best efforts of all involved in the sale process, rumors of a sale will have undoubtedly spread. Therefore, Buyer and Seller alike should immediately take control of the information release in order to disseminate accurate information. Keeping quiet can breed ambiguity, and ambiguity is no one's friend. Don't let further rumors fly.

Telling Seller's employees about the deal

Employees are an important stakeholder in any business, and they deserve to learn about the sale as soon as possible; Seller's employees probably want to know the identity of the new boss! Buyer and Seller both need to address Seller's employees. Those disclosures often occur at separate times, but depending on the specifics of the deal, both parties may want to coordinate efforts and make the announcement at the same time.

Sellers: Informing the employees

When I say employees should learn about the sale as soon as possible, I mean the same day the deal closes! Stat! After the papers are signed and the wire transfers clear, you should assemble the employees (if in one location) and make the announcement. If the closing is finalized after hours, tell the employees first thing the following morning. The key is to control the message and make sure you're the one delivering it. If employees are going to hear the news, better they hear official and accurate news from their leader than unofficial and potentially inaccurate secondhand innuendo (masquerading as news from fellow employees).

Don't wait until all the employees are present. Invariably, someone will be at a sales meeting, out of town, or out sick. Letting the genie out of the bottle and telling some of the employees now is better than waiting a day or two until you can tell all of the employees.

If the company has multiple locations, do your best to assemble as many people as possible and have other locations join by conference call. If a conference call isn't feasible, direct managers in the other locations should deliver the news as soon as possible.

Be sure to keep the proceedings positive. Selling a business can be a very emotional time; after all, owners often view their employees with a parental eye. Expressing and displaying emotions is wholly appropriate, but don't let the meeting become downcast. The announcement should focus on what the employees and new owner will be able to do in the future and not be a pity party for you the Seller as you move on to the next phase of your life. A positive and uplifting message helps eliminate ambiguity and hopefully creates excitement and amity between the employees and the new owner.

Don't bad-mouth the new owner. Be gracious, supportive, and encouraging, and remind the employees that the new owner can take them to the next level. Focus on moving forward; refrain from dredging up times of yore and refighting past battles, especially if the negotiations and sale process with the Buyer were difficult and arduous. Take the high road: Act like a responsible leader as you hand the baton to the next leader.

Buyers: Making a good first impression

If you haven't coordinated with the Seller to make the announcement together, I highly recommend getting in front of the employees as soon as possible; no more than a few days should elapse between the deal closing and your meeting with the employees.

Before meeting with the employees, take the time to understand the local culture of the company. The way you and your colleagues do things may be different from the approach of the people at the newly acquired company. Seek out someone who has lived in the area and ask for some insights about the local culture. You don't want to pander to the employees, but you do want to demonstrate that you are aware of their customs and ways of doing things. Showing that you're cognizant of someone else's views, opinions, and sensibilities is a great way to begin building a relationship.

When speaking with the employees, act like a leader at all times because you're going to be under a microscope. Although talking about your plans for the company is permissible and encouraged (even if those plans differ from the previous owner's plans), refrain from bad-mouthing the former owner. However, don't go overboard and become cloying in your comments, either. Don't dwell on the past too much. Move forward and focus on the future.

Business deals often succeed or fail based on how well an owner is able to connect with the employees. Demonstrating that you are a relaxed, confident, friendly leader with a sense of humor requires walking a fine line. You don't want to be a stiff, jargon-spouting automaton, but you also want to avoid going overboard and becoming overly familiar. Some people have that innate ability to connect with people and others don't, so walking that line may be more difficult for some.

Check out Chapter 18 for more on combining the companies post-sale.

Making a media announcement

After the deal closes, the sale can become public information. Usually, the Buyer controls news releases; in fact, the purchase agreement may define how to disseminate the information to the media.

Refer to the purchase agreement and any confidentiality clauses that may prohibit you from speaking about the deal. Speak with your attorney if you are uncertain about what you can and can't say about the deal.

Typically, Buyer decides how much information to release to the media. Private companies making acquisitions of other private companies usually don't furnish the media with specifics such as revenues, profits, and price paid. Executives with public companies should consult with their advisors before making any written or oral public statements about the deal.

Announcing an acquisition can be a great way for a company to garner some free publicity.

Following Through: The Deal after the Deal

Very rarely do Buyer and Seller conclude a deal, walk away, and never interact again. Even though Seller has his money and Buyer has her company, the two sides usually have some post-closing issues to conclude. The following sections walk you through some of those matters.

Closing the loop on post-closing adjustments

One of the first items that need wrapping up after the deal closes is the post-closing adjustments. The closing day balance sheet often involves some guesswork, and the actual balances may not be available until a few weeks go by. Usually 30 to 90 days after closing, Buyer presents an actual balance sheet as of the closing date to Seller. The parties compare this balance sheet to the estimated balance sheet presented at closing and *true up* (adjust) any differences in working capital.

In most cases, the adjustments are relatively small in relation to the purchase price, and most adjustments can be made by adding or subtracting money from the escrow amount.

However, depending on how the purchase agreement is worded, one side may have to write a check to the other side. Buyer is usually the one writing the check; Sellers usually insist on having any downward adjustments made to the money in escrow rather than paying them out of pocket.

Wrapping up the contingent payments

Depending on the deal, contingent payments such as earn-outs, Seller notes, and Buyer stock may be part of the Seller's proceeds. In the following sections, I provide information on following up on these payments. Chapter 12 discusses the various contingent payments in more detail.

As a Seller, stay on top of a Buyer's obligation to you regarding contingent payments. If the Buyer owes you information about an earn-out or misses a payment on a note, speak with your legal advisors about the best course of action. I don't advocate being litigious, but you may have to sue if you exhaust all other options.

Maximizing the earn-out

Earn-outs can be the trickiest of all contingent payments. Seller is trusting Buyer provide necessary and accurate documentation regarding the specifics of the earn-out. The key to the earn-out is how it's crafted and defined in the purchase agreement (see Chapter 15). Simplicity is the best course of action; avoid using a complex formula for calculating the earn-out. The more complex the earn-out, the more calculations involved and the greater the chance Buyer and Seller will disagree.

For Sellers, the best chance at influencing the earn-out occurs if they remain with the company as an employee and have a direct impact on the earn-out metrics. For example, a Seller can impact an earn-out that's based on top line revenue if he stays employed in a sales position. But if the Seller is leaving the company after close, he probably has little or no control over the earn-out.

Collecting the note

If Seller agrees to accept a note, he becomes a creditor of the company, and Buyer is therefore legally obligated to pay that note (as opposed to an earn-out, which she may not have to pay if the company doesn't meet the metrics). Sellers should make sure the Buyer's books officially record any note.

As with an earn-out, a note is only as good as what you negotiate in the purchase agreement.

Dealing with the stock

The ability to sell stock received in an M&A transaction depends on a few factors: where it trades, any restrictions on selling it, and its *liquidity* or trading volume.

If the stock Seller receives is with a publicly traded company, he can sell the stock on the exchange where it trades after any restrictions are removed from the stock.

If Seller accepted stock in a private company, however, his ability to sell the stock may be limited. Not only may a market not exist for the stock, but Seller may also be expressly prohibited from selling the stock even if he could find someone to buy it.

Dealing with Disputes

If the post-closing matters in the earlier "Following Through: The Deal after the Deal" section proceed without incident (no breaches of representations or warranties, no claims to escrow), the escrow agent releases the escrow money to the Seller at the appointed time.

However, some deals don't proceed in an orderly and uneventful post-closing fashion; Buyer and Seller may have disputes. In the following sections, I give you some guidance on taking care of breaches and disputes that may arise after the deal closes.

A purchase agreement that doesn't lay out the process of adjudicating a disagreement is almost certainly inviting problems. Head to Chapter 15 for more on squaring away the purchase agreement.

Handling breaches

Breaches (in other words, post-closing disputes between Buyer and Seller), come in three basic flavors: violation of noncompete and non-solicitation agreements, discrepancies with working capital, and breaches of reps and warranties. The following sections delve into these issues.

Violations of the noncompete and non-solicitation agreements

One of the biggest concerns a Buyer has is that the Seller will take the money from the sale and open a competing business across the street, perhaps even hiring (or attempting to hire) employees now working for the Buyer. Because of these concerns, most purchase agreements contain *noncompete agreements* preventing Seller from opening a competing business in a certain defined geographic area for a certain defined amount of time, as well as *non-solicitation agreements* barring Seller from hiring or trying to hire Buyer's employees.

If you as a Buyer suspect a breach of these agreements, speak with your attorney. The typical course of action in these cases may include going to court and obtaining a temporary restraining order.

Sellers, don't forget that Buyers effectively derive a portion of the purchase price from the noncompete agreement. Essentially, Buyer is paying you not to compete, so breaching this agreement may affect your valuation.

Discrepancies with working capital

As I note earlier in the chapter, M&A parties make adjustments to the purchase price a few weeks after closing, after the Buyer has an updated balance sheet for closing day. Sometimes, this balance sheet can be a source of disagreement between Buyer and Seller because the Buyer's calculations don't match what the Seller promised. In particular, *working capital* (the difference between quickly convertible assets, such as accounts receivable and inventory, and the bills that are due within 30 days, such as accounts payable) commonly creates disputes.

Some typical areas of dispute between Buyer and Seller include

- ✔ **Bad debts reserve:** Buyer may claim Seller didn't set aside a sufficient reserve against bad debts. In other words, the value of the accounts receivable wasn't as high as Seller claimed at closing.

- ✔ **Inventory valuation:** Buyer may claim Seller overvalued inventory and/ or kept unsalable inventory on the books. Writing off inventory reduces a company's earnings, and if the valuation was based on some measure of earnings, Buyer could claim she overpaid for the business.

- ✔ **Failure to record liabilities correctly:** Often, Buyer may claim Seller didn't properly record employees' accrued (that is, unused) vacation.

If Buyer disputes the value of working capital and asks for a substantial post-closing adjustment, Seller may have to live by the terms of the purchase agreement. This situation can be costly for Seller; a Seller in this predicament should consult with his attorney.

The Buyer's post-closing working capital calculation can be a classic "Seller beware" moment. An aggressive Buyer may create some issues by claiming Seller didn't properly account for certain assets or liabilities.

Balance sheet discrepancies may be due to changes in accounting software and treatment. A Seller may use a relatively simple off-the-shelf accounting package and a local accounting firm. A Buyer, often larger and more sophisticated than a Seller, may use a far more robust accounting program and may employ one of the big-time accounting firms (colloquially referred to as *the Big 4*). This difference in sophistication can lead to a discrepancy in results.

Breaches of representations or warranties

In a typical purchase agreement, Seller provides Buyer with a slew of promises known as representations (reps) and warranties (see Chapter 15). A breach occurs when Buyer disputes one of those reps or warranties. Essentially, Buyer is claiming, "The business wasn't as I thought it was."

Common disputes can include undisclosed pending litigation, financial statements with mistakes or omissions, an undisclosed material liability (such as a large unpaid bill of the company), and illegal immigrant employees.

If Buyer claims a breach of a representation or warranty, she usually makes a claim to money held in escrow (see the following section). But escrow is only Buyer's first recourse. If the breach is egregious enough, Buyer may end up suing Seller.

The purchase agreement defines Buyer's recourse. If Buyer suspects Seller of breaching the purchase agreement, Buyer should immediately speak with her attorney.

Making claims against escrow

The myriad representations and warranties Seller provides Buyer in the purchase agreement forms the basis of what, if anything, Buyer can claim against escrow. In other words, if something Seller says is inaccurate or false and causes harm to Buyer, Buyer can make a claim and recoup money from the escrow account.

If Buyer discovers a problem or suspects a breach by Seller, Buyer usually informs Seller, and Seller has some amount of time to either reimburse Buyer for the damage or to contest the damage. If Buyer and Seller are unable to settle the issue, the issue may go to court.

The purchase agreement lays out the process for Buyer to make claims against escrow as well as the recourse for Seller to dispute those claims. Consult with your attorney about how best to proceed with making a claim against escrow or disputing a claim.

Chapter 18

Come Together: Integrating Buyer and Seller

In This Chapter

▶ Creating a plan to ensure a successful integration

▶ Streamlining the parent and acquired company's products and services

▶ Bringing together operations, accounting, and technology

▶ Handling cultural differences between Buyer and Seller

▶ Instituting and enforcing new rules and accountability measures

*B*uying a company can be a time-consuming, complex, and frustrating process, but integrating that company with the Buyer's existing company can be surprisingly time-consuming, complex, and frustrating, too.

Buyers often think that after the deal is closed, the two entities will somehow naturally fit together with little or no work. But going into the post-closing phase of the M&A process without proper preparation can be fatal to the company. Far too many M&A deals fail for wont of proper planning and realistic expectations.

In this chapter, I introduce you to the world of post-closing M&A integration. I cover some of the operational aspects deal-makers face (technology, products, accounting, and so on) as well as the far-too-often underreported area of personnel issues and personality conflicts. This may be the most important chapter of the book. *Note:* Although this chapter primarily offers advice for Buyers, I strongly encourage Sellers to read it as well. Regardless of what side you're on, the information here can help smooth your integration process.

Don't let your own worldview bias you. Don't expect other people to work and think the same way you and your colleagues do; how would you feel if someone came in making such assumptions about you?

Planning the Integration

Two companies don't integrate unless the managers of those companies work together in a coordinated fashion to figure out how, what, and even whether to integrate. Making the integration issue trickier is the fact that no two integrations are the same.

The following sections break down some of a Buyer's integration considerations.

Assembling a Buyer's transition team

In preparation to take over a company, you should have a dedicated transition team in place. I recommend assembling this team as early as the due diligence phase (see Chapter 14). This team generally includes the following members:

 ✔ A financial person (often the CFO or another high-ranking financial executive) interfaces with the acquired company and answers questions pertaining to banking, payroll, working capital, and so on. The financial person also may or may not be able to handle questions regarding operations (order processing, customer service questions, vendor relations, and so on).

 If the financial person isn't the one to answer operations questions, a separate operations executive should be available.

 ✔ A human resources (HR) person should be available to help the employees of the acquired firm with any paperwork they need to complete (401k, tax information, insurance documents, new hire paperwork, and the like). The HR person also distributes the employee handbook and is on hand to answer questions, which may involve some handholding for some of the employees. A change in ownership can be a shock for some people, and they may need a little extra attention to help them deal with the new situation.

 ✔ You want an IT person available to help the employees of the acquired company with any technological issues (phone, Internet, computers, software, e-mail, and so on). This team member is especially important given the prevalence of computers and the Internet in almost every facet of almost every job today.

Determining the level of autonomy

One of the most basic questions you face as a Buyer after the deal closes is, "What the heck should I do with what I just bought?" On paper, combining two entities may seem easy, but in reality, that integration is much more complex. Further, the level of integration varies greatly from Buyer to Buyer.

✔ Financial Buyers, such as private equity (PE) firms, usually allow the acquisition to maintain a level of autonomy, especially if they're not integrating the acquired company into another firm but rather running it as a standalone business. These Buyers are in the business of buying and selling businesses and therefore aren't in the same industry as their acquisition; although they may make some operational changes, financial Buyers typically let the acquired company run itself.

✔ Strategic Buyers often institute quite a bit of operational integration and may combine some products and eliminate others. Strategic Buyers are often in the same (or a related) industry as their acquisition, thus the level of integration may be very high.

 No matter what type of Buyer you are, after the deal closes, I recommend you do nothing! Let the acquired company operate as before. Take some time to understand the business and how it operates before instituting changes. Instituting huge changes before you fully understand the business can be a recipe for huge problems.

Covering the carve-out bases

If the acquisition is a *carve-out* (a divestiture from another company), you likely have quite a bit of work to make sure the carved-out company is able to operate as a stand-alone entity. Some of the areas of focus include the following:

✔ **Payroll and banking:** Making sure employees continue to receive their paychecks is probably the most important immediate consideration of any Buyer. You need to make sure the carved-out company has a new bank account with enough cash to handle the next payroll.

✔ **Employment paperwork:** In a carve-out situation, employees may actually be technically fired by the former owner and rehired by the new owner. Be ready on day one to process all the new employees who are being fired and rehired. Employees may need to bring in identification and will probably have to fill out paperwork as if they were new hires. Speak to your human resources manager about what paperwork will be necessary.

✔ **Accounting:** Make sure all accounting issues are settled before you close the deal. What accounting package does the carved-out company use? Is it still using the former owner's accounting package, or does it have its own package that's part of the transaction? Are the records from the previous owner available to the carved-out company after the deal closes? Is accounts receivable information accurate and available to the new owner?

✔ **IT and phone systems:** What software systems does the carve-out company need? Who handles the IT system? How about the phone system? If the carve-out is utilizing software from the prior owner, make sure you obtain all necessary software so that employees can conduct work. You may have to install new servers, buy software packages, and buy a new phone and voice mail system.

You may not find having replacement software, systems, and processes in place at the very moment the deal closes feasible; in that case, negotiate agreements with Seller to continue using certain systems and software after the closing. You'll probably have to pay for those services, and Seller will want to place cut-off times for the services.

✔ **Applied overhead:** Many overlook this aspect of M&A. What services did the prior owner perform? I'm talking human resource functions, accounting, legal work, marketing and design work, and so on. Have you fully accounted for these services and put personnel in place to make sure those services continue?

✔ **Management:** Who's going to run the carve-out? Does the company have suitable management in place, or do you need to bring in new management? In either case, you want to inform management at the carve-out of your plans prior to closing.

Communicating with Seller before the close

This area is one of the trickiest parts of the integration. Although you want (and need) to communicate closely with Seller (more specifically, Seller's management) in the weeks and days leading up the close, take care to communicate only with Seller's permission.

Focus your communication on the imperative issues (see the later section "Immediately" for a breakdown), but refrain from delving into post-acquisition planning, especially if that planning involves utilizing Seller's employees.

Don't act like you own the place until you actually own the place! You can plan and communicate with (as permitted) certain employees prior to closing to make sure the integration is smooth and seamless; just remember that Seller's employees don't work for you until you buy the company.

Transition process: Planning the first 90 days

Tasks as mundane as ordering supplies can get lost in the shuffle. The new owner may have different processes for ordering supplies and may utilize different vendors. This basic information needs to be communicated to employees.

Upon closing a transaction, you probably have some ideas, if not a plan, for making changes to the acquired company. But before you actually make those changes, you need to make sure the newly acquired employees are up to speed on the plan. You don't need to (nor should you) dump everything on the employees at once; rather, I recommend rolling out the changes in multiple parts as I outline in the following sections.

The timing of the transition process I suggest here is rather general. Each situation is different, so keep your particular integration in mind as you time out the transition process.

Immediately

You should settle the following tasks and process prior to closing. The moment the deal closes, you need to communicate the following information to the new employees:

- ✔ **Company name, e-mail, phone, and Web site:** Do the employees continue to use the old company name, use the name of the acquirer, or use something else? Will they be using the same contact info, or do they have new e-mail addresses and phone numbers? Will they have a new Web site and/or URL? Do they need to use a particular letterhead and/or e-mail signature? Even if the info stays the same, make sure to communicate the fact to the employees that their contact info is the same.

- ✔ **Payroll:** Make sure the new employees continue to receive their paychecks (or direct deposits). Pay close attention to dates of the all-important day known as payday! People work to earn money, so this area is one you don't want to screw up. If a payday is coming immediately after closing, make sure that payroll is set up ahead of time so you don't miss a beat when paying employees. If you are unable to continue direct deposits for that first payroll due to changing banks (not an uncommon occurrence following a acquisition), you absolutely need to make sure checks are printed and ready to be delivered to the employees.

- ✔ **Contact info of the new owner:** New employees need to know who to contact if they have a question. Following the announcement of the closed deal, make sure all the employees know who to contact at the new owner's company in case they have a question.

✔ **Banking and paying bills:** If you're switching the acquired company to a new bank, that bank account needs to be set up prior to close so the financial people at the acquired company know exactly where to deposit checks and from where to pay the bills.

✔ **Purchasing:** The new employees also need to know whether their suppliers are changing or whether they should continue to purchase raw materials from their old sources.

✔ **Sales team:** In addition to needing to know the basic contact info, sales teams need to know which proposal templates and sales contracts they need to use. Should they continue to use the old documents, or do you have new sales documents?

Within 30 days of the close

You don't need to inundate employees on the day the deal is announced with every single change on the horizon; let them digest the announcement before you begin to make the following changes:

✔ **Operational update:** You may want to change purchasing guidelines, vendors, suppliers, and the like, and instituting those changes within the first month makes the most sense.

✔ **Human resources:** New employee handbooks, new-hire paperwork, 401k documents, insurance documents, and so on should be filled out and completed within the first month, if not the first days, following the close.

✔ **Hiring and firing:** Probably the most difficult of all post-acquisition integration is reducing staff. If cuts in staff are necessary, make those cuts as soon as possible after the deal is announced. It's a painful process, but the sooner it's over, the sooner the business can move forward. You don't want employees wondering (and gossiping) if they're going to be fired or not.

Within 90 days of the close

You can make some changes, such as the following, even later after the close:

✔ **Closing or moving operations:** If you've made some decisions about combining or moving offices or shuttering operations, instituting those changes during the first few months of the acquisition probably makes the most sense. You don't need to do this on the first day (remember, you want to give employees a little bit of time to digest the deal), but getting these sometimes difficult decisions over with sooner as opposed to later makes the most sense.

✔ **IT and software changes:** IT and software changes are another area that you don't need to deal with immediately. After you take care of other changes (such as payroll, HR, and purchasing), you can begin to update or change the IT and phone systems, if necessary.

Culling Products and Services

I can't write a one-size-fits-all guide for combining or culling products and services. Buyers go through countless considerations when deciding whether and what to combine, cut, or keep. Instead, this section gives you some of the criteria you may use when making these integration decisions. For brevity, I'm just going to use the word *product* when referring to both products and services.

One of the first steps is often to compare the acquired products to the parent company's products. Remember your rationale for making the acquisition: If you bought the company in order to pick up new products, you'll likely keep integration of products to a minimum. However, if you bought the company to increase your market share or to obtain new customers or geographies, you may want to take a long, hard look at the product mix of the parent company and the acquired company and determine if all the products fit your go-forward plan. (Flip to Chapter 2 for more info on determining motivations for acquisition.)

Here are a few criteria you may use to compare and contrast the mix of products created by your acquisition:

✔ **Financial performance:** Products that aren't profitable enough or even lose money may be worth cutting. Depending on your situation, you may be better suited utilizing the resources (employees, money, time, office space, and so on) to sell a product that generates a higher profit.

✔ **Quality:** You may choose to eliminate products (existing or acquired) deemed to be low quality. Now that you have the added revenue from the acquired company, you may be able to finally pull the trigger on getting rid of some of your product line's dogs.

✔ **Market overlap:** If the parent company's and acquired company's products compete against each other, you likely need to make some decisions about shutting down or integrating these products to avoid overlap. Some options here include slapping the acquired product's brand name on the parent company's product or vice versa if one product has good brand recognition (see the following bullet). Or maybe you keep the product with higher sales and/or profits.

✔ **Fame:** Using the strongest brand name (be it from the acquired company or the parent company) for all of the products in the combined company may be a good strategy. A household name can go a long way to increase market share.

✔ **Strategy:** Do all the acquired products fit with your strategy? If not, you may elect to shut down or sell off products that don't fit the go-forward strategy of the parent company.

✔ **Housecleaning:** This rationale may be rather simplistic, but after the deal is done you may simply have too many products, such that some of them have to go.

In addition to improving the product mix of the parent company and the acquired company, you may *rationalize* sourcing — that is, reduce the number of vendors supplying the acquired company and/or parent company. The idea behind rationalizing is that you expect better pricing, terms, and service by conducting more business with a vendor.

Combining Operations, Administration, and Finance

As with a company's products and services, the level of integration with operations between acquired company and parent company largely depends on how much autonomy you as a Buyer grant to the acquired company (see the earlier section "Determining the level of autonomy"). In some cases, the level of operational integration may be high because you want to realize savings and streamline operations by eliminating duplicate positions and processes, closing extra offices, and moving employees to one office.

In other cases, you may grant the acquired company a lot of autonomy, sometimes out of necessity: Your executives may not be experts in the acquired company's industry, so you have to rely on the expertise of the acquired company's management team.

One of the reasons companies buy other companies is to realize the benefits of cost savings when the two entities are combined. Here are some of the common areas you as a Buyer may look to change and update:

✔ **Analyzing the technology and software:** You may decide the parent company has more robust IT and software packages than the acquired company and that you want to go with the parent company's system. Avoiding competing and conflicting technology and software helps streamline operations and should help wrangle out some extra savings.

✔ **Changing accountants and improving accounting controls:** Parent companies are typically larger than the companies they acquire; as a result, your parent company probably works with a larger accounting firm than the acquired company does, and you'd probably institute stricter and tighter control over all sorts of accounting functions (paying bills, taking inventory, collecting past due accounts, and so on).

✔ **Eliminating duplicate staff positions:** To cut to the chase, this term means firing people. It's harsh, but it's life; trimming excess staff and duplicate positions is probably one of the ways you expect to improve profitability. Head to "Firing people" later in this chapter for more on letting unnecessary employees go.

✔ **Switching up the management team:** Immediately following the announcement of the deal, you should internally discuss the role of the acquired company's management. To replace or not to replace the management team: That is the question. It's a decision Buyers make on a case-by-case basis. You may find that you want to replace the Seller's management team for any number of reasons: the old team isn't up to snuff or constitutes duplicate positions after mixing in with your management, or you simply have another team you want to run the acquired company.

✔ **Banking and financing:** Post-closing, the acquired company may find that its banking relationship changes. The acquired company begins to use the parent company's bank (or a bank of the parent company's choosing). The financing may also change because the parent may be able to negotiate better terms on short-term borrowing with the combined assets or cash flow of the parent company and the acquired company. *Better terms* is synonymous with lower interest rates.

Some PE firms partner with an experienced executive and acquire a company specifically for that executive. In these cases, Buyer may not want or need the management team of the acquired company to be a part of the company after the deal closes.

Handling Personnel: Successful First Steps for New Owners

M&A is a human activity, and people are involved more than ever after the deal closes. The biggest trick is getting the acquired employees' assorted and disparate goals, aspirations, plans, and motivations in alignment with those of the new owner.

The single, biggest expense of most companies is personnel. If you as a Buyer don't know how to successfully work with and intertwine the multitude of personalities between the two entities, you're in serious danger of ending up with a failed business.

Luckily, the following sections present you with a guide to squaring away the personnel situation right out of the gate.

Addressing cultural differences

For most deals, culture is the biggest issue. No two companies have the same business culture, and geographic differences can exacerbate those cultural discrepancies.

Speaking in very broad terms, the cultures of U.S. companies can differ wildly from region to region. The culture of New York City varies from that of the South. Midwestern states have a different culture from Southern California. Heck, even the culture in eastern Washington State can differ drastically from the culture in the western part of the state.

But what are these cultural differences, and how do they manifest themselves in business and in the integration of combined companies? In my experience, cultural differences go far beyond the simple and obvious differences. Speech mannerisms, for example, are simply cosmetic; in the following sections, I address a few of the deeper cultural differences I've encountered while integrating companies.

Don't assume the culture of the acquired company is the same as your culture. One of the biggest mistakes managers can make is to have what I call cultural myopia, where they fail to even consider cultural differences.

The boss as the all-knowing deity: Large versus small power difference

Geert Hofstede is a Dutch researcher who uses the term *power distance* to describe how members of a society interact with their bosses. (If you're not familiar with Hofstede's work, I recommend you check it out.)

In cultures with a small power distance, subordinates respect the boss but also voice their opinions, which often disagree with the boss's. Subordinates in cultures with a large power distance tend to view the boss as unfaltering and all-knowing; as a result, underlings rarely if ever speak up and give their opinions, especially if those opinions contradict the boss's opinion. They just assume the boss knows everything.

As Buyer, you have to be aware of both your and your new employees' views of power difference; otherwise, you run the risk of creating confusion or misunderstanding. For example, in a previous life, I ran a bunch of retail stores, one of which had a problem with two employees who were frequently at odds.

I questioned the store manager; she told me the two employees in question "hated each other" and constantly fought. When I asked her why she scheduled them on the same shift, she answered, "You never said anything, so I thought it was okay."

Her comment made our differing views of power distance readily apparent. I grew up and spent most of my adult life in Chicago, so I assumed my subordinate would tell me of a problem, or better still, take charge and make the executive decision to not schedule the fighters on the same shifts.

This store was located in rural Georgia. Due to her cultural upbringing, the manager viewed me, the boss, as an all-knowing entity who obviously knew of the problem; because I never said anything, "it was okay" to continue to schedule the fighters on the same shift.

Study the cultural biases and approaches of your new partner. You may have to ask exacting questions in order to get to the heart of the matter. Due to cultural differences, a subordinate may just assume you already know all about a situation and therefore may not tell you the full or accurate truth.

You can use power distance to your advantage. If you suspect a problem (and you don't mind putting on a Machiavellian hat), you may be surprised at what comes out after you simply state, "I know what's going on, so just tell me."

Direct communication versus the bypass method

Another cultural difference that I've observed is in how management communicates with employees. In a very general sense, cultures in Latin America, Asia, and the southern United States tend to use the *bypass method*, which gets to a point in a roundabout way. Those who utilize this method often hear simple statements like "Clean up the wording in that contract" to mean something like "You're worthless; that contract was terribly done."

Instead, when speaking with a bypass method user, you need to say, "You did a great job with that contract. I know you worked really hard; I have just a couple of little things I need you take a look at, and maybe you and I can tweak the language a little bit."

Northern U.S. culture and Western Europe tend to be more direct. Those cultures don't mince words. And of course, New York City is in a league of its own — it's possibly the most direct culture on the planet!

One of your primary objectives is to provide clarity, deepen understanding, and increase commitment. Take the time to determine how best to communicate with your newly acquired company, including employees, the management team, and customers and vendors. Failure to understand the differences of how cultures communicate can cause unwanted and unintended consequences. Do they communicate directly or use the bypass method? Direct communication with a culture used to the bypass method causes irritation, and worse, jumbled and misread communication.

For example, my company once acquired a number of local retail stores that I was charged with integrating into the company fold. I called a meeting with the dozen managers who reported to me, and I proceeded to give a rousing speech about how we were all going to work together and have the best stores in the company and how we were going to improve and operate even better than before my company bought their stores.

I thought I was giving the speech of my lifetime. Instead, I was met with awkward silence until one of the managers said, "You must think we're all stupid."

Here I was smacked in the face with a cultural difference between the northern states and the southern states. My approach to communicating was as I had learned up north. I was direct. I simply said what I wanted to say.

However, my southern colleagues heard something very different. In the South, directness is akin to rudeness. Their takeaway was that I was informing them, in a not-too-polite way, that they didn't know how to run their stores. Because I was directly telling them what do, they viewed me as a rude Yankee know-it-all. So instead of directly telling people what to do, I learned to take the bypass. I got to the same location, but I didn't drive straight through town.

Successful communication involved telling people all the wonderful things they were doing, asking them about their families, talking about fishing or the big football game, and then after a few minutes of polite chitchat, discreetly pointing out something I wanted them to take care of. I'm sure they still thought I was a know-it-all Yankee, but I was able to ingratiate myself and eventually get the result I sought.

Today versus tomorrow

Another culture difference that often pops up as two companies attempt to integrate is urgency — in other words, the speed at which people accomplish tasks. Large, urban areas tend to have a greater sense of urgency about completing tasks. They get things done today. Rural areas often have a slower pace and are more accustomed to taking care of jobs tomorrow; those people may greet your query about an uncompleted task with a befuddled "Oh, you were serious about that?"

Another element in the today-versus-tomorrow issue may lie outside geographical boundaries, in the difference between ownership styles. Owners of privately held companies often aren't as forceful or assertive as owners or executives of larger, public companies. The laid-back culture of the pre-sale owner may be diametrically opposed to the high-charged, over-caffeinated culture of the new owner, and this difference can cause miscommunication and problems.

If faced with an acquired staff's more laid-back view of urgency, don't be surprised by an initial blasé attitude. But stick to your guns. Don't change your expectations. People will figure out quickly that the new owner expects things done differently, namely today.

Resolving conflict

Conflict between the new owner and the acquired company's employees is an occasional and unfortunate disease that pops up shortly after the announcement of the business sale. Initially, you meet with politeness and deference. However, because the employees are likely in shock and may not have yet digested the consequences of the sale, this politeness and deference may be more the result of the survival instinct than sincerity.

The clock is ticking. If you don't communicate fully and accurately with your new employees, those good manners may disappear quickly as skepticism and perhaps hostility creep into your new employees' relations with you.

Starting on the right foot is important, obviously. You want to win over the new employees as soon as possible, but if you've been unable to do that, you may encounter conflicts that need resolving. The following sections provide some tips on dealing with conflict.

Remember who's in charge: You!

Don't be afraid of letting people know there's a new sheriff in town. The sooner you start to institute changes and new rules, and the more resolute you are in applying those changes, the sooner the company will adjust.

Inertia (the flow of how the employees are used to working) can be difficult to change, and your odds of breaking that cycle improve if you offer a better way for employees to do their jobs. Assuming your changes are actually improvements, the employees will quickly forget the old ways after they get used to the changes.

This immersion method can be painful, but you need to be determined and committed. If you waver, people will go back to the old way of doing their jobs.

Part of remembering that you're in charge means stepping up and letting people go if they refuse to go along with the new standards. Although no one likes to fire people, you can't be afraid to pull the trigger if a situation with an employee is untenable. The later section "Firing people" gives you further guidance on letting folks go.

Move forward. Don't allow the employees to get wrapped up in past battles that may have flared during the sales process. Your mantra should be, "That's over; the past is history. I'm here to work."

Set a high bar and be consistent

The best lesson I can give to anyone about implementing new rules and methods is to set a high bar and be consistent with your own actions and expectations of others. When you say you're going to do something, do it. Be on time; don't change plans at the last minute.

People want to be led. Don't afraid of changing the tone and applying fair discipline. Stay the course and demand excellence from others. They'll follow. You'll probably find that more people pull you aside and thank you for the changes than grouse and complain at being held accountable.

In one of my roughest integration processes, I took over a completely dysfunctional business with a culture of zero discipline and accountability (among other problems). I addressed the problems by giving the managers a pep talk and letting them know, in no uncertain terms, what I expected. Management and a number of employees quit en masse rather than abide by the new rules.

As I went about my work to fix the operations, a mother of one of the remaining employees (a high school senior), came to my office, obviously agitated and upset, and began to read me the riot act. Apparently, the daughter had informed Mom that the new boss was mean and cruel and was picking on everyone. The daughter, closely ensconced behind the mother, had a smug smile on her face.

I told the mother I expected my employees to show up for work on time and be ready to work. I expected them to be helpful to our customers and to be well groomed (asking them to tuck in their shirts seemed to cause a major problem). I wanted them to enjoy their jobs and work with their coworkers, and I wanted them to work in a clean environment (hence my insistence that they clean the restrooms and dust and vacuum).

I then asked the mother to tell me which of my rules she found objectionable. The mother's demeanor immediately changed as she informed the daughter, "You're not quitting," and then pointing at me, added, "You're working for him."

Pick your battles

When dealing with conflicts, you may have to prioritize and deal with certain issues before delving into secondary problems. Any business has a certain ingrained inertia in the way it does things, and that inertia can be tough to overcome. Although instituting change throughout the entity may be important, your focus should not be taken away from the basic blocking and tackling of a business: taking care of the customers, sales, inventory, purchasing, and paying bills.

Improving punctuality, following often-ignored minor rules, cutting down on needless office chitchat, and the like may be part of your long-term plan to improve the company, but until the big issues are addressed and fixed, these smaller issues may have to go on the back burner.

Acting like a leader at all times

Getting off on the right foot is important for building any successful relationship, and this is especially the case for a new owner meeting the employees for the first time. Injecting a positive culture into an organization isn't difficult; you simply need to be aware of the power of your words and actions before you step in to the new office. A truly effective leader is careful with every step, word, and action and presents an air of confidence, maturity, strictness, fairness, stability, decisiveness, and honesty, especially right after a deal closes.

Every leader is under a microscope, and the higher up the corporate ladder you are, the more powerful the observation of others becomes. Subordinates take their cue from their managers. As a result, the culture in any organization is directly tied to the actions of department managers, company executives, and ultimately the ownership of the company. Leadership is a double-edged sword: People follow your good examples but they also follow your bad ones.

You have a chance to shape how employees act, the way they think about their jobs, and most importantly, the way they interact with your clients.

If you talk about clients and possible customers with an air of disdain, you infect your employees with that poisonous culture.

Be careful with your comments and jokes. Off-color jokes and rude comments can find their way to the employees. You can easily and unintentionally foster a negative culture through careless and ill-timed comments.

As long as your jokes are appropriate, though, you can also maintain a personality and sense of humor. In fact, reminding employees that laughing and smiling while on the clock isn't a crime is a wise approach. Accomplishment should be the first and most important goal, but setting an environment where people actually enjoy their work is tantamount to success, too.

Making friends

Be a part of the culture of the acquired company. Be willing to partake in local customs, and be sensitive to special events and occurrences in the community. Nothing creates division as much as being (or appearing to be) oblivious and uncaring to someone else's cherished rituals.

Being friendly with employees is important, of course, but don't go overboard and act too familiar. You shouldn't be standoffish or aloof, but employees are looking for a leader, not a best buddy.

To demonstrate the importance of considering local customs, consider this story. A Buyer I worked with years ago acquired a company whose custom was to pay a $100 Christmas bonus to all employees. When the Buyer gathered the employees for an announcement after the particularly difficult acquisition, the employees were worried that the new owner, a large PE firm, would cut that annual goodie.

Instead, the new owner announced the Christmas bonus would continue, and that each employee would also receive a special bonus of $500, paid immediately. Although paying people a bonus is no guarantee of making friends, continuing the annual bonus and adding a special bonus made talking about increasing the accountability of employees and discussing how employees would be compensated and rewarded for achieving goals much easier.

No matter what you do, you're going to irritate someone. You can't manage a business trying to please everyone. Don't worry about it.

Instituting accountability

A new owner often has a challenge with increasing the accountability of the acquired staff. Many companies face a large shock when they go from being owned by a single owner to being part of a larger company or PE firm with increased and more-exacting standards. The following sections cover some areas in which you as a Buyer may need to address accountability in your acquired company.

Focus on the customer

Remember where your money comes from: your customers. As amazing as it sounds, employees can get so busy with the minutiae of their daily tasks that they can take their eyes off the reason why they have a job: the customer!

As a new owner, you may find you need to install a renewed focus on customer service and sales. Tying employees' compensation to increased sales (or customer retention) may be necessary for a company to make sure it doesn't lose sight of the most important part of the business.

A simple test for an executive or owner is to ask employees to explain what the company does. Far too often, employees don't have a strong sense of the company's core business. All employees need to know and understand that what they do and how they interact with clients directly impacts the buying decision of a customer.

Introducing cost-benefit analysis

The flip side to revenue is expense. The difference between revenue and expense is profit, and profit is the only reason we do what we do.

New owners commonly find that the former owner rarely said "no" to the staff. Every idea employees had — good, bad, or indifferent — got a shot. As the new owner, you need to communicate that the company can't afford to take a risk on every single idea because the company needs to remain mindful of costs.

Instead, inform employees that the company is willing to take some chances and will reward employees when the chances pay off. But if that chance-taking results in a failed product or bad marketing program, the cost of that failure may come at the loss of a promotion, raise, annual bonus, or (if the failure is egregious enough) even someone's job.

Communicating rules and responsibility

Part of the process of refining the operations of a company is to make sure the employees know exactly what is expected of them. Clearly communicating new rules, expectations, and goals and (preferably) tying clear rewards to achievement helps improve morale and goes a long way toward establishing the legitimacy of your authority.

Most employees will adjust to a manager who is strict as long as that person is also fair and impartial and holds all employees to the same high standards.

Recognizing hard work earns the right to play

The balance between the goals of a business and a rewarding personal life is important if the managers of the business want to achieve goals. Expecting employees to log long hours and sacrifice only works if you also encourage those employees to take some time for themselves. Count on employees to take vacations and take full advantage of paid holidays, especially if you're demanding changes from the employees. Kick them out of the office and tell them to go home.

Delegate responsibility and authority

Instituting accountability means delegating authority and responsibility and then, ideally, getting out of the way. Don't be afraid of other people's ideas. Delegating responsibility only is a recipe for disaster. If you want results, make sure people have the authority to get the job done. If you're going to hold people accountable, you must give them the leeway to execute their plan.

Firing people

Firing is an unfortunate side effect of business. Although I believe in giving people chances to perform and show they're part of the team, sometimes employees just don't buy in to the new way of operating. If you don't have buy-in from your employees, especially your managers, you may need to ask certain people to do themselves a favor and leave; if they don't leave on their own, you need to show them the door.

Firing people boils down into three basic camps: firing for cause, firing due to job performance, and firing due to redundancies. Firing for cause is pretty straightforward: You're canning the employee because of an explicit bit of wrongdoing. Embezzlement, cooking the books, committing or abetting a crime, and so on are all reasons to fire someone for cause. Firing for cause is the least painful of all employee terminations. The person deserves to be fired.

Letting someone go due to poor job performance is a trickier affair. The person may have given her best efforts to do the job but fallen short of the job's goals and expectations. This situation can be difficult, especially if you personally like the employee. But if you paid a person a base salary of $100,000 expecting her to generate $1 million in sales, and she generated only $10,000 even though you clearly laid out your expectations and gave her the tools to succeed, a change is necessary.

When letting someone go for cause or poor job performance, make the conversation short and to the point. Simply say, "It's not working out; I'm letting you go." Ideally, if you have the personnel resources, you can turn the process over to an HR person and leave the room after you've delivered the news. Don't belabor the process. The HR person should make sure all necessary paperwork is in order, including a severance check if that was part of the fired person's package or expectation.

The final part of the termination trifecta is the most difficult situation: laying off people due to job redundancies, which isn't uncommon in the M&A business. Most managers prefer to avoid laying off otherwise-good employees strictly due to business reasons. Paying severance and/or assisting an affected employee with finding another job can help soften the blow, but firing is unpleasant business.

No one likes to get fired, but don't let that prevent you from making a change when you need to.

Part VI
The Part of Tens

The 5th Wave — By Rich Tennant

"The potential buyer liked our offering memo — particularly the in-depth assessment of our competition, which is who they've decided to purchase instead."

In this part . . .

In this part, the famous *For Dummies* Part of Tens, I discuss some thoughts you should ask yourself before you sign an LOI. I also provide some pointers on avoiding common M&A mistakes. Finally, I give some of my thoughts on bridging valuation differences between Buyers and Sellers.

But that's not all! You also get an appendix full of helpful information, including online resources for many facets of the M&A process, some mock M&A documents, and an extensive list of the info required for due diligence.

Chapter 19

Ten Considerations Prior to Signing an LOI

In This Chapter

▶ Getting a handle on the deal and payment setup

▶ Keeping an eye out for warning signs

Moving forward with an M&A deal means that both sides sign a letter of intent (LOI). Although the LOI is an important step, rushing and carelessly signing an LOI without fully understanding it can create plenty of problems. To help you avoid problems and increase the odds of a successful closing, this chapter presents ten issues to consider before signing an LOI. Check out Chapter 13 for the nitty-gritty on LOIs.

Is the Deal Too Good to Be True?

This caution is especially true for Sellers. That great deal that Buyer is dangling may be nothing more than a Trojan horse, a ruse to lock up you, the Seller, with exclusivity for a period of time before coming back with a lower price after you've been out of the market and are therefore in a weaker position. Even if Buyer isn't trying to pull a fast one, he may not be able to line up the capital needed to actually close the deal he's offering (see the following section).

As a Seller, you need to be brutally honest with yourself about your company's value. Frankly, an experienced advisor can be a huge help here. Does the company really warrant the high price Buyer is offering? See Chapter 12 for more on valuation.

How Is the Buyer Financing the Deal?

Does Buyer have the cash, is she planning to tap a bank line, or is she asking Seller to help with the financing? Does Buyer already have access to sources with cash, or is she planning to shop for investors after signing the LOI?

As a Seller, carefully vet potential Buyers and their fund sources. If Buyer is private and is unwilling to share financials, ask for a letter from her bank stating that the bank supports her acquisition plan.

How Much Cash Is in the Offer?

A great offer with a high valuation may not be what it initially seems to be. Does Buyer pay 100 percent of the proceeds at closing? Is any hold back or any sort of contingent payment (such as notes or earn-outs) involved? Is stock part of the offering price? In other words, does Seller have to jump through hoops to get his money?

Weigh all the merits of each deal and not just the valuation number; an offer with a lower deal value but all cash at closing may be a better deal than a higher valuation comprised of contingent payments, because the former may be more likely to result in your being paid in full.

What Are the Conditions of Escrow?

How much money is held in escrow, and who controls its release? In a very general sense, the amount of money held back in escrow should be 10 percent or less of the purchase price, and that money should be released to Seller within 12 to 18 months. Other considerations include how the reps and warranties are associated with that escrow and who receives the interest from the escrow account. Chapter 15 digs into escrow in more detail.

Is the Deal a Stock or Asset Deal?

The age-old issue in M&A is the stock deal versus the asset deal. Sellers usually prefer stock deals because of preferential tax treatments. Buyers usually prefer asset deals because those deals lower Buyers' risks of *successor liabilities* (legal problems for Buyer as a result of issues that occurred before the company was sold).

Frankly, perhaps the better question here is, "Does the deal type even make much difference to you?" Depending on variables far too numerous and disparate to recount here, Seller's specific tax situation may mean the difference between the tax consequences of a stock deal and those of an asset deal is negligible. And Buyers may not really need an asset deal. If the reps and warranties are strong enough, the successor liabilities issue may not be as large as it seems.

Both Buyers and Sellers should speak with their attorneys about the specific deal at hand and their specific situations when determining what type of deal to accept.

How Does the Deal Settle Working Capital Issues Post-Closing?

Does the deal include a *working capital adjustment* (adjustments made to the purchase price after closing, based on the actual balance sheet values)? A working capital adjustment can be a major lurking surprise, especially for Sellers. Sellers should make sure all current liabilities are in fact current! If not, Seller may face a substantial post-closing adjustment.

Along those lines, Buyers should note whether all Seller's receivables and payables are current or whether she's slow to collect receivables and pay her bills, especially if Buyers are assuming the accounts receivable and accounts payable as part of the deal. Buyers need to be careful about assuming payables that should have been paid months ago. Paying overdue bills is Seller's responsibility! Flip to Chapter 17 for more on post-closing issues.

Is the Inventory 100 Percent Salable?

Inventory can be another pain point for Buyers and Sellers. A Buyer operates under the assumption that she can sell all the Seller's inventory. If the Seller has obsolete inventory, the Buyer may press for a post-closing adjustment.

Hiding obsolete inventory from a Buyer is an unwise plan. A Seller who doesn't address the issue of inventory salability is asking for trouble! Sellers need to bite the bullet and either write off inventory prior to close (thus reducing earnings and possibly the valuation) or brace for a large post-closing adjustment (see Chapter 17).

Who Pays Off Any Long-Term Debt and What Happens to the Line of Credit?

Make sure you're clear on who's responsible for the Seller's long-term debt and any short-term lines of credit. Either the Buyer assumes it or the Seller pays it off.

Seller shouldn't assume Buyer will simply pay off the debts of the business. If Buyer is going to pay off the business's debts, he'll first subtract those debts from the proceeds of the business sale.

What Are the Tax Implications of the Seller's Accounts Receivable?

Another lurking surprise for some Sellers is the taxability of accounts receivable. Taxing authorities may consider a company's receivables as income and therefore tax the receivables at Seller's marginal income tax rates rather than capital gains rates.

Sellers, confer with your tax advisors about the proper tax treatment of your company's accounts receivable as the result of the sale of your company.

Is the Seller Signing a Noncompete Agreement with the Buyer?

Many deal-makers often overlook and underappreciate the noncompete agreements that accompany most deals. These agreements prevent Seller from competing with Buyer for some length of time and in some defined geographic area. (Chapter 17 provides more info on these agreements.)

Sellers need to remember that part of the purchase price is wrapped up in the noncompete agreement. Buyers won't be willing to pay the full price unless Sellers agree not to compete.

Chapter 20

Ten Major M&A Errors and How to Avoid Them

In This Chapter

▶ Avoiding faulty assumptions about M&A

▶ Knowing when to tell others of the deal

A s with many industries, the mergers and acquisitions business is full of errant opinions. People who have never done a deal before can't possibly know what to expect, and as a result, many people harbor false impressions and incorrect assumptions about M&A. Here are ten of those common errors.

Assuming the Deal Is Done after the LOI Stage

The letter of intent (LOI — see Chapter 13) is a key document because it defines the basics of the deal and essentially becomes the foundation of the purchase agreement. Sellers and Buyers alike often make the mistake of thinking a signed LOI means all the work is done.

The LOI isn't the final deal. In fact, the LOI simply ushers in a host of work called *due diligence* and *contract writing.* The heavy lifting of M&A doesn't begin until after the LOI is signed.

Being Unprepared for Due Diligence

In my experience, perhaps the number one mistake Sellers make is being unready for the crush of materials they have to provide for due diligence. A Buyer (rightfully, I should add) expects to gain access to the due diligence materials the moment the LOI is signed. Sellers, perhaps thinking the deal is done after the LOI is signed (see the preceding section), often don't share that same sense of urgency.

Sellers, plan ahead. You should start compiling the due diligence materials the moment you start marketing the company. This way, the moment the LOI is signed, you can provide the Buyer access to the due diligence materials. Check out the appendix for a detailed list of possible due diligence requirements.

Asking for a High Valuation with No Rationale

Many first-time deal-makers make the mistake of thinking, "If I ask for a crazy price, I'll get it." This notion is often compounded by the Seller's own biased, sentimental opinion of his company's worth. Although I'm a big fan of compelling valuations when I'm selling a company, I've never been able to get a compelling valuation without providing the Buyer with the rationale for the valuation.

Buyers have to leap over financial hurdles in order to do deals. They don't have unlimited piles of cash and aren't looking to overspend when making acquisitions. Sellers need to provide Buyers with a rationale for a high valuation. Head to Chapter 12 for more on figuring out a company's true value.

Figuring Buyers Won't Discover Problems in the Financials

Sellers, sticking your head in the sand and hoping the Buyer doesn't discover discrepancies or problems with the books isn't a realistic approach. Buyers hire accountants and auditors to pore through a Seller's financials, and those folks will discover problems. Worse for Seller, Buyer is then in control of how to use that information to her own benefit. As Seller, you're far better off to own up to problems in the financials and share that information with Buyer. This enables you to control the situation and frame the argument.

Underestimating the Other Side's Sophistication

This miscalculation pops up with surprising regularity, typically with Buyers (and specifically, Buyers from large cities). Underestimating the other side's sophistication and abilities is almost always a recipe for problems. Never take for granted your superiority over the other side; you're bound to be unpleasantly surprised.

Be especially wary of those who purposely portray themselves as backwoods rubes. Odds are, they're simply playing you and lulling you into a false sense of superiority.

Failing to Understand Who Really Has the Power

During an M&A process, power oscillates between Buyer and Seller. A huge error by novice deal-makers is to miscalculate their power. Failing to understand the amount of power you have simply increases the odds you'll misread the situation and make a wrong move.

Misplaying a strong hand is bad, but misplaying a weak hand is worse. If you're in a weak position with no other options, you may have to take the deal being offered. In that case, you're not in a position to dictate terms.

Withholding Material Information

Material information is any bit of information such as a lawsuit, an environmental problem, the loss of a large client, and so on, that has a substantial impact on the company. Failure to disclose material information means Seller is acting in bad faith and is effectively deceiving Buyer through the omission of important data. If you offer to pay $300,000 for a home and subsequently discover the house is missing the furnace and half the windows are broken, you're probably going to rethink the offer price. You may even walk away from the deal. The same goes when buying a company.

Seller is obligated to inform Buyer of all material events.

Blabbing about the Deal Before It Closes

Depending on the terms of the LOI, informing outsiders about the deal may be a breach of confidentiality. If one or both of the companies is public, disclosure of this insider information may be considered illegal, especially if someone uses it to buy or sell stock. But it's easily avoidable — just keep your mouth shut.

Even if the Buyer and Seller are private companies, improperly disclosing deal discussions may harm one or both of the companies. The Seller is most susceptible to consequences: Employees may jump if they think they'll lose their jobs post-sale, and competitors can use the information to steal customers from the Seller.

Calling the Seller's Employees without Permission

Unfortunately, Buyers have been known to pick up the phone and call a Seller's employees prior to the deal closing. Sometimes, Buyer even lets slip that he's buying the company and that the employees will soon have a new boss.

Although the cause of this behavior is usually not malicious (in their excitement about doing a deal, would-be Buyers jump the gun and start calling employees as if they've already closed the deal), this conduct is still wholly unacceptable and really just poor form. Tipping off an unsuspecting employee about a deal can cause untold havoc in Seller's business, much like breaking confidentiality can (see the preceding section). Buyers should always follow the chain of command and only speak with those people who know about the deal and to whom the Seller explicitly agrees you can contact. Make sure you go through the proper channels.

Contacting a Seller's Customers or Vendors without Authorization

Another huge no-no for Buyers! Customers are the most important relationship for a Seller, and a Buyer who carelessly contacts a customer and informs her about the pending deal may cause that customer to find a new vendor. This kind of breach can quickly scuttle the deal, as well as harm the Seller.

In most cases, this breach is caused by an overzealous Buyer trying to conduct due diligence. Although determining the strength of the relationship with customers is important, this situation is delicate, and Buyers should tread carefully.

Buyers should refrain from contacting Seller's vendors without permission for the same reasons.

Chapter 21

Ten Possible Ways to Solve Valuation Differences

*V*aluation is always the million-dollar question — well, often the multimillion-dollar question. The stereotypical negotiation impasse has Seller asking for a high price and Buyer offering a low price, with each side digging in their heels and insisting that the other side totally capitulate to their demands. But that strategy rarely results in a closed deal.

In the spirit of getting deals done, in this chapter I provide a few ideas on ways Buyers and Sellers can settle valuation disagreements and move forward to a closing.

Payments over Time

If Seller wants a certain price for the company, Buyer may be willing to pay that price over a period of time. Buyer has the benefit of the *time value* of money (today's dollars are worth more than tomorrow's dollars, so paying today's debts with tomorrow's dollars is a benefit to Buyer), and Seller gets to tell everyone that he was able to get the valuation he wanted.

If Seller agrees to accept payments over time, I suggest using a note to officially and legally document Buyer's obligation to Seller just in case the arrangement comes into question later.

Earn-Out Based on Revenues

The venerable earn-out (see Chapter 12) is a favorite deal component for Buyers because it allows the Seller to prove the company's profitability. If the company achieves the goals Buyer and Seller agree to, Seller gets the earn-out. Keeping the earn-out metric simple and easy to measure reduces the chances of a dispute down the line. Basing the earn-out on revenues is usually the most straightforward approach.

Earn-outs shouldn't be an all-or-nothing proposition. If the company falls short of the earnings goal, perhaps the Seller is still eligible for some of the earn-out. A dollar-for-dollar reduction in the earn-out based on how far short of the projection the company falls is often the solution. Say the earn-out was worth $2 million if the company achieved a certain revenue goal. If the revenue was $1.5 million short of that goal but the earn-out didn't require all-or-nothing success, Seller still receives $500,000 ($2 million minus $1.5 million).

Earn-Out Based on Earnings

This option is a cousin to the earn-out based on revenue (see the preceding section). It functions exactly the same, except that the metric for the earn-out is based on some measurement of earnings. Both sides need to very precisely determine how they'll measure earnings (EBITDA, net income, and so on).

Sellers should be wary of Buyers applying some overhead from the parent company's books to the acquired company's books. This accounting treatment may artificially lower the acquired company's earnings (because now expenses the company didn't incur are eating up its profits), thus reducing or eliminating the Seller's earn-out.

Earn-Out Based on Gross Profit

Another metric for an earn-out is to base the earn-out on the business's *gross profit,* or its profit after deducting the cost of sales but before deducting operating expenses. This method can be a great way to settle a valuation difference in an environment where pricing is falling (thus resulting in lower revenue) and the cost of sales is falling, too. And because the earn-out takes the profit before operating expenses, this technique eliminates the risk of Buyer adding applied overhead to the company's operating expenses, a trick I note in the preceding section.

Valuation Based on a Future Year

A multiyear earn-out may result in Seller not earning all the available money in some of the years. Basing the final valuation on a future year and providing Seller with advances against that future-year valuation helps eliminate that occurrence. Effectively, this strategy gives Seller a make-up clause. If the company falls short of its goals in the early years, Seller can still get 100 percent of the earn-out as long as the company achieves the goals in the final year.

Sellers, make sure the purchase agreement defines all advance payments as nonrefundable. Doing so prevents Buyer from trying to reclaim some of the advance payments if the company falls short of the final goal of the earn-out.

Partial Buyout

If a Buyer and Seller can't agree on a valuation for a full buyout, a *partial buyout* is often the solution. Seller retains an ownership interest and can sell her remaining shares at some future date and hopefully at a higher valuation. In M&A lingo, this later sale is called a *second bite of the apple*.

Most Buyers want a control stake in the business, meaning they acquire more than 50 percent of the company's equity. Depending on the situation (and how the purchase agreement is written), however, Buyer may be amenable to buying a minority position.

Sellers who retain a minority position should make sure a *put option* is part of the deal so that they can sell the remaining equity to Buyer at some future date at some future calculation. If Buyer ends up taking a minority position, Buyer should make sure the deal contains a *call option;* in other words, Buyer can buy the remaining equity from Seller at some future date at some future calculation.

Stock and Stock Options

Stock can be a great way for a Buyer to help finance an acquisition. If Buyer and Seller disagree over valuation, Seller may be receptive to taking stock in the parent company. The situation is often win-win: Buyer has to lay out less cash at closing, and Seller has the upside potential of stock appreciating in value.

Buyer should carefully consider the *dilutive effect* (owning less of the company) that comes as a result of providing equity to Seller. Also, Seller should consider the marketability of that stock; in other words, does the stock trade on a public exchange, and is the average daily volume sufficient enough to allow Seller to unload his position? Flip to Chapter 12 for more on stock deal considerations.

Consulting Contract

Another way Buyers can provide Sellers with added dollars is by including a consulting contract in the purchase agreement. Buyers have the benefit of the Seller's advice and counsel, and Sellers get the benefit of increased deal value.

Sellers, consult with your tax advisor if a consulting contract is on the table. Pushing proceeds into a consulting agreement may result in those dollars being taxed at a higher marginal income tax rate rather than the lower capital gains rate.

Stay Bonus

If a Buyer wants a Seller to stay on board for some period of time after the deal closes, offering Seller a bonus for not leaving can be another way to bridge a valuation gap. Buyer gets the security of knowing he won't have to pay the bonus if Seller resigns early, and Seller knows she'll receive added money by simply staying put.

Buyers, consider including a clause in the agreement stipulating that you can fire the Seller for cause, such as theft, embezzlement, conviction of a felony, and so on. That way, if Seller engages in egregious behavior that harms the company, you can limit damages without having to pay out even more money to the person.

Combo Package

Be creative! Don't think of the ideas in the preceding sections as being mutually exclusive. You can offer a little more earn-out and less stock, or a larger note and a consulting agreement. You can increase the length of the earn-out term or consulting agreement. The only limit is your creativity.

If you consider these options as knobs of a stereo, you can twist the dials in unlimited ways. A creative deal-maker has unlimited ways to bridge a valuation gap.

Appendix

• •

*T*his appendix provides you with extra content to help get your M&A show on the road, including Web sites, sample M&A documents, and lists of the info you may need to gather for important M&A stages.

Online Resources

All M&A deal-makers need some extra help, so to that end I've compiled some resources, advisors, and private equity firms in this section.

Groups, associations, and networking organizations

M&A, as with most industries, has some networking and professional associations. If you're thinking about pursuing a career in M&A, I suggest acquainting yourself with the following groups:

- **Alliance of Merger & Acquisitions Advisors:** www.amaaonline.com
- **Association for Corporate Growth:** www.acg.org
- **Association of Professional Merger & Acquisition Advisors:** www.apmaa.com
- **Global M&A Network:** www.globalmanetwork.com
- **Institute of Mergers, Acquisitions, and Alliances:** www.imaa-institute.org
- **Merger Network:** www.mergernetwork.com

Virtual data rooms

M&A deal-makers today utilize online data rooms for due diligence (see Chapter 14). Here are few of the commonly used rooms:

- ✔ **Firmex:** www.firmex.com
- ✔ **Merrill Datasite:** www.datasite.com
- ✔ **Share Vault:** www.sharevault.com
- ✔ **V-Rooms:** www.v-rooms.com

Periodicals

The following sections help you satisfy your nose for news. The first section lists some good sources of M&A-specific news, while the second provides some of my favorite sources for more-general business news.

M&A periodicals

- ✔ *Buyouts:* www.buyoutsnews.com
- ✔ *The Deal:* www.thedeal.com
- ✔ *Deal Reporter:* www.dealreporter.com
- ✔ *Debt Wire*: www.debtwire.com
- ✔ *Dow Jones LBO Wire:* www.dowjones.com/privatemarkets/lbo.asp
- ✔ *Mergers & Acquisitions:* www.themiddlemarket.com
- ✔ *Merger Market:* www.mergermarket.com
- ✔ *Thompson Reuters:* www.thomsonreuters.com

Business periodicals

- ✔ *Barron's:* www.barrons.com
- ✔ *Bloomberg:* www.bloomberg.com
- ✔ *CFO:* www.cfo.com
- ✔ *Financial Times:* www.ft.com
- ✔ *Forbes:* www.forbes.com

- *Fortune:* www.money.cnn.com/magazines/fortune
- *Inc:* www.inc.com
- *Investor's Business Daily:* www.investors.com
- *Wall Street Journal:* www.wsj.com

Advisors

A deal-maker needs suitable counsel from lawyers and accountants. Some firms that focus on M&A transactions, especially for the middle market and lower middle market, include the following:

Accounting and auditing

- **Baker Tilly:** www.bakertilly.com
- **BDO Seidman:** www.bdo.com
- **Crowe Horwath:** www.crowehorwath.com
- **Deloitte:** www.deloitte.com
- **Ernst & Young:** www.ey.com
- **Grant Thornton:** www.grantthornton.com
- **KPMG:** www.kpmg.com
- **PriceWaterhouseCoopers:** www.pwc.com
- **RSM McGladrey:** www.mcgladrey.com

Law firms

- **Baker McKenzie:** www.bakermckenzie.com
- **Horwood Marcus & Berk:** www.hmblaw.com
- **Morrison Foerster:** www.mofo.com
- **Quarles & Brady:** www.quarles.com
- **Ulmer Berne:** www.ulmer.com
- **Ungaretti and Harris:** www.uhlaw.com
- **Vedder Price:** www.vedderprice.com
- **Wildman Harrold:** www.wildman.com
- **Winston & Stawn:** www.winston.com

Private equity firms

Private equity is one of the usual suspects when it comes to finding a Buyer for a company. The United States alone has hundreds of private equity firms. Here are just a few of them.

- **Audax Group:** www.audaxgroup.com
- **Beecken Petty O'Keefe & Company:** www.bpoc.com
- **Eos Partners:** www.eospartners.com
- **Frontenac Company:** www.frontenac.com
- **Gemini Investors:** www.gemini-investors.com
- **Geneva Glen Capital:** www.genevaglencapital.com
- **Harbour Group:** www.harbourgroup.com
- **H.I.G. Capital:** www.higcapital.com
- **Huron Capital Partners:** www.huroncapital.com
- **LaSalle Capital Group:** www.lasallecapitalgroup.com
- **Linsalata Capital Partners:** www.linsalatacapital.com
- **Longroad Asset Management:** www.longroadllc.com
- **Mason Wells:** www.masonwells.com
- **McNally Capital:** www.mcnallycapital.com
- **Monomoy Capital Partners:** www.mcpfunds.com
- **Pfingsten Partners:** www.pfingstenpartners.com
- **Prairie Capital:** www.prairie-capital.com
- **Prospect Partners:** www.prospect-partners.com
- **Saw Mill Capital:** www.sawmillcapital.com
- **Sverica International:** www.sverica.com
- **Svoboda Capital Partners:** www.svoco.com
- **Trivest Partners:** www.trivest.com
- **Wynnchurch Capital:** www.wynnchurch.com

Regulatory agencies

An M&A advisor should be registered with the Financial Industry Regulatory Authority, Inc (FINRA). Visit FINRA's Web site (www.finra.org) for more information. The Securities Investors Protection Corporation (SIPC) is a federally mandated entity charged with protecting investors from fraud, so you should be familiar with it as well. Check it out at www.sipc.org.

Online business references

A few good sources for business information include the following. These sites don't necessarily focus on M&A, but they provide great information and research tools for M&A-related work nonetheless.

- **Biz Stats:** www.bizstats.com
- **Capital IQ:** www.capitaliq.com
- **Deal Logic:** www.dealogic.com
- **Ibis World:** www.ibisworld.com
- **Investopedia:** www.investopedia.com
- **OneSource:** www.onesource.com
- **US Census Bureau – Business & Industry:** www.census.gov/econ

Teaser

In this section, you find a mock teaser. This sample document can give you a basic idea of what to expect in a teaser; Chapter 7 covers teasers in more detail.

Business Sale Opportunity

Industry: Telepathic Pet Feeding and
Grooming

Revenues: $75 million
Adjusted EBITDA: $12 million
(Fiscal year end 12/31/2010)

Location: Dothan, AL

The Company is a provider of telepathic feeding services to dogs, cats, fish, birds, and other non-exotic pets throughout the United States. Through long-term contractual relationships, the Company exclusively manages the feeding services for 1,500 federal, state, and county facilities across 25 states, which have the capacity to feed approximately 135,000 pets. The Company's focus is on privately-owned pets. Approximately 75% of the total pet population served by the Company is in private homes. Due to the long-term contractual nature of the Company's customer relationships, the Company has approximately $150 million of revenue under contract through 2015, 90% of which will be generated by the end of 2013.

The Company has also developed a patented product for scheduling and conducting wireless pet grooming services. The product enables pet boarding facilities to provide pet cleaning services over long distances by using real-time videoconferencing and shampooing. Ownership believes this is the future of telepathic pet grooming.

Key Investment Considerations
- **Leading Provider of Comprehensive, High-Quality Services:** The Company provides its customers with industry leading technology for the real-time telepathic feeding of pets. In addition, the Company provides first-class customer service in all of its facilities, which is key to achieving contract renewals and generating long-term recurring revenue. The Company's customer service includes: (i) site administrators who work directly at the facilities for the Company's larger customers, (ii) 24/7/365 on-call support for all facilities, (iii) remote or onsite training for the employees of a facility, and (iv) monthly, detailed reports.

- **Long-Term, Recurring Customer Relationships:** The Company's customers are very loyal and entrenched. Due to its customer service, the Company has only lost 50 customers since 2000, and 1,400 of its 1,500 existing customers have renewed the Company's contract on at least one occasion The balance of the Company's customers renew their contact while still in the initial term of their first contract. The average tenure of the Company's existing customers is approximately six years.

- **Cost-Efficient Operations:** Management has designed the Company to operate as a low-cost provider in the industry, which has enabled the Company to generate attractive margins. The Company's cost-efficient operations include: (i) a focus on privately-owned non-exotic pets, which tend to have a lower costs of service, (ii) an active promotion of debit card and prepaid wash cards to reduce bad debt and collection expense, and (iii) good relationships and competitive contracts with long distance telepathic pet feeding and cleaning providers.

- **Attractive Growth Opportunities:** In order to accelerate its growth, the Company is (i) increasing its sales and marketing efforts, (ii) launching a remote, hosted solution from which it can profitably serve smaller pets, and (iii) launching a robust, Web-enabled platform to enhance monitoring, recording, and reporting capabilities for its facilities.

- **Favorable Industry Trends:** The telepathic pet feeding and grooming industry has experienced growth every year for the past 25 years, and management believes it will continue to grow in future years. Several drivers of this growth include (i) increasing pet populations, (ii) increasing need for owners to have well-fed and clean pets, and (iii) the inability or unwillingness of many pet owners to actually feed and groom their pets.

- **Experienced Management Team and Employees:** The Company's workforce is led by an experienced management team with an average of 17 years of industry experience.

- **Attractive Financial Performance:** The Company expects to grow its net revenue from approximately $82 million in 2010 to $112 million in 2014, while increasing Adjusted EBITDA from approximately $12 million to $19.5 million over the same period. Additionally, the Company expects to increase its Adjusted EBITDA margins to approximately 17.4%.

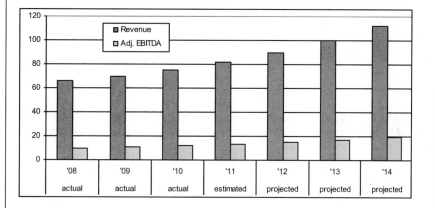

For more information or to review the offering document, please contact:

Fred Milton
Managing Director
Zero-Sum Investment Banking
123 Main St
Ste 9000
Chicago, IL 60699
555-555-5555

Indications of Interest

The following sections offer a couple of sample indications of interest (IOIs), one from a financial Buyer (private equity firm, for example) and one from a strategic Buyer (a company). The specific language of an IOI depends on the specifics of the deal, of course, but the basics are often very similar. For more information, head to Chapter 9.

Financial Buyer Indication of Interest

October 3, 2011

Frederic von Friedman
Senn Investment Banking, Inc.
123 N. Howard St
Chicago, IL 60699

Dear Fred:

Farmside Private Equity Partners is pleased to submit this indication of interest outlining our thoughts on acquiring 100% of the stock of Circuitous Therapeutic Information, Inc. ("CTI" or the "Company"). Based upon the information contained in the Confidential Information Memorandum, as well as the conversations we have had with CTI's advisors, Senn Investment Banking, we are prepared to acquire CTI based on a debt-free valuation between $25 to $28 million.

We are very excited about the prospect of buying CTI and further establishing it as a leading provider of information for the circuitous therapeutic industry. We like CTI because of its tremendous growth, excellent margins, and its growing end market of resellers of circular medical devices. Farmside's sole focus as a leveraged buyout firm is the acquisition of leading lower middle market companies. Once acquired, we seek to find ways to create additional value by growing the business, often through add-on acquisitions but also through new office openings, capacity expansions, or increased marketing or R&D expenditures, as appropriate. We do not run the companies ourselves, but seek to work in partnership with existing managers, who are encouraged to invest on the same basis as Farmside and are given the opportunity to increase their stake through performance-based options.

Farmside expects to finance this acquisition with a combination of senior debt and equity. We anticipate 40% to 50% of the purchase price will be in the form of equity provided by the $100 mm Farmside Lower Middle Market Fund III. The debt financing for the transaction will be obtained from one or several of the many debt providers with whom we have established relationships. Given our experience in financing acquisition transactions, we do not anticipate any difficulty in obtaining the funding needed to acquire CTI.

Farmside Private Equity Partners is one of the largest private equity firms focused on the lower middle market. Farmside specializes in buying industry leading companies with enterprise values of less than $150 million, and partners with strong management teams to build companies through acquisitions and value-added growth. Since 1985, the firm has invested in over 200 transactions with a total value of $3.9 billion. We currently own a portfolio of 75 companies in the U.S. and Europe with total aggregate sales of over $3.1 billion, EBITDA of $355 million and 14,000 employees.

We are one of the most active acquirers in the marketplace, having completed 85 transactions over the past four years. Farmside has the ability and resources to quickly close transactions, usually in less than 60 days, thanks to its large pool of capital under management ($2.3 billion in nine funds), large staff in 14 offices (New York; Newport, RI; Cleveland; Virginia Beach, VA; Douglasville, GA; Monroeville, PA; Park Ridge, IL; Seattle; Dothan, AL; Tampa; San Diego; Guam; Amsterdam; and Eureka, SD), and long-standing relationships with partner lenders. Farmside constantly produces high returns for its investors. Our limited partners include some of the largest pension funds, university endowments, funds-of-funds, insurance companies and banks. Not only are proud of our record of one of the most successful buyers of lower middle market companies, but we place a high value on honesty, integrity, and professionalism. More information on Farmside Private Equity Partners can be found at our website.

This letter is not a commitment to acquire the company. Our proposal is subject to the satisfactory completion of due diligence, which will include, but is not limited to, a thorough review of the Company's financial, legal, tax, environmental, labor, and pension records and agreements, and any other matters as our auditors, tax and legal counsel, and other advisors deem relevant. To conduct due diligence, Farmside and its advisors will need access to the operating management of the Company and be permitted to inspect all offices of the Company. The proposal is further subject to the negotiation and execution of definitive purchase agreement. This letter is provided to you with the understanding that it will not be shown to anyone other than directors and officers of CTI and their agents who have a need to know.

Farmside's investment committee has approved the submission of this indication of interest and will be required to give its final approval prior to the execution of a definitive purchase agreement. Farmside's investment committee is an internal committee composed entirely of Farmside partners. No approvals are required from any outside parties.

Thank you for giving us the opportunity to express our interest in acquiring CTI. We are eager to speak with the management team as soon as can be mutually arranged to learn more about this opportunity. In addition to myself, the Farmside team will be lead by Moe Townsend, partner; Shep Daltrey, managing director; Larry Entwistle, vice president; and Curly Moon, associate, all in our Eureka SD office. We are available to discuss any aspect of this letter with you at any time. If you have questions or comments, please feel free to contact me at 555-555-5555.

Sincerely,

Caroline Cochran
Managing Director

Strategic Buyer Indication of Interest

October 5, 2011

Frederic von Friedman
Senn Investment Banking, Inc.
123 N. Howard St
Chicago, IL 60699

Dear Fred:

Thank you for providing us the opportunity to consider the acquisition of Circuitous Therapeutic Information, Inc. ("CTI"). We have reviewed the Confidential Information Memorandum, discussed the opportunity with our senior leadership, and concluded there may be an interesting growth opportunity given the strong fit between the markets, customers, and products of CTI and Zanzibar Medical Documentation Corporation (Zany).

We have a strong strategic interest in this business, the financial capacity and experience to complete this transaction (we are active buyers typically acquiring 5 to 10 businesses per year), and, therefore, are pleased to provide this preliminary and non-binding indication of interest.

Purchase of Assets: We propose the acquisition o f substantially all of the assets of CTI free and clear of all liens, claims, encumbrances and interests pursuant to a definitive Asset Purchase Agreement.

We would intend to assume only those current liabilities which are related to the normal working capital needs of CTI or as specifically agreed to in the definitive Asset Purchase Agreement. We would not intend to assume any interest-bearing debt of CTI.

Valuation: Assuming the historical and projected financial information provided in the Confidential Information Memorandum is substantially accurate, we propose a valuation of $27 to $29 million.

Consideration and Financing: Consideration would be in cash. We have no financing requirements or contingencies as conditions precedent to the closing of the Transaction. Zany is a very profitable, privately held corporation with annual revenues in excess of $5 billion and with adequate cash reserves to consummate the Transaction without borrowing funds.

Acquirer: The acquiring entity would be Zanzibar Medic al Documentation Corporation or an affiliate of Zany established specifically for the Transaction.

Conditions to Closing: Please note that completion of the Transaction would be subject to (1) Zany's completion of and satisfaction with its due diligence process; (2) the negotiation and execution of satisfactory documentation of the Transaction which is expected to include normal and customary representations and warranties; (3) receipt of approval from Zany's Board of Directors; and (4) the absence of any material adverse change in the performance or prospects of the business.

Required Approvals: As noted above, closing of the Transaction would be subject to receipt of approval from Zany's Board of Directors and, further, any regulatory approval required under the Hart-Scott-Rodino Antitrust Improvements Act of 1976.

Ongoing Operations of the Company: From the date of acceptance of this proposal until closing of the Transaction, we would expect CTI to conduct all of its operations in the normal course of business.

Confidentiality: This document contains confidential information intended solely for the recipient named herein. The information set forth in this document may not be reproduced or disclosed by the recipient without the prior written consent of Zany. This condition is deemed accepted unless the recipient returns the original of this document together with a notice of rejection within 24 hours of receipt without (1) having made any copies or extracts of the information contained herein; or (2) having disclosed the information to any other person.

Contact: To discuss this proposal further, please contact Mathew Stockman, Vice President of Corporate Development.

We appreciate your consideration of this proposal and look forward to discussing it further with you and the leadership team of CTI. We look forward to learning more about them and their vision for their business. Lastly, we look forward to sharing information about us, our mission and values, and the fine group of companies that make up Zany.

Sincerely,

Matthew Stockman
Vice President of Business Development

Zanzibar Medical Documentation Corporation

Letter of Intent

This section shows you a sample letter of intent (LOI). As with all M&A documents, the exact letter you use depends on your specific deal, but this example can give you a jumping-off point.

November 11, 2011

Circuitous Therapeutic Information, Inc.
c/o Frederic von Friedman
Senn Investment Banking
123 Main St
Chicago, IL 60699

Dear Fred:

I am delighted to submit a nonbinding letter of intent (this "LOI") on behalf of Pixie Capital Partners LLC ("Pixie" or "Buyer") regarding a proposed acquisition of substantially all of the assets of Circuitous Therapeutic Information, Inc. ("CTI" or "Seller"), pursuant to terms and conditions anticipated to be generally as described herein (the "Transaction"). Buyer would assume only certain liabilities of CTI as set forth herein and would not assume or be responsible for any other liability or obligation of CTI.

After meeting with CTI on October 31, I believe Pixie represents an ideal partner for creating liquidity for CTI's owners. The company's circular medical device information focus is an excellent match for my team's background, and I believe Pixie can lead a successful transition of the business and ensure a healthy future for the company, its employees and its customers.

The purpose of this LOI is to set forth a proposed structure for a Transaction. This LOI is not intended to contain all matters upon which agreement must be reached in order to consummate the Transaction.

1. Proposed Transaction Structure. Pixie (or its assignee) proposes to acquire all of CTI's assets free and clear of all liens, claims and encumbrances, and assume its operating liabilities, in an asset purchase transaction. Pixie would pay total consideration of $30,000,000 (the "Purchase Price"), representing a multiple of approximately 5.0 times the Seller's projected 2011 EBITDA of $6,000,000. The Purchase Price would payable as follows:

(a) $18,000,000 in cash at the consummation of the Transaction (the "Closing");

(b) $3,000,000 in cash, to be held in escrow until no later than 12 months after Closing to allow for any post-acquisition adjustments based on

    (i) shortfalls in working capital at Closing or

    (ii) final 2011 EBITDA below management's projection of $6,000,000; and

(c) $9,000,000 in the form of a subordinated seller note (the "Seller Note"), with a 3-year term bearing interest quarterly at 8.0%.

Note that this structure provides approximately 60% of the Purchase Price in cash at Closing (and 70% in cash within 12 months), subject to certain adjustments. The 12-month period is chosen to allow for completion of the 2011 audit to finalize the calculation of the 2011 EBITDA.

2. Adjustments to Purchase Price. The Purchase Price will be subject to the following adjustments:

(a) amounts below or in excess of net working capital at Closing of $2.0 million would adjust the Purchase Price on a dollar-for-dollar basis.

(b) amounts below or in excess of the Seller's projected 2011 EBITDA of $6,000,000 would adjust the Purchase Price proportionately.

Reductions in the Purchase Price will reduce the amount of escrow released to the Seller, with any reduction in excess of the escrow amount decreasing the principal amount of the Seller Note. Increases in Purchase Price will increase the principal amount of the Seller Note.

3. Consummation of the Transaction. The Transaction will be subject to execution and delivery of a definitive agreement (the "Definitive Agreement"); as well as to additional terms and conditions set forth herein. The Definitive Agreement will contain representations and warranties, covenants, conditions and indemnification provisions that are customary in transactions of this type.

Among other things, execution of the Definitive Agreement will be subject to Pixie's completion of, and satisfaction with, its due diligence review, satisfactory transition of CTI's agreements with its various key suppliers and vendors, and is contingent on execution of a satisfactory non-compete agreement by members of CTI's management team.

Buyer and Seller each intend to use all reasonable efforts to cause negotiation, execution and delivery of the Definitive Agreement and any related agreements to occur as soon as practical, which Buyer estimates to be approximately 60 days after acceptance in writing of this LOI. Closing would be held simultaneous with the execution of the Definitive Agreement.

4. Fees and Expenses. Each party shall bear its own legal fees and expenses incurred in connection with the proposed transaction. Buyer shall not be responsible for any broker's, finder's or other such fee incurred by the Seller in connection with the Transaction, and the Seller shall indemnify Buyer for all amounts expended in investigating, defending against or satisfying any such claim brought against Buyer. Each party shall be responsible for all costs and expenses, including, without limitation, attorney's fees in connection with the Transaction

5. Conduct of Seller's Business. Until such time as the Transaction shall have been either consummated or abandoned, Seller shall continue to conduct its business in a manner consistent with its operations prior to January 1, 2011, without substantial change to the nature, composition or amount of its assets or liabilities, without any disposition of any of its assets other than inventory, or without changes in any operating procedures or personnel inconsistent with prior practice which may be detrimental to the business' long-term health.

6. Due Diligence. Pixie and its representatives shall be afforded full access to and the opportunity to review all of CTI's business and operations, including, without limitation, CTI's offices, intellectual property, technology, equipment and inventory, senior management, books and records, financial forecasts and similar data relating to CTI's operations and business prospects. In addition, Buyer shall be afforded access to and able to speak with CTI's employees,

customers, vendors and suppliers in a manner to be mutually agreed upon by the parties hereto.

7. Exclusivity. In order to induce Pixie to pursue the Transaction and to incur the costs and expenses related to its due diligence and the closing of the possible Transaction, neither CTI nor any of its members, employees or advisors (the "CTI Team") shall, prior to January 31, 2012, directly or indirectly:

(a) negotiate for, solicit or entertain any offer, inquiry or proposal for, or enter into, any transaction that has the purpose of a business combination, sale of debt or equity, a financing transaction of any type, or any other transaction comparable or similar to the Transaction (any of the foregoing, a "Competing Transaction");

(b) provide information to any other party regarding CTI (except in the ordinary course of business); or

(c) enter into any agreement, arrangement or understanding regarding a Competing Transaction. CTI shall promptly notify Pixie if CTI or the CTI Team receives any such offer, inquiry or proposal and the details thereof and shall keep Pixie informed with respect thereto.

8. Public Disclosures. Prior to consummation of the Transaction, none of Pixie, Buyer, Seller or the CTI Team (or any of their respective affiliates, representatives or agents) shall, directly or indirectly, without the prior written consent of the other parties hereto, make any statement or public announcement, or make any release to trade publications or the press ("Public Disclosures") with respect to the Transaction, this LOI or any of the matters expressed herein.

Notwithstanding the foregoing, nothing herein shall prohibit CTI, the CTI Team, Pixie or Buyer from disclosing any information or making any Public Disclosure if, based upon the advice of counsel to the disclosing party, such disclosure or Public Disclosure is required by applicable law or regulation.

9. Confidentiality. Unless and until the transaction contemplated hereby shall be consummated, Buyer and its affiliates shall maintain the confidentiality of all trade secrets and other confidential information relating to Seller or the Assets, except for (i) disclosure to Buyer's legal counsel and accountants, (ii) disclosure which, in the opinion of Buyer's legal counsel, is required by law, and (iii) disclosure to prospective investors and lenders to Buyer. If the proposed transaction contemplated hereby shall be abandoned, then at Seller's request Buyer shall return to Seller all documents supplied to Buyer by Seller which contain any such trade secrets or other confidential information, including all copies thereof.

10. Binding Agreement. Except for the provisions of paragraphs 4 through 9 hereof, which shall constitute binding obligations, this LOI shall only serve as evidence of the intent of the parties hereto and shall not constitute a binding agreement of Pixie, CTI or the CTI Team.

11. Entire Agreement. This LOI constitutes the entire agreement between the parties hereto regarding the subject matter contained herein and supersedes all prior and contemporaneous undertakings and agreements between the parties hereto, whether written or oral, with respect to the subject matter herein.

12. Governing Law. This LOI shall be governed by and construed in accordance with the laws of the State of Delaware, without reference to principles of conflicts of law.

If the foregoing is an acceptable basis for proceeding and you are in agreement with the proposals set forth in this LOI, please indicate your approval by signing and returning to me an acknowledgment copy of this LOI. This LOI, unless extended in writing by Pixie, shall expire, become null and void and may not be accepted if not accepted and acknowledged by you prior to 5:00 p.m. central time on Friday, November 18, 2011. We look forward to working with you toward a successful and mutually beneficial Transaction.

Sincerely

Carrie Etherson
Managing Director

Due Diligence Checklist

The information in this section is a very detailed listing of typical due diligence information, split into common categories. Not all items apply to each situation, of course, but this appendix can give you an idea of the breadth and depth of needed materials. Flip to Chapter 14 for more on the due diligence process. Many thanks to Kinsella Group for supplying this list!

Note: Reporting period refers to the most recent financial period.

Corporate information

- Copies of the company's Articles of Incorporation, including all amendments.
- Copies of the company's bylaws and all amendments.

- ✔ Copies of the company's corporate minute books (including minutes of meetings of the shareholders, boards of directors, and committees thereof).

- ✔ Copies of correspondence with shareholders, including proxy solicitations and annual reports, during the reporting period.

- ✔ Listing of shareholders (including name, address, and telephone number) and number of shares held by each.

- ✔ Listing of all directors and officers (including name, address, and telephone number).

- ✔ Copies of all shareholders' agreements, voting trust agreements, or other restrictive agreements relating to the sale, transfer, or voting of shares of capital stock of the company or any of its subsidiaries.

- ✔ Certificate of Good Standing from the Secretary of State of the state where the company is incorporated.

- ✔ Listing of the jurisdictions and copies of annual reports for each during the reporting period:

    - Where the company is incorporated or qualified to do business.

    - Any other jurisdiction where the company owns, stores, leases, or licenses properties or assets or has employees, agents, or customers.

- ✔ Schedule of the company's assumed names, division names, or other names under which the company is conducting or has conducted business and copies of registration.

- ✔ Schedule of any corporations, partnerships, joint ventures, or other entities in which the company has a material interest or is affiliated.

- ✔ Listing of all federal, state, local, and foreign governmental permits, licenses, and approvals (excluding those listed elsewhere herein) either held or required to be held by the company for the conduct of business.

- ✔ A schedule of all law firms, accounting firms, consulting firms, and similar professionals engaged by the company during the reporting period.

Operations

- ✔ Listing of all existing products or services and products or services under development.

- ✔ Listing of major operations discontinued during the reporting period, or expected to be discontinued.

- ✔ Copies of all correspondence and reports related to any regulatory approvals or disapprovals of any of the company's products or services.

- ✔ Summary of all complaints or warranty claims.

- ✔ Summary of results of all tests, evaluations, studies, surveys, and other data regarding existing products or services and products or services under development.

- ✔ Samples of all sales and promotional material utilized in marketing products and services (catalogs, brochures, sample kits, and so on).

- ✔ Copies of all articles and press releases relating to the company published during the reporting period.

- ✔ Schedule of any volume or sample rebate programs or special deals with customers (discounts, terms, and so on).

- ✔ Copies of any contracts or agreements with customers, whether formal or informal, including pricing arrangements, incentive programs, inventory/supply arrangements, quality criteria, warranties, and so on.

- ✔ Copies of the company's quality and any similar manuals.

- ✔ Schedule and copies of any customer quality awards, plant qualification/certification distinctions, quality certifications, or other awards or certificates that are reflective of superior performance.

- ✔ Copies of internal and external quality audits performed during the reporting period.

- ✔ Detailed listing of all business application software, vendor and version, number of licenses, and approximate acquisition date.

Financials

- ✔ Accountant-prepared financial statements for the reporting period.

- ✔ Most recent interim internal statements with comparable statements to the prior year.

- ✔ Auditor's letters and replies for the reporting period.

- ✔ Credit report, if available.

- ✔ Description of any change in accounting methods, policies, or procedures during the reporting period.

- ✔ Description of the company's internal control procedures.

- ✔ Description of the company's policy for capitalizing assets, including internal costs for internally constructed assets.

- ✔ Description of depreciation and amortization methods.

- ✔ Copy of the general ledger for each year-end of the reporting period and most recent month-end.

- ✔ Copies of any projections, capital budgets, and business/strategic plans.

✔ Copies of any analysis of fixed and variable expenses.

✔ Copies of any analysis of gross margins.

✔ Listing of all bank accounts and safety-deposit boxes, including authorized signatories.

✔ Accounts receivable aging at each year-end of the reporting period and each month-end of the current year.

✔ Detailed breakdown of the basis for the allowance for doubtful accounts.

✔ Listing of bad debts during the reporting period.

✔ Analysis of all accounts receivable currently in dispute and/or greater than 90 days old.

✔ Schedule of prepaid expenses with backup documentation and accumulated amortization.

✔ Schedule of deferred income at most recent year-end and month-end.

✔ Schedule of security deposits at most recent year-end and month-end.

✔ Schedule of all indebtedness and contingent liabilities.

✔ Accounts payable aging at each year-end of the reporting period and each month-end of the current year.

✔ Description of accounts payable year-end and month-end cut off policy and procedures.

✔ Detail of accrued expenses as of the most recent year-end and month-end.

✔ Detail of any customer advances, deposits, credit balances as of the most recent year-end and month-end.

✔ Listing and detail for all related party transactions during the reporting period.

✔ Listing of any adjustments to EBITDA and provide substantiation for those adjustments.

Sales and marketing info and documents

✔ Complete customer list, including name, address, telephone number, and contact name.

✔ Listing of major customers (by major product line, if applicable) and percentage of sales to each for each year-end of the reporting period and the most YTD. (A *major product line* means any product or service of the company contributing 5 percent or more of the revenues of the company. A "major customer" means the top 50 customers [by sales volume] of the company.)

- ✔ Schedule of open orders.

- ✔ Copies of all supply or service agreements.

- ✔ Description or copy of the company's credit policy.

- ✔ Listing and explanation for any major customers lost, or who have notified the company (orally or in writing) of a proposed adverse change or modification to the relationship during the reporting period.

- ✔ Copies of all surveys and market research reports relevant to the company or its products or services.

- ✔ Schedule of the company's current advertising programs, market plans and budgets, and printed marketing materials.

- ✔ Schedule and description of the company's major competitors.

Real estate and facilities

- ✔ Schedule of the company's business locations.

- ✔ Listing of all owned or leased real estate including location, date, term, termination rights, renewal rights, rent amount, unusual provisions (for example, purchase options), and existence of defaults or breaches.

- ✔ Copies of all real estate appraisals, leases, deeds, mortgages, title policies, surveys, zoning approvals, variances, or use permits.

- ✔ Listing of current and pending construction in progress, including date commenced, expected completion date, and further required financial commitment to complete.

Fixed assets

- ✔ Schedule of fixed assets, owned or leased, to include description, date acquired, price, depreciation years, accumulated depreciation, net book value, and location.

- ✔ Copies of any equipment appraisals performed during the reporting period.

- ✔ Copies of all U.C.C. filings.

- ✔ Schedule of sales and purchases of major capital equipment during the reporting period.

- ✔ Schedule of unpaid balances and open purchase commitments for any capital equipment.

- ✔ Listing of any surplus or idle equipment and the dollar value of such equipment.

- ✔ Copies of any vehicle registrations.

Inventory and costing

- ✔ Inventory listing (by location if applicable) including item description, item number, date, units, and cost for the most recent year-end and month-end.

- ✔ Description of practices regarding inventory aging, valuation, and obsolescence and any methodology changes during the reporting period and the related effect on reported performance.

- ✔ Details of inventory reserves and/or write-offs during the reporting period.

- ✔ Summary of physical inventory count results (by location if applicable), including explanation of significant book-to-physical adjustments for the most recent year-end and month-end.

- ✔ Details of any consigned inventory arrangements.

Purchasing and suppliers

- ✔ Listing of major suppliers and dollar volume of purchases from each for each of the last three fiscal years. (A *major supplier* means the top 30 suppliers [by purchase volume].)

- ✔ A separate list of any supplier to the company where practical alternative sources of supply are not available.

- ✔ Schedule of open purchase orders, to include item number, description, quantity, price, and value.

- ✔ Summary or copy of the company's purchasing policies.

- ✔ Copies of any supplier contracts or descriptions of any significant supplier agreements.

Intellectual property

- ✔ Schedule of domestic and foreign patent registrations and applications identifying each patent by title, registration/application number, date of registration/application, initial expiration, and country of registration.

- ✔ Schedule of all trademarks, trade names, and service marks held or applied for, including maintenance and status on registrations, applications, and licenses.

- ✔ Schedule of all copyrights held or applied for, including maintenance and status on registrations, applications, and licenses.

- ✔ Schedule and copies of all consulting agreements, agreements regarding inventions, and licenses or assignments of intellectual property to or from the company.

✔ Schedule of domain name registrations, including status on renewal.

✔ Description of methods used to protect trade secrets and know-how.

✔ Description of any material trade secrets or know-how held by the company or provided to or by the company under any agreement.

✔ Copies of any work-for-hire agreements.

✔ Schedule and summary of any claims or claims threatened by or against the company regarding intellectual property.

✔ Copies of any communication to or from third parties relating to the validity or infringement of the company's patents, technology, trade secrets, trademarks (service marks), trade dress, and copyrights.

Human resources

✔ Organizational chart by department showing all positions within the department. All open positions should be noted as such.

✔ Listing of employees including hire date, job title/position, job description, and current pay rate.

✔ Copies of all employment, consulting, non-disclosure, non-solicitation, or noncompetition agreements between the company and any of its employees.

✔ Résumés of key employees.

✔ Summary and copies of executive compensation plans, including salaries, bonuses, commissions, vacations, club memberships, and so on.

✔ Copy of the company's employee handbook, including all employee benefits and holiday, vacation, and paid time off policies.

✔ Copies of all documentation for qualified and nonqualified retirement plans; any IRS determination letters; the most recent Form 5500, 5500-C, or 5500-K; and for each multiemployer plan, a statement of the employer's "withdrawal liability" within the meaning of ERISA section 4211.

✔ Copies of collective bargaining agreements.

✔ Listing and description of benefits of all employee health and welfare insurance policies or self-funded arrangements.

✔ Schedule of costs associated with the aforementioned plans during the reporting period.

✔ Summary of all employee problems within the reporting period, including alleged wrongful termination, harassment, and discrimination.

- Summary of any labor disputes, requests for arbitration, or grievance procedures currently pending or settled within the reporting period.

- Listing of company-provided vehicles, including individual assigned to the vehicle.

- Schedule of worker's compensation claim history for the reporting period.

- Schedule of unemployment insurance claim history for the reporting period.

- Copies of all stock option and stock purchase plans and a schedule of grants.

- Copies of all OSHA examinations, reports, or complaints during the reporting period.

- Copies of all policy and/or procedure manuals.

- Description of all performance bonus plans in place and listing of bonuses paid during the reporting period.

Debt and financings

- Schedule and copies of all promissory notes, bonds (including industrial development revenue bonds), commercial paper, loan/credit agreements, indentures, and other agreements or instruments relating to the short-term and long-term borrowing of money involving the company and existing at any time during the reporting period.

- Schedule and copies of any guaranties, repurchase obligations, and other arrangements whereby the credit of the company is obligated for the indebtedness of a person (including one of the company) and subordination and inter-creditor agreements involving the company.

- Schedule and copies of all security agreements, pledge agreements, mortgages, and other agreements or instruments whereby the properties or assets of the company are subject to the indebtedness of a person (including one of the company).

- Schedule and copies of any letters of credit, financial surety/performance bonds or similar credit support devices outstanding for the benefit of the company and related reimbursement or indemnification agreements.

- Copies of any compliance certificates, including borrowing base certificates and covenant compliance calculations, supplied to any creditor during the reporting period.

✔ Copies of material correspondence with any creditor during the reporting period.

✔ Schedule and details of any existing defaults under credit arrangements and any events that have occurred that, with the giving of notice or the passage of time, will become such a default.

Environmental

✔ Copies of any environmental reviews or inspection reports relating to any of the properties owned or leased by the company during the reporting period.

✔ Copies of any applications, statements, or reports filed or given by the company with or to the Federal Environmental Protection Agency, any state department of environmental regulations or any similar state or local regulatory body, authority, or agency.

✔ Copies of any notices, complaints, suits, or similar documents sent to, received by, or served upon the company by the Federal Environmental Protection Agency, any state department of environmental regulations, or any similar state or local regulatory body, authority or agency.

✔ Copies of outside reports concerning compliance with waste disposal regulations, hazardous or otherwise.

✔ Listing of hazardous substances, including, but not limited to, asbestos, PCBs, petroleum products, herbicides, pesticides, or radioactive materials, used in the company's operations.

✔ Listing of permits, licenses and agreements of the company relating to air or water use or quality, solid or liquid wastes, hazardous waste storage or disposal, or other environmental matters.

✔ Description of the company's disposal methods.

✔ Description of any adverse environmental or occupational safety or health condition or concern of the company not previously requested.

✔ Listing and description of any environmental litigation or investigations.

✔ Listing and description of any known Superfund exposure.

✔ Listing and description of any contingent environmental liabilities or continuing indemnification obligations.

✔ Copies of all correspondence, notices, and files related to the Federal Environmental Protection Agency, state, local, or similar foreign regulatory agencies.

✔ Copies of all annual reports, manifests, or other documents relating to hazardous waste or pesticide management during the reporting period.

✔ Copies of the workplace safety and health programs currently in place, with particular emphasis on chemical handling practices.

Taxes

✔ Copies of all federal, state, local, and foreign tax returns during the reporting period and for all open years.

✔ Copies of state sales tax returns during the reporting period and for all open periods.

✔ Copies of any audit and revenue agency reports.

✔ Copies of any tax settlement documents for the reporting period.

✔ Copies of all employment tax filings for the reporting period.

✔ Copies of real estate, property, or any other tax filings for the reporting period.

✔ Copies of any tax liens.

✔ Listing of returns and years thereof that have been audited by any tax jurisdiction and copies of related determination letters.

✔ Listing and description of any pending or threatened disputes with regard to tax matters.

✔ Copy of Form 2553 (S-corp Election), if applicable.

Contracts

✔ Schedule of all subsidiary, partnership, or joint venture relationships and obligations with copies of all related agreements.

✔ Copies of all contracts between the company and any officers, directors, 5 percent shareholders, or any of their respective families or affiliates and a written description of oral agreements or arrangements between the company and any related party.

✔ Copies of any license, sublicense, royalty and franchise agreements, or equipment leases involving the company.

✔ Schedule of all distribution, agency, manufacturer representative, marketing, and supply relationships and obligations with copies of all related agreements.

✔ Copies of any letters of intent, contracts, and closing transcripts from any mergers, acquisitions, or divestitures during the reporting period.

✔ Copies of any options and stock purchase agreements involving interests in other companies.

✔ Copies of all standard forms and agreements used by the company.

✔ Copies of all non-disclosure or noncompetition agreements to which the company is a party.

✔ Copies of any agreements affected in any manner by a change in control of the company.

✔ Copies of all management contracts involving the company.

✔ Copies of any brokers or finders agreements applicable to the company.

✔ Copies of any hold harmless indemnification or similar agreements of the company.

✔ Copies of any contracts relating to other material business relationships, including, but not limited to

• Copies of any current service, operation, or maintenance contracts.

• Copies of any current contracts for purchase of fixed assets.

✔ Listing of all contracts and agreements subject to renegotiation.

✔ Copies of all contracts and agreements not previously requested.

Insurance and risk management

✔ Schedule and copies of the company's general liability, personal and real property, product liability, errors and omissions, key-man, directors and officers, worker's compensation, and other insurance policies currently in effect.

✔ Listing of risk management advisors and copy of recent coverage/exposure reviews.

✔ Description of the current status of the payment of premiums related to insurance, including a specific description of any premiums which are subject to retroactive adjustment.

✔ Schedule of insurance claims filed during the reporting period.

✔ Schedule of the company's loss experience per insurance year during the reporting period.

✔ Listing of areas of self-insurance and schedule of related costs during the reporting period.

✔ Listing and description of any outstanding premium adjustments (audits, retros, and so on).

Litigation and contingent claims

✔ Schedule of all litigation, arbitration, and other proceedings to which the company is a party or by which its properties are bound and all pleadings and other material papers related thereto existing at any time during the reporting period.

✔ Listing and description of all pending or threatened claims, lawsuits, arbitrations, or investigations involving a claim for relief against the company, any subsidiary, or any of their respective officers or directors.

✔ Description of settlements of litigation, arbitration, and other proceedings during the reporting period and copies of settlement agreements, releases, and waivers related thereto.

✔ Description of bankruptcy proceedings in which the company is a creditor or otherwise interested.

✔ Description of any contingent liability of the company not referenced herein or in the financial statements provided hereunder, including those arising from or out of

- Contracts and agreements.

- Price redetermination, renegotiation, or escalation clauses.

- Sales subject to warranty or service agreements.

- Sales to foreign buyers.

- Product liability.

- Unfunded pension liability, other retiree health or insurance benefits, or similar matters.

- Antitrust, Robinson-Putmon, or other trade regulation matters.

- Equal opportunity/anti-discrimination matters.

- Environmental matters.

- Any other matter which, in the judgment of the company, is significant with respect to the company or which should be considered and reviewed in making disclosures regarding the business and financial condition of the company.

✔ Listing of unsatisfied judgments, orders, and decrees to which the company is subject.

✔ Copies of all orders, injunctions, judgments, or decrees of any court or regulatory body applicable to the company or any of its properties.

✔ Copies of all agreements whereby the company agrees to indemnify or hold harmless another person or entity for claims against that person or entity.

✔ Schedule of any litigation involving an officer or director of the company concerning bankruptcy, crimes, securities law, or business practices at any time during the reporting period.

✔ Description of any investigations of the company, pending or threatened, by any governmental authority.

Governmental filings and reporting

✔ Copies of any governmental licenses, permits, and authorizations of the company not otherwise provided hereunder.

✔ Copies of all filings with, and notices to or by, governmental agencies or authorities by or to the company during the reporting period not otherwise provided hereunder, and all material documents and correspondence, including those of or in connection with Hart-Scott-Rodino, Securities and Exchange Commission, Blue Sky Administrators, Internal Revenue Service, Equal Employment Opportunity Commission, Food and Drug Administration, Environmental Protection Agency, any state or local environmental agency or authority, Occupational Safety and Health Administration, Immigration and Naturalization Service, Federal Trade Commission, or National Labor Relations Board.

✔ Description of any complaints, investigations, or other informal or formal proceeding involving the company by or before a governmental agency or authority, and copies of all material pleadings, filings, correspondence, or other papers related thereto.

Index

• J •

Apple & Macs

iPad For Dummies
978-0-470-58027-1

iPhone For Dummies,
4th Edition
978-0-470-87870-5

MacBook For Dummies, 3rd
Edition
978-0-470-76918-8

Mac OS X Snow Leopard For
Dummies
978-0-470-43543-4

Business

Bookkeeping For Dummies
978-0-7645-9848-7

Job Interviews
For Dummies,
3rd Edition
978-0-470-17748-8

Resumes For Dummies,
5th Edition
978-0-470-08037-5

Starting an
Online Business
For Dummies,
6th Edition
978-0-470-60210-2

Stock Investing
For Dummies,
3rd Edition
978-0-470-40114-9

Successful
Time Management
For Dummies
978-0-470-29034-7

Computer Hardware

BlackBerry
For Dummies,
4th Edition
978-0-470-60700-8

Computers For Seniors
For Dummies,
2nd Edition
978-0-470-53483-0

PCs For Dummies,
Windows
7 Edition
978-0-470-46542-4

Laptops For Dummies,
4th Edition
978-0-470-57829-2

Cooking & Entertaining

Cooking Basics
For Dummies,
3rd Edition
978-0-7645-7206-7

Wine For Dummies,
4th Edition
978-0-470-04579-4

Diet & Nutrition

Dieting For Dummies,
2nd Edition
978-0-7645-4149-0

Nutrition For Dummies,
4th Edition
978-0-471-79868-2

Weight Training
For Dummies,
3rd Edition
978-0-471-76845-6

Digital Photography

Digital SLR Cameras &
Photography For Dummies,
3rd Edition
978-0-470-46606-3

Photoshop Elements 8
For Dummies
978-0-470-52967-6

Gardening

Gardening Basics
For Dummies
978-0-470-03749-2

Organic Gardening
For Dummies,
2nd Edition
978-0-470-43067-5

Green/Sustainable

Raising Chickens
For Dummies
978-0-470-46544-8

Green Cleaning
For Dummies
978-0-470-39106-8

Health

Diabetes For Dummies,
3rd Edition
978-0-470-27086-8

Food Allergies
For Dummies
978-0-470-09584-3

Living Gluten-Free
For Dummies,
2nd Edition
978-0-470-58589-4

Hobbies/General

Chess For Dummies,
2nd Edition
978-0-7645-8404-6

Drawing
Cartoons & Comics
For Dummies
978-0-470-42683-8

Knitting For Dummies,
2nd Edition
978-0-470-28747-7

Organizing
For Dummies
978-0-7645-5300-4

Su Doku For Dummies
978-0-470-01892-7

Home Improvement

Home Maintenance
For Dummies,
2nd Edition
978-0-470-43063-7

Home Theater
For Dummies,
3rd Edition
978-0-470-41189-6

Living the
Country Lifestyle
All-in-One
For Dummies
978-0-470-43061-3

Solar Power Your Home
For Dummies,
2nd Edition
978-0-470-59678-4

Internet

Blogging For Dummies,
3rd Edition
978-0-470-61996-4

eBay For Dummies,
6th Edition
978-0-470-49741-8

Facebook For Dummies,
3rd Edition
978-0-470-87804-0

Web Marketing
For Dummies,
2nd Edition
978-0-470-37181-7

WordPress
For Dummies,
3rd Edition
978-0-470-59274-8

Language & Foreign Language

French For Dummies
978-0-7645-5193-2

Italian Phrases
For Dummies
978-0-7645-7203-6

Spanish For Dummies,
2nd Edition
978-0-470-87855-2

Spanish
For Dummies,
Audio Set
978-0-470-09585-0

Math & Science

Algebra I
For Dummies,
2nd Edition
978-0-470-55964-2

Biology For Dummies,
2nd Edition
978-0-470-59875-7

Calculus For Dummies
978-0-7645-2498-1

Chemistry For Dummies
978-0-7645-5430-8

Microsoft Office

Excel 2010 For Dummies
978-0-470-48953-6

Office 2010 All-in-One
For Dummies
978-0-470-49748-7

Office 2010 For Dummies,
Book + DVD Bundle
978-0-470-62698-6

Word 2010 For Dummies
978-0-470-48772-3

Music

Guitar For Dummies,
2nd Edition
978-0-7645-9904-0

iPod & iTunes For
Dummies, 8th Edition
978-0-470-87871-2

Piano Exercises
For Dummies
978-0-470-38765-8

Parenting & Education

Parenting For Dummies,
2nd Edition
978-0-7645-5418-6

Type 1 Diabetes
For Dummies
978-0-470-17811-9

Pets

Cats For Dummies,
2nd Edition
978-0-7645-5275-5

Dog Training For Dummies,
3rd Edition
978-0-470-60029-0

Puppies For Dummies,
2nd Edition
978-0-470-03717-1

Religion & Inspiration

The Bible For Dummies
978-0-7645-5296-0

Catholicism For Dummies
978-0-7645-5391-2

Women in the Bible
For Dummies
978-0-7645-8475-6

Self-Help & Relationship

Anger Management
For Dummies
978-0-470-03715-7

Overcoming Anxiety
For Dummies,
2nd Edition
978-0-470-57441-6

Sports

Baseball
For Dummies,
3rd Edition
978-0-7645-7537-2

Basketball
For Dummies,
2nd Edition
978-0-7645-5248-9

Golf For Dummies,
3rd Edition
978-0-471-76871-5

Web Development

Web Design
All-in-One
For Dummies
978-0-470-41796-6

Web Sites
Do-It-Yourself
For Dummies,
2nd Edition
978-0-470-56520-9

Windows 7

Windows 7
For Dummies
978-0-470-49743-2

Windows 7
For Dummies,
Book + DVD Bundle
978-0-470-52398-8

Windows 7 All-in-One
For Dummies
978-0-470-48763-1

DUMMIES.COM®

Wherever you are in life, Dummies makes it easier.

From fashion to Facebook®,
wine to Windows®, and everything in between,
Dummies makes it easier.

Visit us at Dummies.com

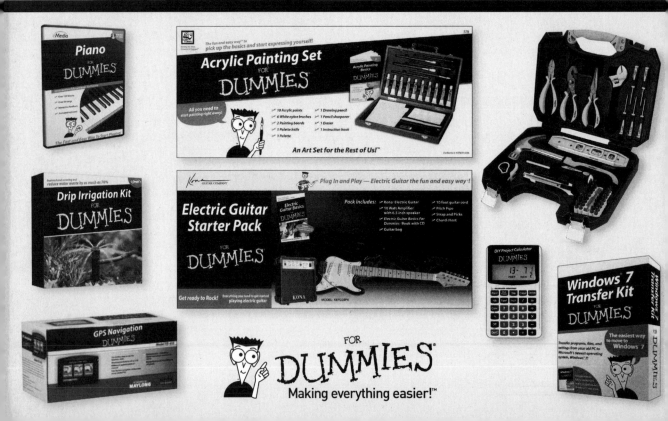